MW00954997

Paulo and the Magician

As always, Ken, for all your love + kindness, Many blessings + thanks, Bernard

Paulo and the Magician

A Guide to Inner Peace

Bernard H. Groom

Booksurge Publishing
2009

Copyright © Bernard H. Groom 2009

All rights reserved. No part of this book pay be reproduced by any mechanical, photocopy, photographic, or electronic process, or in the form of a phonographic recording; nor may it be stored in a retrieval system, transmitted, or otherwise be copied for public or private use – other than for "fair use" as brief quotations embodied in critical articles and reviews – without the prior written permission of the author.

For further information, contact:
Booksurge Publishing
1-866-308-6235
www.booksurge.com

A Course In Miracles® and *ACIM*® are registered trademarks of the Foundation for A Course In Miracles.

Library of Congress Control Number: 2008908431

ISBN 10: 1-4392-0784-4
ISBN 13: 978-1-4392-0784-0

Printed in the United States of America

To order additional copies, please contact us:
Booksurge Publishing
www.booksurge.com
1-866-308-6235
orders@booksurge.com

To all of us who stood before the Great Door
and hesitated before entering,
and now look back across the threshold…
Toward Home.

Contents

PART 3

PART 4

Further Acknowledgements

Author's Note

Dear Reader,

Welcome to the world of *Paulo and the Magician*!

When I first began this work some seven years ago, I had my mind set on a short allegorical story. Just a short little fable.

I began with an intention, a desire to share with others the magic and beauty I had discovered in working with the text known as *A Course In Miracles*, in my opinion the revelatory book of the highest Gnostic spirituality and philosophy of our era. I thought the best way to accomplish this would not be by producing a formal text book, but by using a blend of fable and story. In this way, I could perhaps create an imaginary world richly filled with symbols and metaphors that would transport the reader into these very experiences *A Course In Miracles* (A.C.I.M.) had offered me through the beauty of its language and the gentleness of its words.

As the writing progressed, however, it appeared more and more unlikely that I would be able to convey the essence of the philosophy of A.C.I.M. – its explanation for our world and our daily experiences within it – in just a short novel. There seemed indeed so much to say, and a true picture of our world would not have been complete, I felt, without the passages I subsequently came to add. Please forgive me if I did the original intention of the book an injustice. The proper meaning and nature of our individual reality on earth is perhaps still not fully captured within this final finished version. On the other hand, I do believe the reader can begin his journey here, the journey that will take him through his own gentle experiences back to the remarkable spiritual Home we all share – back to Paulo's City of Light.

Nevertheless, I would like to express a word of caution at this point. At first sight the reader might be tempted to believe he understands the individual concepts within this book quite easily. The reader may even be reminded of other works or thought systems. Or the ideas might appear as simplistic, given the fairy-tale style in which they are expressed. But, in the experience of many of those who have attempted working with *A Course In Miracles*, putting these concepts together in right perspective is all *but* a simple task. After all, understanding the true nature of being from *outside* the perception of this material universe can be nothing less than a lifelong task of struggling against lifetimes of pre-conditioning. It is in fact a goal that obstinately refuses to materialize while we still firmly believe that these individual selves we see in the mirror every morning are truly the anchor point of our existence. So I would encourage the reader to be patient with his work through the ideas contained within, and, above all, not to underestimate the obstacles we contain to transforming our deeply held beliefs about ourselves and the world we live in.

A Note on the Philosophy

I have mentioned that the concepts presented here are a representation of the principles of *A Course In Miracles*. Still, the reader familiar with the work of the early Christian Gnostics will most likely find a certain resonance with many of the ideas presented within this book. Similar to the philosophy of the early Christian Fathers in various respects, *A Course In Miracles* follows an adamantly Gnostic principle of creation, maintaining that this material world is *not* the work of a metaphysical God-Father entity. However, A.C.I.M. then goes on to explain, unlike the Gnostics, that only that which the true God created (a unified celestial realm of wholeness without opposition or separation) could in fact be real at all. Hence, the logic of A.C.I.M. goes, this material universe of multiplicity is not the real world or our real home, and is, in fact, illusion.

An illusion, yes, but one that seems exceedingly real in our senses – *but why?* By explaining the origin of the physical world as the result of a powerful decision in our collective mind (the decision to separate ourselves from our original state of celestial 'wholeness'), A.C.I.M. informs us that everything within our range of daily experience today is nothing more than the mental out-picturing of this cosmological division, a division which continues to be played out not in a physical world of *fact*, but *within* the greater Mind.

True to its mission of deliverance, *A Course In Miracles* does not leave us to wander in this shadow-land of ignorance and suffering without help, but provides us with a number of concrete solutions to our dilemma. It presents us notably with a number of powerful psychological techniques to resolve the enigmas and troubles that abound in our daily experience (techniques described within this book), and the way, of course, to begin the real journey of turning our minds toward Home.

A Note on Mythology

The beauty of Gnosticism in general, and particularly of *A Course In Miracles,* is its ability to provide us with a powerful alternative to the myths supplied to us by the Judeo-Christian tradition. We live in a world of myth, whether consciously aware of the symbols in our personal mythology or not. I believe it is only by identifying the myths that currently run our lives, then consciously choosing the mythology we wish to rule our sub-conscious, that we can begin to turn our minds toward Truth and Happiness. But while we remain unaware of the symbols that dominate our psyche, we cannot possibly be in a position of power to choose.

As a result, this book seeks to give power and choice back to the decision-maker within each of us, to that part of the individual capable of being honest about her life, of being willing to discover her personal mythology, and of consciously choosing her path toward happiness. I hope, and trust, you will find that this book represents an honest alternative to the various models available to the modern philosopher-seeker, specifically a path that offers a sincere promise of finding better understanding of our existential condition and greater peace through applying its principles. And hence I invite the reader to enjoy, to reflect, and to try her or his hand at one or two of the ideas contained within if she or he feels so moved.

Many blessings, and happy reading!

Bernard H. Groom
Salviac, Lot
France
2009

Acknowledgements

Aside from the many people who have crossed my path as informal guides and teachers to whom I shall always remain very grateful, I would like to extend a special, heartfelt thanks to Dr. Kenneth Wapnick, founder and director of the Foundation for *A Course In Miracles*.

People working with A.C.I.M. have invariably, at one time or another, come to the conclusion that they do not fully grasp the subtler meanings or entire vision of this complex work. In my case that moment of self-honesty occurred nine years ago, provoked by a passage through a challenging divorce and change of work situation. I came at that time upon Kenneth's extensive work on A.C.I.M. (having battled alone with the material for eleven years) and could only say that from that day forth my life has taken wings, in every sense. His comprehension of the spiritual and psychological nature of our world should not be underestimated, and anyone seriously interested in being helped along the Gnostic path Home can very profitably share a part of his life with this great man's teachings. My debt to him cannot be repaid in so few words, and I thank him from the bottom of my heart.

A Word on Errors

In every way possible, within the confines of a story, the author has tried to represent the correct metaphysical principles, perspective and psychology of *A Course In Miracles* in this work. Many sections were re-written several times over the space of eight years in order to come ever closer to a more precise expression of A.C.I.M's basic tenets, without losing the fable-like quality intended for the work. Nevertheless, if errors have slipped in, then they are purely the author's.

A Word of Advice to the Reader

The author would also like to advise the reader that the material within this book may at times provoke a strong emotional reaction. The powerful symbolic language of the story in effect can make an unexpectedly strong impression on the sub-conscious mind. If he or she feels at any time over-whelmed by such feelings, then he or she should apply the principle of good sense and put the book away for another time, or skip chapters.

About the Author

Bernard Groom first encountered *A Course In Miracles* in 1987 in New York City while working on Wall Street. He subsequently worked as a corporate trainer in Europe before moving to a country village in the Southwest of France. He has since been studying and writing on questions of spirituality while learning the building trade. Bernard is Australian-born and has a M.A. from The Fletcher School of Law and Diplomacy, Boston.

Paulo and the Magician

Part 1

− Chapter One −

Beware of Strangers

The Domain, the year 1255

Paulo bolted straight from the market place and down the lane as fast as his legs would take him. Heavy footsteps pounded after him, the sound of hob-nail boots slapped hard on the cobble-stones and echoed in the narrow street off the half-timbered houses, pursuing the boy like a premonition of danger.

Suddenly, a merchant stepped out of an alley leading a small horse by the halter, and Paulo instinctively swerved to duck behind the animal; but he failed to see the long wooden cart it was drawing, loaded down with copperware and brass trinkets. He slammed against the side of the cart, tipping it violently, upsetting pots and ewers and basins in a deafening heap onto the cobbles.

"Holy Maker! What on earth do you think you're doing, boy?"

The furious merchant let forth a barrage of insults above the metallic din of clanging pots and vessels, but the boy picked himself up and kept running.

The heavy footsteps fell closer behind him and Paulo tried losing the pursuer in a frantic dash to the left through a high stone archway. The path led into a small courtyard where he often used to play; from there he knew he could make a sprint through a small side passage and down to the river, across the stone bridge, along the bank, and eventually into the safety of the deep woods and the Forest.

But now it led only to a dead end.

Paulo ground to a halt in mid-stride and gazed stupefied before him at the passage on the other side of the square that was normally open. But today a wooden scaffolding had been erected across the exit from the square, and a number of busy workmen were repairing some dilapidated stonework on the adjacent building. The boy dropped his shoulders in desperate resignation and just stood there, waiting for the blow from behind.

Heavy feet pounded up to him and within seconds two strong hands gripped him hard by the shoulders and span him around. Paulo stared down at the ground, bracing himself, wincing before the blow actually came.

But nothing happened.

The man's hard breathing beat in his ears, and Paulo could feel a hot sweat start to trickle down his back. He tensed further, gripping his hands, and grit his teeth till his jaw hurt, and waited.

Still nothing happened.

After a minute of terrified silence he painfully raised his head, slowly opening his eyes, and dared to look at his pursuer. But he was not what the boy expected.

Not at all.

In that instant, staring into the quiet face of the tall stranger looking down at him, the whole world turned around for Paulo. Nothing was ever to be the same again.

He stared transfixed as the purest, calmest eyes he had ever seen looked down upon him, the eyes of the gentle stranger in whose depths he found only the most sincere kindness and caring. Eyes that only moments ago he was sure were carrying an onslaught of condemnation and punishment.

And after a few more moments he heard a deep, gentle voice ask him: "Would you like now to know the *Truth*, my young friend. Would you like me to explain the simple Truth to you, would that help?"

The tall stranger had spoken, but Paulo hadn't understood. The words seem to hang in the air about him with some meaning he was missing, like an opening toward a mysterious place; a question, coming from a far away wisdom that the boy couldn't possibly yet fathom.

Paulo shrugged his shoulders. He had no answer.

"Then let me ask, do you wish to be happier now? Do you wish to feel a little more peace, and freedom, in your life?" the kind voice asked sincerely. "It is the same question, and will also lead you to the Truth."

The young boy couldn't move. He didn't think of running away now; he didn't think of fighting anymore. Only one desire filled his heart and drowned out all the sadness: the desperate wish to believe the fantastic promise offered to him by the strange man.

"Yes, I do. I really would like to be happier now," Paulo replied thoughtfully in a quiet voice, hardly a whisper, after several moments.

The stranger spoke with Paulo for some long minutes then, and the rich, magical words that reached his ears made his spirit sing with hope, and engraved themselves in shining letters on his heart forever.

When the stranger had finished, he walked calmly away without looking back, leaving the boy alone in the courtyard feeling completely bewildered.

After a moment, Paulo looked down at his hand and at last opened his tightly clenched fist. There, in his grimy, sweaty fingers was still the bright silver ducat; the same silver coin he had stolen from the man in the market place just minutes before – an eternity ago – when he had come to make his purchase of wood at his kindlin' stall.

But this was no ordinary stranger, and this was no ordinary meeting.

Without having the slightest awareness, Paulo had just made his first hesitant step on the journey back to the magnificent Golden City lying just the other side of the Domain. All the villagers would make the journey, one day. But none knew it, and certainly none had any idea when the journey would begin…

CHAPTER TWO

A Haunting Dream

The year 1256

"Wake up, now, Paulo! *Wake up!*"

Paulo sighed loudly under the sheets and opened his eyes. Reluctantly he threw back the scratchy wool bed covers and cringed as a draft of cold air flooded in. Then with exaggerated effort he extracted one foot, then another, from the warm place deep in the mattress, and placed each one carefully and purposefully on the rough cold floor of the cottage.

Perching bird-like on the rough edge of his wood frame bed, he gazed inquisitively around the little stone farmhouse from the sleeping alcove. Slowly and in detail he inspected it, running his eyes high and low over the furniture and walls, as if discovering his home just now for the very first time this morning.

"*Paulo!*" a shrill voice punched the air from the kitchen. "I don't want to have to call you a second time, boy!"

The words echoed loudly inside the hollow spaces of his still sleepy mind, and the young boy blew out a long whistling breath.

"And go take your breakfast – *now!*" the woman's voice finished commandingly.

"Yes, mama…" he called in return. "*All* that you wish, mama – *whenever* you wish," he muttered sourly under his breath.

She strode into the main room from the kitchen and glared at him disapprovingly. *Why does he have to test my patience like that?* she wondered, not for the first time.

Hesitating a moment, she continued her preparations. She set the pitcher of milk in her hand on the long eating table, a chipped terracotta jug filled with the thick white liquid, as well as a little wicker basket filled with rough slabs of a dark brown bread. A blazing fire lit the massive stone fireplace and the burning logs filled the room with flickering light, and glinted in the woman's eye.

Paulo's gaze followed his mother's form as she retreated back into the kitchen, and he quickly stole another look around the cottage from his bed alcove before she returned. He frowned.

What's wrong? Things look so much different this morning, he spoke to himself, muddled, shaking his head slowly as if to clear it.

Everything's so unfamiliar.

And then after another minute, he convinced himself of the great wisdom of finally rising and getting started with his regular morning routine.

Methodically, he pulled on his favorite old work breeches, the ones with the worn brass buckles, his checkered flannel shirt (the thick one that better kept out the damp), and ankle-high leather boots laced with twine. Lastly he made sure that the little black purse filled with protective magical herbs and tied tightly with its string was still in his satchel. Though mama kept crying out all the while to hurry, he took his time preparing himself, trying to work out what exactly had changed so much around him since only the night before.

Still bewildered, he sat himself to eat. A hole was busy gnawing away inside his empty stomach, and he set himself to filling it in preparation for the heavy work day he knew lay ahead.

The worn chestnut farm table was dark and shiny with years, decades, maybe a hundred years or so of polishing and use. It dominated the main room and this morning, as usual, was arrayed with a spread of fresh goat's cheese and honey, along with the heavy rye bread and the pitcher of warm goat's milk that his mother had put there earlier. He gripped the jug's massive handle and poured himself a glass, watching the curious way the creamy liquid swirled to the top and savoring the rich farm odor.

Normally he had to milk the goats himself, but this morning it had been his brother's job, along with preparing and lighting the fire. Fredo had woken at five o'clock to do all his chores, and tomorrow it would still be dark and cold outside when Paulo woke alone and set to tending the animals and preparing the many tasks for the day. This morning, he sighed gratefully, he could just rest.

Despite himself, Paulo took his time eating, chewing slowly the dark bread laden with chunks of the fresh white cheese. Staring deep into the heart of the glowing fire, he was lost in thought. That past night he had had a wonderful dream, an exceptional dream, its potent feeling still haunted his mind and confused his senses, and now he struggled to remember it. He had dreamed – he was quite sure – that he was leading another life somewhere else, as someone else, in some sort of remarkable and splendid, princely land. Now, waking this morning in the old farm cottage with his mother and brother in the harsh, unendingly gray world of the Domain, his life as Paulo, the market wood seller, felt odd, ill-fitting and … well, strangely dream-like.

Mama bellowed again from the kitchen: "Paulo – are you *still* day-dreaming, son? Now finish up, go along, and get to the woods. I want you back here before lunch!"

She stuck her head out of the kitchen doorway and interrogated the boy with a stern look. "And *don't go too far* – you hear me? I don't want you collecting wood too far from Towne now, *understand?*"

Paulo knew precisely what that meant; he rolled his eyes and shook his head slowly in disbelief. He dropped his bread back on the table, picked up the oil-cloth roll tied with a rope hanging on its hook by the fireplace, slung it over his shoulder, and then his mother pushed him toward the front door.

Once she had returned inside and slammed the door, the boy started off unhurriedly down through the garden, shoving and kicking untidy bushes and wet leaves out of his way as he went. He leaned against the wooden gate till it creaked open, and turned right onto the cobblestone path.

As was his custom every morning, Paulo took the road not in the direction that led towards Towne, whose pointed gable rooftops and jutting fortress towers he could just make out dark and grim against the rainy-gray western horizon; but instead he made his way eastwards to the line of tall distant trees gently swaying in the early morning glow. Toward the Forest.

The cobbled lane led first past the neighbor's vegetable fields with its neat and orderly rows of carrot, leak and radish. It then ran alongside a course of low thatched worker's cottages before reaching the end of the hamlet and finally disappearing into the depths of the Domain woods. And most importantly, as far as Paulo was concerned, into *quiet*.

Paulo was always glad to be out. The Forest had over time become a special place for the boy, a place where he had learned how to be alone, and free. There was nothing to be afraid of in the depths of those magical oak and chestnut groves, he felt, though really quite unlike most people. Everyone else seemed to be scared of something dangerous and unspoken out there, and never ventured far enough to discover its secrets.

Paulo was somehow different.

There were in fact places the boy went that other people would never even think of going: they were just too scared, though he wasn't at all. Even the ancient, unwritten laws of the sacred and all-powerful *Maker* didn't impress him much, and so his path would often take him as far as the very edges of the Forest, despite the many prohibitions the Town Hall had specifically passed. He would simply keep on walking past where everyone else stopped, and then they would just stare at him, and shake their heads solemnly in disbelief.

They would sometimes cry out (no doubt with all the best intentions in the world) as he passed them merrily by, "By the holy Maker, Paulo Vitali, you listen now! People disappear in those woods out there, and never come back! You're going to get yourself, and us, into some terrible trouble one day that way!" and many other ridiculous things, but he didn't really care. In his mind there wasn't much to be afraid of out there so close to the outer edges. So close to the Deathlands Beyonde, that unspeakably dangerous place just the other side of the deep woods.

If truth were told, he actually felt quite the opposite way about the Forest. Far away from Towne, lost and alone in the heart of the woods, he had found it to be gloriously quiet and peaceful. Moreover, he was able to do his wood collecting that much more easily simply because none of the other kindlin' sellers ever searched as far as him. *That* was certainly something to be grateful for.

Way at the extremity of the Forest, as far as one could possibly go and just short of the Beyonde, Paulo had discovered there was always abundant wood for harvesting, and he was always able to fill his sheet of oil-cloth quickly and neatly with as much kindlin' as he needed. Afterwards, he brought the wood to the market place and sold the bundles at his stall to the Townspeople to start their hearth-fires.

Maybe his customers didn't like where he went to find his wood – but they were certainly always glad to buy it from him.

You see, Paulo's kindlin' was particularly easy to sell. It was perpetually cold and damp in the Domain, and since it rained frequently, the Townspeople needed to light a fire in the hearth almost every day. And yet, strangely enough, the wood Paulo brought to market was always of the best and driest quality of which he was particularly proud. People sometimes wondered from which part of the Domain his tinder came, as exceptionally dry and fire-worthy as it was, but they were never truly in a great hurry to find out: they were simply too scared of the deep forest to really want to know where he got it.

Paulo had, in fact, a well-kept secret:

The wood was always the best and driest in the most forbidden places, near the far, extreme limits of the Domain. Why? It was actually quite simple: because that's where it rained the least! No one else could possibly know this, and no one else was ever likely to find out, since none of the other Townspeople ever went there, but the weather was always much sunnier and more pleasant at the far edges of the Domain nearby the exterior Fortress Wall than closer to the center of town.

Paulo didn't understand why, and he certainly lost no sleep trying to figure it out. He liked the far outer reaches of the Domain in the heart of the woods even if no one else thought it was safe or a good idea to go there. Despite what his mother told him daily about staying close to Towne, and despite what everyone told him about the inevitable Maker's wrath, he felt there was always a good reason to go to the far outer reaches.

And today, he was thinking, was certainly not going to be any exception.

CHAPTER THREE

Silver Sounds in the Forest

Another misty-gray morning was dawning slowly as the boy paced faster down the stone-laid path, and made his plans for the morning's wood harvest. A desire for discovery had lodged in his heart, and (despite his mother's warnings) Paulo was drawn today to the idea of going all the way to the outer defenses to find his kindlin' supplies.

Arriving at the forest's edge, he turned left as usual off the high road, onto the deeply rutted cart track that skirted the overgrown tree-line. But then, shortly after, he began a careful search amongst the brush and bracken and took no more notice of the old worn cart-way. There was in fact a thin trail, difficult to see by any but those who were really searching, and known only to very few people, that led to the right off the cart-way, and, quick as lightening, the boy parted the thorny bushes and plundered inward.

The narrow trail entered immediately into the thick forest, passing through dense stands of ancient box-wood and around thickets of impenetrable briar-hedge, before winding its way amongst the trunks of taller trees and over carpets of soft, damp leaves.

As the underbrush and bracken began to thin, his vision into the heart of the lush woods became clearer and clearer. He was aiming towards a patch of daylight he could see gleaming brightly somewhere in the distance between the tall shapes of trees, and he marched on doggedly.

With every further step he took, the weather slowly transformed, the dampness of the early forest giving way to crisper, drier leaves, the deep and solemn quiet disturbed only by their pleasant crackling noise as they crunched underfoot. Minutes later the skies strove to lighten and then finally parted above him, breaking up the strands of low cloud and streaming down a pale but bright and hope-bearing sunshine. Instantly the forest came alive before his eyes, dancing with hundreds of flashes of mottled browns and greens splaying around him on the leafy carpet. And the young wood seller wandered on, among the sun-speckled trees and under slanting shafts of yellow light and through trails of glowing mist, toward the far end of the Domain.

Even before the Fortress Wall was in view, Paulo could already find good wood on the ground around him; but he knew that just a little further all the perfectly dry kindlin' he could possibly want would be available within simple arm's reach. And so marching on, in a short while he found the sign he was looking for: a steady horizontal line that appeared faintly amongst the trunks of oak and beech in the distance, the signal that he was now approaching the Fortress Wall, the barrier delimiting the end of all the known Domain: the final and unchallenged protection the Towne maintained against the hidden dangers in the Deathlands.

And so it was here, just short of the Wall, just far enough to keep a respectable distance between himself and the ghostly barricade, that the wood seller finally set to his collecting. At first, he busied himself with his work, placidly ignoring the stony barrier that lay just at the edge of his vision, breaking and clumping all sorts of small branches into piles, tying each one with an individual string, then neatly placing the bundles one by one onto the oil-cloth. Just out of range, the Wall sat there calmly.

The wood he found here was really very good wood, able to light a fire without any real problem. Even better, exceptionally good wood did, in fact, exist, but it could only be found set tight up against the stone wall. It was just that Paulo often didn't have the courage to harvest right up alongside it. Something about the

Wall still made him feel uneasy and anxious in the back of his mind, despite the fact that he had never personally seen any particular reason to be afraid of it. Perhaps because of all the terrifying stories the Townspeople constantly whispered to themselves about it in the market place.

He looked at the ancient fortification now, and wondered.

There was a powerful, unbreakable barrier that ran for many, many miles, he knew, all the way around the extremity of the Domain. It was old beyond anyone possibly recalling its first construction, and separated the Towne from the nether-world beyond, though no one had ever explained to him exactly what the Wall was actually a defense against.

Once, before his father died, Paulo had ventured to ask him what kind of wild animals or evil foes lay on the other side. His father's face had instantly blanched and he had stood up, trembling, as if to strike the boy, but he had said nothing. His mother had then intervened and silenced him. "No one ever, *ever*, asks what's out there in the Deathlands of Beyonde," she had said tersely. "It's an extremely evil, *accursed* place," she had hissed at him, he remembered.

To the boy all this seemed more than a little bizarre, but everyone else appeared to think it was quite normal. He only knew that it felt good and free near the Wall, and that was all that really mattered to him. And, right now, he felt as happy and peaceful as he had ever been in the Domain.

Spotting a particularly interesting branch, he began breaking it up into several bundles, the noise of the sharply cracking wood interrupting for just an instant the chattering of some birds in a nearby tree. The day dawned glowingly around him, the sun tingeing the low distant clouds in a shiny warm pink, and he noticed the profound tranquility that filled his beloved forest at these magical times, working alone with no other thought than quietly accomplishing his tasks.

'How strange, being afraid of coming all the way out here,' he now thought to himself, sighing. He looked far around him, breathing deeply the crisp, fragrant air, and could only find the most wonderful peace and stillness.

'Just look at what everyone's missing… Why on earth don't I come out here more –'

Then he froze.

Something very peculiar was now happening around him. He had heard a noise, or had he? No, he was *sure* there had been a sound. There was definitely something or someone else out there in the Forest with him now… This had never happened before.

'*What's going on?*' he muttered under his breath, listening intently.

Something was indeed out there with him, something really strange, and he tensed. It was only a noise for the moment, he couldn't see any movement, just a sound really, but it was a distinct, penetrating sound.

The boy relaxed a little when he saw nothing immediate happening and after a moment dropped his defensiveness – it didn't appear threatening in any way, not for the moment. No, certainly not *threatening*. In fact the sound seemed if anything really quite gentle and pleasant after all, he thought, whatever it was.

"A lovely kind of song, that's what it's like," he said aloud to himself, drawn further into the mysterious melody. It seemed to float all around and somehow shimmer strangely about him in the misty cool air.

He looked around but found nothing that could be filling the woods with such beautiful singing. The trees were quiet, there was no breeze that morning, and the leaves were all still: it wasn't his forest that was chanting so prettily to him. So he turned himself from one direction to another to locate the source of the wonderful silvery music.

Over there to the right sat the forest, the tall silhouettes of trees sedate and silent in the rising morning. And over there on the left, just the massive bulk of the stone wall that hugged the horizon.

Paulo closed his eyes and pivoted slowly on the spot, turning around and breathing gently and rhythmically, listening. He frowned slightly. Something seemed so extremely familiar in the delicate, gilded tones that reached his ears, though he was at a loss for the moment to tell precisely what it might be. Like a misty echo, the song floated and whispered in his memory; a clear bell ringing softly now, coming seemingly from nowhere in particular. Then slowly, following the tendrils of sound reaching out to him, he turned toward its source, and found himself looking directly toward the gray-stone wall. He paced forward toward it, and listened.

'Yeah – *that's it.*'

It was quite obvious now, the silver-sound was indeed coming from the stone wall, or rather from the other side of it … from the *Beyonde*.

He covered the last few steps to the wall and held out his hands toward it. Hesitating an instant, he placed his hands lightly on its rough, pitted surface which was hard and cold under his fingers. He closed his eyes and quieted his breathing, and drew himself further inside to listen.

And there it was, the sound, clear as crisp, pure dawn-light. There was something so fascinatingly melodious and familiar in the wonderful noise. It seemed to remind him of something especially lovely, but something long-forgotten, or unremembered. For some while he stood there, contemplating the peaceful, tender intonations that filled his ears, and began to feel things move deeply inside him. Something in the notes was so profoundly reassuring, so calming, something that made him drift off now to a distant place, to another utterly *extraordinary* place –

The sun abruptly appeared from behind a cloud and shone powerfully upon his spot till he felt its heat intense on his back. The light built further in majesty and illuminated the gray stone

wall until it began to glow brilliant-white beneath his hands …
and his thoughts blazed outward.

The breath caught suddenly in his lungs.

In just a second, an instant of time, an image flashed through
Paulo's mind, of a magical, astonishing place of sunshine and
happiness. Streams of crystal-clear water flowed through fields of
brilliant wild flowers all swaying gaily in a warm summer breeze.
A rainbow sky of pink, violet and azure-blue arched overhead, its
luminous, serene radiance reflected in the contented faces of all the
people he found there. Joyful faces, laughing and smiling, beamed
as he passed to and fro now, running from one merry greeting to
another. Brothers and sisters they were, of one magnificent family,
all exchanging gifts and presents that went on and on forever. It
was a world of plenty and peace, and one of an exceptional feeling
of all-embracing Love.

"That's where I wanna be," he said hoarsely, just above a
whisper. "That's where I've got to get to." The intense desire took
him by surprise. It just came by itself: it felt like the most natural
thing.

He woke from the image, shaken, and presently became aware
of a subtle but distinct change in the notes of the ever-present
song. He lowered his eyes toward the ground, trying to decipher
the new sounds that were becoming more precise, sharper and
more specific. And in moments he was sure he could make out
what appeared to be individual words within the melody.

The Silver-Song continued, but he was convinced that
embedded within it there was something, or someone, trying to
give him a message. He listened: it wasn't a mistake, there were
words, and they seemed to be calling him. Entreating him. Then it
became clear after a moment that what they were pronouncing
was *his name*.

"*Paulo…*" a calm, mysterious voice resounded now gently. The
words were calling him, inviting him towards something, and yet
strangely it all felt completely familiar. After a moment of
listening, the specific nature of the message became clearer: "*The*

Door," the voice entreated him firmly, "…you must find your way to *the Great Door*."

Paulo's eyes opened wide with astonishment, although the mystical voice remained kind and reassuring throughout.

"Paulo, *you must go to the Great Door*," he heard once more. The young boy's heart filled with peace, as if he had heard something extremely hopeful, though it wasn't clear at all what specific door or place the beautiful voice might be referring to.

For some moments longer the sun shone brightly on the wall, then slowly faded.

"*Go to the Door…*" he heard the voice say faintly once more before finally disappearing.

Paulo removed his hands from the stone wall, now cold and dull once more, raised his head and looked thoroughly around him at the forest. No, there was no one who might have been playing tricks on him – there *had* been an extraordinary presence out there somewhere. He *hadn't* imagined it all.

The feeling of peaceful wonder and profound hopefulness remained with him as he tied up the wood bundles in the oil-cloth and began to prepare himself for the morning's market. The words of the sedate, gentle voice echoing all the while in his mind as he worked.

'The *Great Door*,' he pronounced slowly to himself. 'What could that possibly be, and *where*? I bet I can find out something about it in the market place.'

And so, hefting the wood load on to his shoulders, he wound his way back along the secret trail, through the forest, and toward the town, speaking to himself as he went:

'How incredible! Just think of it, some kind of a magical door! But why on earth would there be a special door, and where could it lead to? Through the Wall maybe, out to the Deathlands? How spooky! Why else would the voice be coming from the other side? Yes, that *must* be it – a door to go out there into no-man's land! But could it be possible? Think of the unbelievable adventure!'

'No – *danger!* That's what you mean, Paulo!' Several dark and bleak thoughts erupted from out of nowhere in a corner of his mind. 'Not adventure but *danger.* Listen to me now, there can be nothing good in this – only evil. Just think of the immense *danger*, Paulo!"

He heard the words whispering somewhere in the back of his mind, but he was altogether too excited and too intent on uncovering the mystery of the magical portal to pay much attention. He continued to lug the wood wrapped in its oil-cloth along the high road, through the sprinkling rain starting to fall, and then up the wide stone steps that led from the river directly into the busy town square.

Market day was just unfolding, and Paulo positioned himself quickly in his regular place next to the fish stall.

Chapter Four

A Dark and Evil Place

Paulo gazed around at the bustling scene before his eyes, at the hundreds of Townspeople going about their morning shopping routine throughout the market place. The square seemed to be particularly lively that day: stallholders everywhere were peddling all manner of colorful articles and produce. People of all shapes and sizes, nature and character, many carrying baskets full of vegetables and other goods, were wandering from stall to stall or chatting politely with the soldiers scattered here and there amongst the throng.

Paulo's eye was caught suddenly by two hands raised in the air on the other side of the square. They started to wave back and forth in his direction, and Paulo stuck his hand up and waved back in a sweeping gesture of "hello". Antonio, about Paulo's age but a little taller, nodded and smiled from behind his stall then turned his attention back to serving a customer. Francesca, Antonio's younger sister, handed him a small wood crate containing two chickens which he then gave to the shopper. She turned, flashed a grin and mouthed *hello* in Paulo's direction, then returned to serve the many customers lining up.

Paulo heaved a breath.

Their stand is always so successful, he whistled out loud to himself, shaking his head slightly; but for Paulo the reason was only too obvious. It was clearly because Francesca happened to be the friendliest, and the prettiest, girl by far in the entire village. He found her sparkling blue eyes quite the loveliest thing he'd ever seen, much lovelier even (he was willing to admit) than the sunrise in his forest on a clear day. It had often occurred to him that working on the farm with Francesca and selling chickens by her side would be so much better than being alone and selling wood. But for the most part he tried to content himself with just collecting and selling his kindlin' to his customers.

"Here you are, ma'am," Paulo said and placed a bundle of tinder in a shopper's basket.

Paulo wore a friendly smile for everyone, for those who bought wood from him, and even for those who just passed by. He was fond of people on the whole and he tried sincerely to be nice, but he found it wasn't always so easy to please them. There were some people whom he found nearly impossible to appreciate: the Mayor, for instance, who was typically so unscrupulous with the market people and often drove Paulo quite crazy. Then there were some people who were just unhappy and unpleasant all the time, no matter what, and there was just nothing you could do about them. He tried to smile at them, regardless.

Some people made an effort to smile back at him but most of the faces he looked into every day seemed mostly unhappy, and worried. It was especially confusing for the boy because mama had always told him that they should be happy and grateful for everything the Maker had given them. Most of these people actually looked quite miserable on the whole, he found.

During a moment of quiet, Paulo dug he hand into his satchel and found his beloved pouch filled with magical herbs. He always did this when he wanted to do some serious thinking.

My customers…

They came essentially to buy his wood, but then some would also often stop at his stall for a few minutes to chat. Occasionally this could be pleasant, a nice break in the day; but most often people just used their time with him to complain about some difficulty or problem in their lives, and that could really annoy him. It seemed that there was always some type of situation or another that was making them miserable.

Mr Salvatori, for example, a solitary and strange old gentleman from a nearby village, would stop by and his first words would *inevitably* be, "It's awfully damp, don't you think, Paulo? And, you know, I'm really not feeling so well today." Not that Paulo could do anything about either of his problems, but the old man thought it necessary to tell him about them every day nonetheless.

Later in the day Mrs Belladonna would no doubt come by and exclaim, like always: "That shoemaker (or any other shopkeeper, for that matter), I'm sure he takes more than he should. A real thief, he is!" And then she would tell him, *again*, about her lazy daughter, Maria, who did nothing but sit at home, eat sweet pastries, and make her life impossible.

Paulo didn't really care much about her daughter, or the shoemaker. He had his own problems to deal with, like keeping his wood piled neatly under the oil-cloth so it didn't become wet, and making sure his customers didn't make a quick-footed purchase and leave without paying.

Mr Bravuro, dressed in his fancy fur-trim coat, would probably rush over some time later in the morning in a hurry as always and declare, "I don't have much time, dear boy, please hurry. My wife is waiting." Apparently his wife always thought he was spending too much time, and money, at the market. "Come, come, how much will that be then today? Do come along, lad, be quick now."

All sorts of crazy problems…

He would try to smile with his customers, though often he thought people were actually pretty stupid for having so many difficulties; and he wondered how it was that everyone was supposed to be so happy, and really no one was at all.

When Mr Bravuro hurried by to pick up his bundle of kindlin' he took a risk and asked:

"Sir, I've heard there's a special door in the Domain. Is it true? Do you know if there's a place they call 'the Great Door'?"

The gentleman nearly dropped the coins he was counting in his hand and a dark pall fell on his face like a heavy curtain. "What…?

You have no business asking about such things, Paulo Vitali! Where on earth did you–" he cut himself off.

Paulo was taken aback by the gentleman's tone and stared back at him.

Mr Bravuro sought to control himself. "My boy, let me rather say that the Door is really no place for you to go." Then he said sadly, pleadingly, "Paulo, there is no Door anyway … not anymore. Not since…" he said without finishing his thought.

"– It is a very dark and evil place now. Please, leave it alone. *Just leave it alone!*" he whispered, strained, so as not to be overheard. He turned and left abruptly, scurrying away even faster than he had come.

When the gentleman had left, Paulo exhaled loudly and wiped his brow, thoroughly confused.

He couldn't imagine what might be behind his customer's odd behavior. His anxious words echoed insistently around the boy's mind as he stood behind his wood stall and served the following shoppers. '*A dark and evil place*…Where could that be now? In any case, wouldn't it be better to stay away, if it's really dangerous like he says?'

He thought more about the problem. 'Am I going to pay attention to what he says anyway? That's what I'm supposed to do. But then I'd never find out the truth. I'm sure it's okay to want to know the truth; that can't be so bad. No, that can't be bad. So, okay, where could there be a dark, evil place here in Towne that I haven't yet seen?' he asked himself.

And in thinking about all the places he had ever explored in the old town, and those he had never dared, he immediately knew where it had to be…

Once market was over the boy set off, and stole secretly to the other side of town, past the Town Hall and then into the former merchant's district. A large faded sign painted on some timber boards had been fixed to a rusty iron lamp-post. It read in large blood-red letters: "Off Limits". There, through an opening between two tall, narrow half-timbered buildings Paulo entered into what he knew was an abandoned, forbidden quarter where he had never seen anyone go, or anyone come from.

'If there's a secret door somewhere, this *has* gotta be where it's located,' he considered. It was the only area of the village that everyone seemed to avoid particularly and that no one ever spoke about at all.

The narrow cobbled street, already dim because of the tall, looming houses on both sides, became gloomier and more dismal the further he marched. The young wood seller glanced upwards on both sides of him, then back over his shoulder, and thought of turning back to safety and returning to the familiar surroundings of the market place, but forced himself to continue. There was no doubt he was trespassing into a very ominous place, one which must have struck true terror into the townsfolk at one time: every house that lined the narrow street had been abandoned already long ago, doors were thrown open and battered flower boxes lined the filthy sills of every empty window.

Paulo walked the entire length of the street, carefully avoiding looking directly into the eerie, cavernous windows of the houses he passed. Nothing moved there, which seemed even more disturbing. Instead he kept his eyes riveted in front of him, and after a few more paces he observed at the end of the row of houses the street widening into what seemed to be a square. Some distance still before the end, he found a door recess which provided some shelter which he slipped into, then stole a look around the corner.

From this vantage point, looking into the far side of the square, he could distinctly make out a group of guards. Many guards were there, more soldiers in fact than he'd ever seen in one place in his entire life. A whole squadron, perhaps. All of them, it appeared, seemed to be seated upright in tall, straight-backed wooden chairs, which was certainly very strange. They were big men in heavy metal armor and leather cladding, and the boy could see glinting in the dim light an array of polished swords, spears and other sharp weapons that lay poised and ready on the ground at their feet.

Paulo whistled softly through his teeth. *"What on earth are all these guards doing here?"* He was far more scared than he was willing to admit at that moment, and very confused.

He had often seen soldiers before in the market place, but never so many as this. He had no special fondness for the Domain guards since their principal job seemed to lie in constantly reminding him to conform and behave correctly, and to remember to be grateful for all the Maker had given him, which wasn't a great deal as far as he could see. The guards made everyone feel as if they had done something terribly wrong, and made a habit of telling the villagers they would have to do even better if they wanted to be found worthy by the Maker.

Paulo had never had a problem with them in the past, and now he looked at them warily. *"This must be an exceptionally important place indeed,"* he murmured to himself.

He peered out from the doorway again. The soldiers, he saw, were sitting with their heads bent peculiarly to the side, resting on their shoulders in a most unguard-like fashion.

That's odd… Hey, I think they're actually sleeping!

He reflected a minute, then a broad grin spread slowly across his face. *This is great! The Great Door must be behind them … if they're asleep then they won't see me – simple as that!*

Before stepping into the open, Paulo found the magical herb pouch in his satchel and gripped it tightly for reassurance. He hesitated. Powerful, persuasive words broke through into his thoughts:

"Stop – Paulo! Don't you think you'd be much safer if you left this place at once? Look at the guards, look at how big and mean they must be … why, they could squash you in an instant if they wanted. And mama is waiting for you and you don't want to be late – you know how angry she gets when you're late … She wouldn't want to know you've been around here, *that's* for sure. Yes, you'd be much better off getting out of here right now!"

He carefully put the herb purse back in his satchel and his eyes returned to the place behind the guards. He studied the pros and cons of the situation: 'That's where the mysterious Great Door has to be, the door to some kind of incredible danger. But that's also the passage that might just lead me out of here, into a new land, away from this miserable place to something else. To something *new. That's* the path to peace and freedom,' he reflected; 'I just *know* it.'

Still, he cogitated, there was real reason to doubt the wisdom of his plan. After all, what would people say if they ever found him there? *They'd die of fright and probably lock me up right away.*

Then after a moment of further doubt he sighed inwardly: '*Freedom*'. The word seemed to come softly into his mind. '*That's* my goal.'

It seemed for just a moment that the gentle, silver-gilded voice from beyond the Wall accompanied him. And so, despite his fear and doubt, Paulo made the big decision and stepped out from his recess in the doorway and went closer to judge his chances.

He took several hesitant paces forward, then a few more.

The door must still be ahead a little further, not too far really, he reassured himself, though in the back of his mind he now felt a growing fear that he would never be able to make it that far. There was still no movement among the guards; they continued snoring quietly, their heads rising and falling on their shoulders in time with their breathing. *Only a little further,* he persuaded himself, and took another step.

"My, these soldiers are *unbelievably* big!" he heard a stunned voice inside him say unexpectedly.

"Look at this one in front, he's got to be the Chief Guard ... he's as big as a mountain!" He halted a moment, then began again his slow, cautious advance into the square.

The next instant a truly terrifying thought invaded his mind: "What if mama ever found out I was here – she'd be absolutely *furious!*" He drew a sharp breath, and suddenly his eye was caught by a movement amongst the soldiers.

The Chief Guard had unexplainably trembled from head to foot, shaking himself in his sleep, and was grunting loudly. His great head dropped forward over his chest, the iron visor of his helmet was tilting downwards from its open position until it finally fell and smacked closed – *SNAP!*

The narrow courtyard was instantly filled with the loud clanging noise of metal on metal. At this point Paulo stood just twenty paces from the guard's post.

'No!' Paulo shrieked inside, 'If he wakes and finds me here, I've had it!'

The Chief Guard, still half-asleep, lifted a leather-gloved fist and pushed up his visor, returning it to its upright position. He opened his eyes and peered through narrow slits.

Paulo froze, utterly immobile.

The Guard opened his eyes wider and sniffed the air – *something wasn't right*. He straightened up in his seat and strained his meaty neck to stare about him into the gloomy courtyard.

Paulo dared not breathe, trying to remain invisible, hoping his desperately beating heart wouldn't give him away.

The guard, unsatisfied, dislodged his massive frame from the chair and now raised himself to his full, towering height. His armor clanked as it shook, and his face came to morbid, eerie life under the open helmet, showing deep red battle scars along both cheeks.

Paulo's skin went damp with a cold sweat.

The soldier's head moved slowly from side to side, scanning all corners of the courtyard, and then to Paulo's horror his eyes focused directly before him and found the boy standing perfectly still like a marble statue in the middle of the square. His sight narrowed to a vicious, evil glare, and Paulo felt a piercing cold shiver flow instantly down his spine; his legs became stone and locked in place, uncontrollable – and stuck.

Paulo gaped open-mouthed at the guard as he stood there incapable of moving; the soldier glowered malevolently back at him. Then the guard contorted his face into a hideous grimace which made his scars puff and gorge with blood. He opened his mouth as if to bellow and displayed to the boy a mouthful of putrid, rotting teeth: yet still Paulo couldn't budge. The giant soldier then jerked a sudden motion forward as if to begin his attack – that finally unlocked Paulo's legs and he set them into motion at great speed.

Paulo sprinted back into the door recess where he waited just an instant to calm the severe trembling in his limbs. From there he made a wild dash back through the alley, and scampered as fast as he could through the town.

He then ran without stopping down to the river, across the bridge and all the way to his home at the edge of the woods.

CHAPTER FIVE

A Well-Defended Secret

Later that evening, and just before dinner, Paulo asked his mother the one question that still burned in his mind. He breathed deeply and summoned all his courage: "Mama, what's the place they call 'the Great Door'?"

She froze in her preparations and swept her face around to meet his, her eyes glowing fiercely like two hot coals. *What other trouble is he going to get me into now?*

"How many times do I have to tell you to stop asking absurd questions like that, Paulo?" she growled at him. "Who told you about it, anyway? It's not your time." She bored him through with a steely look. "Let me tell you now once and for all, the Door is none of your business, and you have no reason going over there, either. You stay away from there … d'you hear me, boy?"

Meanwhile Fredo looked timidly out from behind the kitchen door.

She glared at Paulo suspiciously. "You haven't been spending time on the outer fringes of the Domain, again, have you? I've *told* you not to go too far from town. Strange things happen out there … it's not good for you."

"No, mama," he said, lying, "I promise I haven't been too far."

He didn't want to frighten his mother. It seemed to Paulo there were some things that were a serious problem for his mother, that scared her a great deal. And he understood she was scared for him, too, even though he wasn't afraid at all.

The three of them ate in silence, and no more was said about the secret Door.

Paulo glanced cautiously at his mother while he ate his soup, and he knew she was wondering about him again. Paulo knew that people thought he was a strange and rebellious child, simply because he liked to do what no other children liked to do. He didn't mind playing with the other boys and girls in the village, but that's not really what interested him the most. He liked to be by himself often and explore the woods, and that wasn't normal for a child of his age. But Paulo was a good boy, and on the whole well-natured, so his mother didn't make a fuss about his peculiar behavior.

That hadn't always been the case.

He had been a lot of trouble before, after his father had died, and his mother often had to get angry to control him; and in many other ways it had been very difficult for her. But then just the previous year there had been a sudden and real change in his behavior, and Paulo had begun to fight less. All had been well since. In fact, things had been substantially better ever since he had started to do well at the market. He managed better with his customers, and they were pleased with the wood he found, so there was little to complain about on the whole.

After dinner, Paulo was cleaning the kitchen with his brother, and was still too curious. "Fredo, please, why don't you tell me what this special place is, this 'Great Door' that no one speaks about? I'm sure you know."

"*Shh!*"

Fredo looked around anxiously. He closed the kitchen door silently. "Do you think mama wants to know you're still asking questions like that? She'd be incredibly angry, you know!"

"Yes, but I'm just curious, that's all. I just want to know what's the big secret about this scary place."

Fredo put down the wooden platters in his hand and checked again to see if his mother could be listening. "You really don't know yet what the Great Door is – no one's told you?" He could see from Paulo's face that he truly didn't.

"OK, I'll tell you; but then you have to promise me you'll stop asking your stupid questions, alright?" Paulo nodded in agreement.

"The Door you're talking about is an *unbelievably* evil place. It's … it's the secret passage we all passed through when we escaped into the Domain from the Kingdom of Death – that's what it is."

He saw Paulo straining to catch his every word, which delighted him no end, and so he ventured to share more of the story, although his brother wasn't yet officially of age.

Fredo continued, "You remember what Papa told us before he died about the Dark Lord? You remember the story he told us about how we were imprisoned in his wicked land, but then found a way to escape? And then the Dark Lord discovered that we'd outsmarted him and he'd become incredibly angry at us? We'd finally managed to escape after so many years of his tyranny alright, but then the problem was that we'd nowhere to go to.

"Well, listen now; I shouldn't be telling you this, but here's the rest of the story: There we were, all alone, and we were in a desperate fix; and that's just when the blessed Maker suddenly appeared and promised he could save all of us. Well, weren't we ever happy! So he made the Domain for us, a safe and secure place where we could live forever after; and he offered a safe and special life to each and every one of us who followed him within. He brought us all the way on the road from the Dark Lord's Kingdom up to the protective Wall he'd built, and he invited us to enter through the Great Door, the place that's hidden on the other side of the Town Hall –"

Paulo interrupted. "But that doesn't explain why everyone's so afraid. Why're there all those guards? Why's it so well defended?"

"I'll tell you – just listen! After we entered, the Maker saw that the Dark Lord had become crazy angry, and jealous, too, that we'd found a safe place to hide and live. The Maker, who's ever so smart and cares for us so much, he knew that the evil Lord would try by every means to come after us to kill us. So he closed the door and then barred and blocked it so solidly that he could never come through to get us. Then he had to make sure no one would ever put themselves or anyone else in danger by trying to get out, and so he placed all the sentry guards in front of it: that way our lives would be safe forever."

Paulo listened, wide-eyed and thoroughly fascinated. "Oh, so that's the reason no one ever talks about the entrance anymore, because they think there's no door since it's been blocked up for such a long time, is that it?"

"That's right," replied Fredo. "No one talks about the Door anymore because it's the passage to *certain death,* and has been blocked up anyway so no one need ever talk about it. Just imagine, the Dark Lord is just on the other side, waiting to get through with hordes and hordes of wild beasts and demons and dragons to invade the Towne, and kill every living soul..." Fredo was glaring hard at Paulo, his eyes wide with fear, and his muscles taught. "But now I've already told you more than is wise for you, and for me, too. So finish up your work and get to bed, and just forget that I ever told you any of this. Mama would be very angry if she ever found out; she just *hates* to hear talk about these things."

"But Fredo, do you really believe all this?" Paulo asked pensively. "I think it's actually all quite strange. Do you really believe it's the gateway to certain death? That sounds just too bizarre to me. Fredo, are *you* scared ... are you really scared of the Dark Lord?" Paulo wanted to think that his brother was braver than that.

"Of course I'm scared – and you should be, too! Now that's enough; you've got to stop bothering me with your dumb questions and finish the dishes!"

Later Paulo went to bed but he couldn't sleep. He lay on his straw mattress for a long time wondering about all these remarkable mysteries: a door into the Deathlands Beyonde, back into the land of the Dark Lord, a place of great danger, filled with dragons and strange beasts ... but a place that no one had seen again for many, many years, ever since they had arrived ... and a door that no one ever spoke about anymore, pretending it didn't even exist!

But then why's there that gentle singing sound, the Silver Voice, calling from the other side of the Wall telling me to go to the Door? I mean, what reason could there be to go to a door that's shut tight anyway? And why would a nice voice like that be telling me to go to a place that's so deathly dangerous? There's *got* to be something else going on behind all this, but *what?*

He eventually fell fast asleep wondering about all these remarkable riddles.

The next day as usual Paulo was at the market place, selling his wood and quietly observing the people around him.

'They really don't look very happy,' he noted to himself, not for the first time, watching the shoppers who came and went at the stalls.

'No, they really don't look very happy, *at all*. But why, if all the townspeople have everything they want and they feel safe and good here, like they all say? After all, that's why the Maker made the Domain – isn't it? – to escape the Dark Lord and to live happily and safely forever after. But no one here looks happy *or* safe.' When he looked closely and honestly at the faces passing in front of him, he thought, in fact, they looked definitely unsatisfied and quite stressed.

It was toward the end of the market that Francesca strolled by helping a customer with her packages. She passed not a few feet from his stall, and Paulo couldn't help himself. He turned, and not knowing quite what to do, just grinned foolishly at her. She looked away immediately, but then an instant later glanced back at him; there was the beginning of an uncomfortable moment as the two looked at each other, and then she smiled and continued walking.

Well, maybe one day… Paulo mumbled to himself.

After market, Paulo was preparing to take the path home to the cottage on the edge of the woods, then angled slightly in the other direction, toward the Town Hall. "What if…?"

He hesitated. "Maybe just one more peek at the Door … before going home to do my chores. That couldn't ever hurt anyone – could it?"

The cobbled streets became dark and dismal again as he passed behind the Town Hall and into the forbidden quarter, and then even gloomier as he made his way down the narrow passage, until he found again his place in the doorway recess. The guards' heads lolled bizarrely on their shoulders just like yesterday, and he heard a faint snoring sound.

'Ah, I've caught them napping again: what great luck! I'm sure they won't see me today if I approach more quietly and confidently, he said to himself. They really don't look so bad when they're sleeping; and anyway, what harm can one little boy do?'

He straightened himself, gathered his courage, and quietly and determinedly stepped out of his hiding place and began to march towards the guards, trying all the while to focus on a view of the door.

The distance between himself and the guards became shorter and shorter, and the place behind the squadron from where he figured he would be able to get a view of the door came closer. Another step, then another. "Confidently now, Paulo," he said to himself. "Keep your head." And the guards remained perfectly asleep.

He marched further on, more reassured now, and found the one thought he most needed: *Freedom*. He let the word drift through his mind, and he breathed more relaxed.

'Just a few more steps…'

But then as he came upon the guards, the armor-clad soldiers suddenly loomed much bigger in his sight than he expected. In fact, they were much larger and more imposing than he could have ever imagined when seen up close, and could no doubt seriously hurt someone if they wanted to. Especially someone small, like him.

"Aren't they *incredibly* dangerous-looking from here!" The thought just escaped from his mind without conscious control.

And thus it was that, preoccupied by the guards, Paulo failed to look down where he was walking at the moment when it was so terribly crucial: the large round pebble lay in front of him just as if waiting for him to come by; and before he could react his boot had made hard contact with the smooth stone which sent it slithering rapidly and noisily across the rain-slick cobbles – directly toward the group of sleeping guards.

'*No!*'

The boy stopped short and the breath froze in his lungs; but it was too late.

The pebble continued sliding blithely on its pre-destined path, and then with a dull "whack!" struck the foot of the Chief Guard's wooden chair.

An instantaneous clanking and grinding of metal armor filled the air, and the giant soldier jerked himself to his feet, towering over the boy. The guard instinctively opened his mouth wide as if to roar, and Paulo could see deep down inside the rotting gullet, and he bellowed a monstrous, fetid cry – "*WHO GOES THERE?!*"

Poor Paulo was terrified and before his stupefied eyes the other guards woke one by one and rattled themselves alive. They jumped immediately into battle stance and drew their long steel swords, and raised their square shields before their face-guards. Then, spotting their target, they marched as one on the petrified boy.

Paulo, however, had decided to take matters into his own hands. He didn't freeze, he didn't flinch, but found the strength and courage to move. And he ran. He ran as fast and hard as his worthy young legs would carry him … but *toward the Door*.

He knew the door was just there, just the other side of the guards, and he wasn't about to let anyone stop him now from seeing it; not as he had come this far. He might never come so close again, and since he wanted so badly to know the truth he was willing to risk a lot of trouble and maybe even his life, because then he would know. He would know!

Three enormous guards sprang in front of him, shouting and gesticulating wildly, swishing their swords and spears back and forth, but Paulo was too determined to be diverted. He dodged around them and ducked under their spears and kept running, setting the guards in a mad chase after him.

Now he could look forward and began to see, yes, almost see… He pushed further, pursued by the horde of furious guards.

He could now begin to see what looked like a passage, an opening, in the Wall. Yes, he could make out what had to be a door, some type of archway, it looked like. But there appeared to be something peculiar, something strange in what he beheld. Something odd, he saw before him now. And something entirely, extremely, *wrong…*

"But it's not *at all* like they said."

He stopped dead before the great archway, unable for a moment to find any words or to comprehend what he was really seeing. Then he gasped, "I can't believe it – it's open! Just look at that door, it's not closed at all… Holy Maker, *it's open!* The Great Door is actually – *OPEN!*"

He could plainly see the passage they called the Great Door, a magnificent huge stone archway, very wide and tall, with enormous heavy wooden gates hanging from massive iron hinges, and something glowing mysteriously at the top. But the gates were open, not closed at all. He stared through the gates, and there outside he saw *sunshine*. In fact it was a bright and magnificent day out there in the Beyonde – it looked even sunnier and brighter than in his forest.

"*Ow!*" He winced painfully as a guard aimed a hard cuff at his ear.

"You've no idea what you're talking about, boy!" sneered the Chief Guard. "The Door's been closed and blocked for years – we should know, we're the elite Guardians of the Passage to the

Deathlands. The Door is closed and barred to protect the villagers from the packs of giant killer wolves and the rampaging hordes of the Dark Lord's servants spawned out there in the Beyonde… you should've been taught all this. Now you'll be taken back to your parents and, believe me, you're going to pay dearly for this foolishness."

Paulo was utterly confounded; he couldn't understand what on earth was going on.

The guards threatened him and frightened him, but they didn't hurt him further. He was still in awe and wasn't even bothered when the guards pushed him away from the Door and back along the dim cobbled alleyway. He only saw adventure and freedom, and no longer even paid attention to the fact that he had been caught at an extremely forbidden place.

One of the guards accompanied him all the way back home.

"Mrs Vitali, this won't do at all!" the guard told his mother when she answered the door. She looked down confused at Paulo who stared back sheepishly at her from underneath the guard's gauntlet. "What have you done this time?" she demanded angrily in a tight voice.

"He has been exceptionally ill-behaved, disturbing the Domain's defenses against the Dark Lord at the Great Door," declared the soldier loudly, enough for the entire neighborhood to hear. "What kind of attitude have you instilled in him? He has no respect for what's good for him, and no fear of the dark powers that can destroy us all. This is a serious warning, you will have to do something about this boy, or there will be real trouble next time."

His mother pulled Paulo into the doorway and gripped him hard by the arm. She kept her eyes low, and replied, "Believe me, kind sir, there will be no next time. I'll make quite sure of it."

"We will hold you to your word, madam."

And with that the giant guard turned and left, the eyes of the neighbors peering out from behind shutters and curtains as he clanked past them on the cobbled path back toward Towne.

She closed the cottage door and faced the boy, shaking her head. "You'll be the death of me yet, I know it."

Paulo feared the worst and felt angry. She didn't even ask him for an explanation. She should know about the door and everything. The guard wasn't right at all. But it didn't seem like the right time to tell her about it.

His mother's face then turned red with fury and she turned him around and hit him hard several times. She told him that it was absolutely unacceptable to return anywhere near the Door, or he would be prohibited from ever staying in Towne after market.

That night Paulo lay in bed without any supper, feeling the emptiness of his stomach and the pain of his sore behind. But these things didn't matter at all:

I've seen the Door! No one else has seen it. No one even speaks of it anymore. And what's more amazing – the door back to the Kingdom, where we all once came from – it's *open*.

"Fredo, Fredo, you awake? I've got something to tell you, something extremely important. Some great news"

"Go to sleep! You'll get me into a lot of trouble as well. Please, don't bother me, and do go to sleep!"

"But, Fredo, it's *really* important. The guard's right, I was at the Great Door today. And you know what, I actually saw it, I really did. But you'll never believe me. You know that everyone swears it's shut tight, well it's actually open. It's *open*! It's not closed like everyone says."

"Oh, no, that's *terrible* news. How can that possibly be good news? That means the Dark Lord can come anytime and kill us all. Oh, that's frightful, dreadful news. Now I won't be able to sleep at all. No, you must be wrong, it can't be true. You're right, I don't believe you. Not at all."

Fredo grabbed his satchel from under his cot and found his purse of protective magical herbs and immediately felt comforted. "No, the Maker *promised* that the entrance was closed and blocked, so we *must* be safe. I know the Dark Lord can never come through and get us here."

"Fredo, I *have* seen the Door, and it *is* open," Paulo repeated firmly. "But what's more amazing still, and this is perhaps stranger than all – on the other side, outside the Door, it looks beautiful. It looks truly fantastic! I saw sunshine and flowers and trees, wonderful trees and flowers and fields, as far as your eye can see. It wasn't horrible and deathly at all, like everyone says!"

"Please, Paulo, I beg you to stop." Poor Fredo couldn't put up with this anymore. "You'll get me into so much trouble. And I have so many other things to worry about already. Please, stop talking such nonsense and go to sleep." Fredo pulled his pillow over his head and started counting out loud to himself: "One, two, three…"

"Fredo, why're you so scared? Stop talking to yourself like that. Oh, you're such a scaredy cat. Why can't you just be a little brave for once?"

"Nine, ten, eleven, twelve,…" Fredo's muffled counting droned from under the pillow.

"Fredo?"

Paulo just lay in bed but he wasn't disappointed. He was still too excited: it was *open*! Everyone was so wrong – who would have thought it? There was indeed an outside world, and one that looked truly exceptional, not evil or frightening at all. How could they be afraid of a place that looked so lovely? What could possibly be so wrong with it? I mean, all that sunshine couldn't be bad. And why was everyone acting so strangely?

Anyway, what's most important, he thought, there really was something else, something other than the perpetual dimness of the Domain.

If only I could get another look at it – but *how*?

Chapter Six

The Boulder's Attack

The next morning Paulo strode quickly into the deep Forest, his feet moving in step with a powerful new resolution in his mind. The collecting, piling and tying of his wood into the necessary bundles was done in record time, so he could then get down to the real work of the morning – a thorough inspection of the Domain Wall.

Long stretches of its length unrolled as he paced alongside it, and now that he took the time for a careful study, he noticed with surprise that there were, in fact, big cracks in its structure here and there that had somehow never been quite so obvious before. At one point, a part of the wall was completely split from top to bottom where a big crack had developed, and where some large stones had already been dislodged and lay scattered on the ground.

He looked at this spot carefully.

"If I'm ever gonna see the outside, if I'm ever to know the truth about what's going on, to find out everyone's big secret, then I'll just have to make my own passage through the Wall. And this looks like it'd probably be the best place to do it – This'll have to do."

He thought for an instant just how incredibly scared and furious the Townspeople would be if they ever found out exactly what he was up to – making a hole in the Domain's sacred defenses – and then got down to work. The loosest stones he could pull out with his bare hands without too much trouble, pulling them out of the dusty, crumbling masonry. They came out without too much difficulty which was all the more amazing, he thought, since the wall had always appeared so tremendously heavy and solid to him in the past.

Paulo pushed and pulled the more difficult stones, sweating profusely and covering himself in dust, and becoming increasingly excited at the prospect of breaking through to the far side, to the fabulous sunlight he knew was shining just beyond. Many stones now lay on the ground around him and the split was already much larger than when he had begun. After a while he sat back on the grass to rest a moment. Looking up at his work, he noticed traces of an intense blue sky already visible in the distance beyond the wall and the split he was making.

"I've just *got* to see what's on the other side of this stupid thing!" he shouted to the woods, setting back to work.

And so stones were torn out of the wall in great numbers, some of the larger ones hitting the soft earth with a heavy and resounding 'thud'; and soon the ground was strewn with rocky debris such that anyone passing by would have had no doubt at all that someone in the vicinity, in an act of spectacular confusion, or insane treason, was definitely planning to break down the Towne's defensive Wall against the Deathlands, or to escape from the Domain, depending on how he looked at it, of course.

Paulo stood back again to survey his progress: that morning had allowed him to make a decent start, but the job would have to be continued tomorrow, he concluded, because now it was really time to go to market.

That night he could hardly sleep at all – he was just too worked up. Tomorrow he would cross the Fortress Wall and discover the other side, *the unseen Kingdom!* He would finally put an end to all the secrets and his questions. And maybe he would even find out where the Silver Voice was coming from and why it had been calling him.

"Fredo, listen! I tell you something, tomorrow I'm going to visit the other side! You know – *Outside*!"

Even in the dim evening light it seemed that Fredo blanched. "No, Paulo, please don't tell me such dreadful things. I don't want to know anything about what you're doing. Here we are safe at home in the Domain, and you want to ruin all that. I swear you're going to get us all killed!"

Paulo raised his eyebrows in disbelief and pulled up the covers, thoroughly ignoring his brother's whining. This was simply all too remarkable; there were just so many exciting things happening, and he went through a long list of all the things he had discovered recently as he lay in bed and began dozing. A warm drowsiness enveloped him as his thoughts turned to far away enchanted lands and magical songs and wild beasts and mysterious portals and … suddenly his eyes blinked wide open, and he smiled. A certain girl with sparkling blue eyes was dancing through a wonderful dream.

The next morning, Paulo made his way back toward the heart of the deep Forest where the weather, as expected, became progressively brighter and warmer. He felt so good there, he remarked to himself, sighing contentedly as he walked, and wondered how much better it might be on the other side of the Wall. A shimmering morning mist strayed between golden sunbeams and dark chestnuts, and he wandered through its sharp coolness, over leaves that eventually began to crackle dryly under his boots, directly toward his deconstruction project in the Domain's defensive barrier to the Beyonde. Visible in the distance through the breach, he could see an exquisite blue sky.

He set immediately to work; there was no time to lose, and so much still to do. Setting his oil-cloth to the side, he extracted a small hammer and chisel from his satchel he had brought to help with the more difficult stones. Rocks tumbled off the barricade, sliding and jostling to the bottom, collecting in great numbers till a great pile of rubble started to form. After a while he took a few steps backwards and checked the wall.

Just one enormous rock now seemed to be blocking his path; just one very heavy block of stone set solidly in place, supporting a large remaining portion of the wall. "If I could just get that one little stone out," he spoke to himself, "the rest would come down quite easily, and I'd have a clear passage straight through this wall to the other side. In fact, it could all be done quite simply really."

He climbed high up into the breach and put a hand around the giant rock to see if it could be moved and indeed it seemed somewhat loose in the wall. But then he stopped. "This is actually pretty stupid," he spoke to the woods. "If that big stone comes free, why, this whole section of the wall above it might just come down on me, squashing me flat as pan-bread."

He got down off the wall and lay back on the grass, staring at the monster stone. This was an important decision. "Should I try to remove the giant rock and run the risk of getting badly hurt?" There was no clear answer.

What should I do?

Then he heard the gentle silvery voice penetrating from the other side of the wall. It appeared somewhat louder now, obviously because of the stones that had already been removed. "Take your time, Paulo," it counseled. "It might indeed take longer, but just be gentle and this obstacle will come away easily at the right moment. Just work slowly, and be gentle and patient."

Paulo thought this was reasonable enough advice, and decided to start with the smaller surrounding stones first. This would take a lot more time, he saw, but would clearly be much safer than ripping the boulder out on its own.

The smaller stones came away without too much difficulty, but there were in fact dozens and dozens of them, each one requiring some prodding to pry loose, and it was clear he wouldn't be finished anytime soon.

"But this is going to take absolutely *ages*. Why can't I get there *today*? Look, there's no reason why not – I just have to get rid of this big stupid old rock, and that's that."

He negotiated his way back up the wall, squared himself against the boulder, and put his hand around the big stone once again, and gave a sharp, hard tug. The boulder started to move, shifting and grinding its enormous bulk slowly out of the wall; small stones began to cascade down, filling his hair and mouth with a fine dust; then a few bigger stones started to plummet down on him, nearly knocking him off balance. But as he looked above to control the downpour, he saw with horror that the entire section of wall above the rock had now loosened itself and was tipping dangerously forward toward him.

"*AARGH – !*"

His scream filled the forest and a furious panic overcame him. He shoved against the massive rock, praying that he would be able to stabilize it back in place; and the boulder began to slow its movement and then, wedging his shoulder against it and pushing with all his might, he managed to push the rock somewhat back in position. Slowly he loosened his shoulder, and the wall and the boulder sat there – unmoving.

Paulo's panting shook his body; he trembled from head to toe and could feel the beginnings of a serious pain in his shoulder. Keeping both eyes riveted on the boulder to make sure it was really still, he hopped down off the wall.

"Boy, that was *really* close. I didn't think I could get hurt doing this. Why on earth did this happen?"

The kind voice spoke from just beyond the wall, "Slowly, Paulo ... *gently!* There's absolutely no need to rush; when the stone is ready, it will come away cleanly. There is no reason to use force. If you use force you will only scare yourself, and maybe even hurt yourself. When you are ready, you will find a way to remove it easily ... Just come back another day."

Paulo gratefully accepted the wise advice this time and left with his tools and wood for the market place.

He felt safe at his stall: the same old activity, the same old square, where no boulders could come crashing down on him unexpectedly. He waved at Francesca who he saw, for some reason, was alone at her stall today. She smiled and waved back and he immediately started to feel his spirits lift.

After the rush of the morning's first customers, and once he had a moment to relax and breathe, he gazed around the market square once again, watching people hectically going about their buying and selling. He heard the persistent thoughts running through his mind:

This is all just so busy. Look at them: these people can't see anything in their lives but their fish, their chickens, their vegetables and shoes. How stupid! Where I'm going tomorrow it looks so much better. Yes, tomorrow I'll leave this place and see something completely new! And so much nicer. But first I must work.

There was Mrs Belladonna who was still glad that Paulo was honest while all the other merchants were so thoroughly crooked. And of course there was her daughter, Maria, who was still a true misery in his life. Obviously that would never change.

Then there was Mr Salvatori who informed him ever so seriously about the unpleasant weather and his weakened state of health. Paulo made an effort to look sympathetic, grimacing at all the right moments. The gentleman appreciated Paulo's smile and attention, and left quite happy with his dry wood that always started his fire so nicely.

Mr Bravuro came by in a hurry at the end of market and Paulo didn't want him to know about his disaster at the Door, being caught and everything.

"Paulo, I hope you're not thinking of such hazardous things still. You don't know what kind of trouble you can get into. Do not be deceived by appearances, my boy. Simple things like 'doors' and 'walls' can sometimes be much more dangerous than you think." He sounded very concerned for the boy, and eyed him paternally from over his spectacles.

Paulo smiled, and nodded respectfully.

"Yes, sir," he said, and kept his thoughts to himself. *What would he do if he ever found out what I'm really doing? He'd have such an attack!*

At the end of market, Paulo closed his stand, folding his empty oil-cloth and throwing the roll over his shoulder, and left to return home. Francesca was busy loading her cart on the other side of the square, and as he passed her by (it seemed to be a good path to take), he tried to give her what he hoped was a particularly becoming smile, though actually he felt pretty awkward.

He turned in the direction of the river, but the next instant the air was pierced by a high-pitched cry from behind him. He span around instantly and saw Francesca lose her footing, toppling backwards on the ground under the weight of a large crate of chickens.

He dashed over to her and grabbed the heavy cage filled with the squawking birds, then held out his hand. She took it gladly, raising herself to her feet, and carefully brushed the dust off her skirts. She looked a little dazed, then distressed. "It won't be so easy now, since Antonio must stay at the farm to help father," she murmured.

Paulo helped her place the rest of the crates on the donkey cart, and pulled the reluctant animal down the road some distance to get the two of them started. He felt clumsy and tried to chat about nothing in particular, saying something about the drizzle and damp, and he was just thinking he must sound to her every bit like Mr Salvatori, always going on about…

Suddenly, Francesca turned to him and looked Paulo straight in the eye. He looked back at her nervously and felt himself getting warm in the cheeks. She hesitated a moment, opening her mouth as if wanting to say something. Then without warning she reached over and kissed him quickly on the cheek.

'Thank you,' she mumbled, then turned and skipped quickly down the road before Paulo could even think of responding. The young wood seller stood immobile some minutes, feeling something strange, something like the dance of a thousand stars turning and spinning deep inside him.

CHAPTER SEVEN

Tricked!

The next day Paulo returned to his work site in the forest after collecting his wood, and observed the piles of stones that littered the ground and the beginning breach in the wall with the blue sky beyond. The boulder was still there, blocking everything: vast, dense, and looking entirely, thoroughly immovable. The last obstacle, he breathed, to his vision of a brand new world.

He sat on forest floor for some minutes, and just stared up at it. "I will get you down – I *will*." The rock seemed to stare back at him belligerently. "When I get you out and visit the other side, everything in my life will be totally different. There'll be nothing to stop me from leaving this place, once you're gone. No more customers – just think of that!"

Then for the first time he actually wondered what it was really going to be like and what he would find. "No customers? Uh … how nice is it really going to be out there?

"I mean, it sure *looks* nice through the hole, with the blue sky beyond and all … but how could I really know for sure from here? After all, Mr Bravuro said that appearances can be deceiving – how can I know it's a nice place, but *before* I go?"

He thought about the problem some more, and his mind seemed to get cloudy with confusion. "What if it's not actually so great over there as I think? I don't believe in those stories of dragons and wild beasts and all, not really, but still… What if it's just another prison, like here. What's even scarier, what if I can't come back. I mean, what if this is the last time I'll ever see the

Domain? Maybe I'll never see my family again, Fredo, or mama. Or, even worse, maybe even Francesca!"

"My customers, too…" The wood seller thought more about his customers and began to worry for them. "How'll they find their dry wood without me? How could they light their fires to keep warm? They count on me, that's clear, since my wood's always the best in the market. I know they're difficult and all, but they're going to be awfully disappointed if I'm not there to give them their wood." He was a special and important person in their lives, it was clear, and that was something to think about before he made the big decision to leave for the other side.

He stared again at the Fortress Wall, so hard and cold, and then further into the distance beyond it at the bright sunshine on the other side.

"But it must be so warm there, and that song is so lovely; there must be something nice behind that melody, behind that lovely Silver Song." He could almost hear it again, singing sweetly, gently, so familiar, reminding him of… of… something he already knew. "*But what?*"

No answer came.

"Should I, or shouldn't I? It's all so confusing!" he said flatly in frustration.

In a state of desperate quandary, he shoved his hand into his satchel and found the pouch of magical herbs, gripping it tightly, and asked for an answer. Immediately potent and persuasive words stormed through his mind, casting aside all his previous thoughts:

'Your customers *do* indeed need you, Paulo – you're important to them. How on earth do you think they'll be able to get by without you? And what about Francesca, you know she means a lot to you… she'd be *so* disappointed if you left. This is indeed an immensely stupid thing to be doing.'

Some dark creature spoke loudly and convincingly in his mind, and its harsh and grating voice fed him now with more powerful doubts. 'In any rate, how can you really be so certain it's so nice over there? Do you really know where that strange beguiling voice, that slippery 'silver' voice, is coming from, and what it might be leading you towards?'

And, suddenly, a terrifying question grew in Paulo's mind:

"Am I being tricked… betrayed? Is that it, I'm being tricked after all? Tricked into going to the other side – is that possible? That'd be a… a catastrophe!"

As the feeling of deep distrust infiltrated his thoughts, the morbid voice doubled and tripled in his ears and the sun was suddenly swept from his forest, leaving the boy in intense shadow. A strong wind rose abruptly from out of nowhere, and within minutes had driven to a furious pitch, shaking the trees till they began to quiver from every twig and branch. But Paulo hardly even noticed these extraordinary changes: he was already in the midst of a wild and frantic storm; inside him a maelstrom was already raging.

The boy stood dead still, his breath cut short, his heart pounding violently in his chest. He clenched his eyelids shut and everything inside him turned deeply black, the inner turmoil feeding him ideas of the darkest nature.

All of a sudden he shrieked, "That's it – *that's it!* It *has* tricked me! The Silver Voice *sounds* nice, but that's just to get me to come to the other side. Everyone's been right all along, it really *is* dangerous and evil on the other side. How could I have been so dumb, so incredibly stupid? And the nice-sounding voice and warm sunshine is just to get me to go over there, and once I'm there I'll be trapped forever. The Dark Lord's hordes of monsters will pin me down and then he'll come himself and get me and, and –" a truly terrifying thought blazed into his mind, "– and then he'll *eat* me!"

Paulo trembled uncontrollably in every limb.

He gasped at the violent storm already raging around him. The branches tossed by the wind whipped furiously through the air and the tall trunks swayed dangerously back and forth, threatening to topple on him at any moment. The once-friendly oaks and chestnuts now stood out like fierce soldiers come to haul him away, and suddenly Paulo felt very small and very vulnerable.

'I've made a horrible mistake, a dreadful, dreadful mistake. This is terrible! A crime, such a terrible crime I've committed! Maybe I've made a hole in the only defense the Domain ever had against the Dark Lord, and now he's coming to take my family and me away. He'll kill my brother and my mother and me, all because of my stupidity!'

A feverish voice shouted malevolently in his ear, 'Evil, despicable boy, look at what you've done! This is indeed a great crime. Now there's no hope, all because of you and your stupid curiosity. Did I not try to warn you of this all along?'

Paulo turned to one side and then another, terrified. *'Where do I go? What do I do?'* he asked repeatedly, now quite frantic. All he saw was the dark, dark night of the storm and all he felt was a terrible, crushing sense of guilt and sin. Then the sinister voice in his ear replied: 'Listen to me, I know precisely what you must do: hurry back to the safety of Towne! Leave the Wall and the treacherous Silver Voice from the other side, there is only danger here! What a crime – horrible boy. Leave quickly now, return to Towne, return at once to the village.'

Paulo repeated, 'Yes, yes! That's right. Back to the village!'

He swooped up his wood and dashed through the forest, the bundles of jumping kindlin' leaving large bleeding scratches across his back.

'Run! Run! Stupid boy, there is only danger here,' he heard once more. *Yes! I'll be safe in Towne* – and Paulo ran without stopping or looking behind him all the way back to the village and the market place.

CHAPTER EIGHT

A Different Day

Several weeks went by and the young wood seller was content. He had decided to forget all about the mysterious Silver Voice and the silly images of a new and foreign world on the other side of the Wall, and became very busy with his work and life. The days slipped by, collecting and selling his wood and working at home: all was routine and predictable. All was now quite safe and familiar.

The market was the same, the same faces and busyness. Francesca was now selling ducks at her stall, in addition to the eggs and chickens, and Paulo imagined how wonderful it would be to work on a farm with animals like these; everyone knew that farm work paid well, and his family would certainly appreciate the extra income. Perhaps that would even allow him one day to buy a cotton-fill mattress to replace his musty old straw bed. That'd be nice.

Mama, he knew, was expecting him to be able to help more financially. She had told his brother it was time to leave his job working in the fields, to go work for the blacksmith and learn about iron tool-making. It was especially hard work, and his brother came home exhausted and filthy every day; but everyone had to work hard, mama said. His father had worked hard in the fields every day until he had died, and his mother was busy working hard all the time, too.

Paulo now looked around the market square at the villagers coming and going, and groaned inside. 'Life isn't very hopeful, he was thinking. But at least it isn't terrifying, like the Outside!

Maybe the Towne and the Domain are all we know, but at least they're safe and familiar. Yep, certainly safe. And familiar. That's good enough.'

He stopped short.

'But then, if everyone's so safe and content, why do they all still look so worried? … When on earth is it ever going to get *clearer*?'

Week after week, Paulo continued to go to the market place and sell his wood, and generally try to find happiness in his plans and little pleasures, but it just wasn't that easy.

Mr Salvatori stopped by one day and was prompted to say:

"Your wood isn't quite so good anymore, Paulo. My fire doesn't light so easily. Is something wrong?"

The gentleman sounded genuinely interested, so Paulo felt it would be alright to take a risk. "I'm not going anymore to the place where I used to get the wood, sir. That's the reason."

In fact, Paulo hadn't returned to the deep Forest near the Wall since his intense bout of fear. Of course, it was more difficult to find dry wood closer to town, because it rained more often there.

"Is there a problem with where you were going to get the wood? Were you stealing it? I'm sure you weren't. Was there something to be scared of in the Forest where you went?" the gentleman asked sincerely.

"Well…" Paulo didn't actually know how to answer the question; he couldn't say for sure whether there was really something to be scared of out there, or if he had just made it all up. "– Well, not really. I just decided to stop going there. That's all."

"But you were doing a great service for all of us, you know. It's quite an important job, helping people light their fires. I don't think you should stop unless you really feel you have to. Anyway, good luck, Paulo. I think you're a good person, and I will keep buying from you."

The gentleman left with his damp wood and a smile.

Early the next morning, Paulo lay in bed staring at the ceiling. It was still dark outside, and he was already late for getting up to milk the goats. *"Paulo – get to work!"* His mother's impatient cries filled the house from one end to the other.

A long, heavy groan escaped from the boy's insides.

Just another day, he thought, just like all the rest. "How can I possibly make today different?" he muttered to himself. "There *must* be another way, there *must* be something else."

He felt a gentle presence enter his thoughts, and suddenly the long-forgotten enchanted Silver Whisper spoke to him inside his mind. "Yes, Paulo, there is much, *much* more than everything you currently know. Come, discover with me, trust me, I'll show you … I won't let you down."

Paulo wondered, thinking about this mysterious peaceful voice that came to him so strangely. Could it *really* be trying to trick me? Is it truly dangerous, is that possible?

Then abruptly he knew the right answer to his questions, and he knew his path.

After his morning chores, he ran lightly from the house into the woods, along the trail and all the way to the big split in the wall. Only once more did he think about the possible danger of passing through to the unknown world on the other side, then his hands went quickly to work.

Very gently, he removed all the small stones he could that surrounded the giant boulder, and then piled them and other rocks underneath the big stone to make a long slide like a ramp. Next, he found a long, strong branch on the ground nearby and he took this to wedge behind the big stone.

Standing well clear of the rock and the dangerous section of wall, he started to push against the branch like a lever. Then, pushing more firmly, very easily and slowly the enormous rock plucked itself from its anchor-point and tumbled with a whoosh down the ramp of small stones till it reached the bottom and rolled safely away. The entire section of the wall above it tilted forward as it had done before, and now collapsed harmlessly in a heap of dust at the foot of the wall.

"*Yahoo*, I did it! It was so incredibly easy, after all!" he shouted to the woods.

He faced the Forest that had been his faithful friend for so many years, and looked at it carefully, perhaps for the last time. Then he turned full of confidence and hope, and faced the opening that was the doorway he had made with his own two hands, the opening to all things new and possible.

Standing before the opening in the Wall, he could already feel the warm fragrant air coming from the other side, and he breathed in deeply, filling his lungs with the delicious odors wafting toward him from a different world. Without hesitating he scrambled up the ramp of small stones and high up into the breach in the Wall, and gazed out toward a bright new horizon.

"Oh, my God!" he heard himself say. "It's so *beautiful!*"

CHAPTER NINE

Unexpected Encounters

Paulo jumped off the wall, and landed on a thick bed of soft green grass which he instantly noticed was filled with thousands of little yellow and pink star-like wild flowers. With his feet planted firmly now in the land of Beyonde, he looked carefully all around him, absorbed and fascinated beyond his imagining by the sparkling world surrounding him.

Above him, elegant trees stretched their branches into a broad, leafy canopy, and warm sunlight filtered through the gently swaying boughs, splaying all around him in dazzling patterns of gold and green. A summer morning's breeze whispered through the leaves, bringing delicious smells of green things, ferns and herbs and flowers fresh and completely new to his senses. Turning his face skyward, Paulo lingered under the trees and let a ray of light caress his face, soothing away all his previous cares and questions. After another moment, he turned and began striding through the trees, determined now to discover all he could about his magical new environment.

The woods here were not dense or dark, he noticed; in fact, the trees were spaced delicately apart, making it easy to stroll over the thick grass that formed wide alleys and passageways that disappeared into the distance, and he wandered through the sun-lit glades without a care in the world. He thought an instant how he'd been so anxious on the other side, apprehending the loss of all that was familiar and dear to him, and he could only smile at his fear. And, for the moment at least, there didn't seem to be a dragon or wild beast in sight, anywhere! It was such a pleasure seeing his friends, the oaks and chestnuts and beeches, on this side of the Wall, too. He thought it was like his Forest, but somehow much, much better.

Yes, in many ways it looked the same, he thought, but the Forest on the Outside seemed so much more peaceful and magical, like there was nothing here that could ever be a problem … as if there was nothing here that could ever possibly hurt him.

Paulo walked faster, eventually trotting, and then broke into a swift run, overjoyed to be in such a glorious, remarkable place. He ran harder, faster, and shouted out loudly as he rushed wildly past trees and flowering bushes, calling greetings to plants, stumps, shrubs and all manner of things that he passed along the way. Brightly colored birds chirped merrily from high branches and he looked up and cried, *"Hello there!"* They didn't seem too surprised, and just looked at him curiously.

The woods ended with a sparse fringe of ash and beech and gave way to broad rolling fields, an expanse dotted with wild flowers, hundreds of flowers of types he'd never seen before. Paulo set off, pushing his feet through their fresh morning dew which sparkled on every stem and petal, and wandered further out into the open meadow. From this point on, the field began to slope in a deep wave away from him, and Paulo picked up speed, then threw himself onto the ground with abandon, rolling over and over amongst the deep sweet grasses.

When he lifted his head he halted abruptly.

"Oh, my Lord…"

He was staring fixedly at the horizon, beholding a most remarkable vision.

A bright golden haze enveloped a tall hill some leagues off and, reposing serenely in the middle of the diffused light, was the most extraordinary city he had ever seen. The shapes of houses, buildings and towers met his eyes, all glowing brilliant shades of silver, violet and blue, and all sparkling in the morning sunshine. Soft green hills surrounded the City, and a golden path curled through the lush valleys and all the way up to the gates at the entrance to the City.

Paulo stood rooted to the spot and gazed at the remarkable vision for what seemed an eternity.

It feels so … familiar, he breathed. Something about this strange distant city called to him, stretching its golden rays into his heart, only to find a little kernel of the same brilliant light already buried there inside him, now glowing. The rising sun gleamed off the distant hill and a warm breeze carried the scent of magic and something else wonderful, like hope.

He strolled across the field looking for a comfortable tree to sit beneath, and some shade. Crossing his legs and extending his hands out behind him, he lay back in the pleasant coolness offered by the great oak's broad branches. From this position, he had a perfect view of the shimmering image on the horizon, and closely observed the subtle play of colors on the far hill and pondered on all these marvelous things.

'And to think this amazing place has been here all this time, he mused, just behind the Wall, and I've never even known about it. And to think that I was going to give up altogether on my wish to see the Outside – that would've been the greatest tragedy!'

In that instant, he *knew* his dream of real happiness and joy was true; there *was* something else – it hadn't all been just a vague wish or a silly dream. It'd take some time to get there maybe, but he'd one day get to the magical Golden City, he just knew it. And that was all that counted. Gazing out at the horizon, the Domain was already starting to seem far, far away, the gray sky and wet cobbled streets of the market place and his miserable customers appearing like phantoms from a bad dream.

Then suddenly – *"Cra-aack!"*

A monstrous noise erupted from the branches right above him, and Paulo swiveled his head toward the sky. Something large and heavy came plummeting through the oak's limbs toward the ground, and he jumped to his feet.

Dragons!

Paulo turned to run but the toe of his boot caught on a knobby tree root and he fell head first, landing face-down in the thick grass. An enormous object broke free of the branches, dropped out of the tree and landed with a tremendous thud on the ground.

Immediately a voice spoke out from somewhere behind him: "*My word*, that's quite a drop there, isn't it? Didn't quite realize… I will have to mind my step next time, won't I? Deary me… Well – look who we have here! Hello there, young man! *Did I scare you?*"

The words rang out laughingly and friendly, and Paulo lifted his face from the grass, and turned to see from whom, or what, they were coming. He climbed shakily to his feet and took a few steps backward in amazement. With a long white beard, dressed in a dark blue robe with brilliantly flashing gold and silver stars, an elderly gentleman eyed Paulo with warmth and kindness from underneath a strange long felt hat. Paulo stepped back another pace, suspicious.

"I see you're quite confused, my boy," the peculiar man said. "And perhaps a little scared, too? That's a pity, quite a pity, and so tremendously unnecessary. But it's quite normal, quite normal I assure you, for First-Timers from the Otherside, believe you me. Yes, indeed, I imagine you're somewhat confused…

Indeed Paulo was scratching his head.

"Allow me to introduce myself, young man. My name is Toroth Cithar Zephahro Thompson, the Third, of course. *At your service.*"

He took a slow, deep bow that looked very graceful and impressive, but then the tall felt hat on his head came tumbling off, revealing a bald spot among his bright white hair. Paulo found himself giggling despite his fears, reassured by the man's warm and light manner.

"But you can call me 'Zeph' for short. It's much easier, don't you think? Not as impressive, of course, but much more efficient among friends."

Suddenly the boy caught his breath. He understood – that was it! It was *the* voice, the *Silver Voice*, that he had heard from the other side of the Wall. He tried to exclaim but was unable to find the words. "But you're not ... you're not –"

Zeph was already answering him, "I'm not what, my lad? *Not scary, not frightening?* You don't think so, eh?" He was trying to sound indignant but was clearly only playing.

"Not scary enough, eh? Well, just look at *this* –"

The man, who it was obvious to Paulo was certainly a very respectable magician, or wizard at least, then brought his thumbs to the sides of his mouth and pulled hard toward his cheeks. He rolled his eyes toward his nose and flapped his ears with his fingers, making an extremely ludicrous face for such a wise looking person. Paulo laughed all the harder.

"So you don't think that's scary? Alright, I agree, I have some work to do on my scary-face. But getting down to important matters…"

He pulled himself fully upright, looking quite regal and official, and crossed one hand over his chest. "I would like to say on behalf of everyone here in the Kingdom of Happiness, how we are indeed so *very frightened* to have you here."

Paulo stared in surprise, and the wizardly-looking gentleman scratched his beard.

"No, no, I've got it all wrong again – No, we're very *delighted* to have you here. Yes, that's it, we're *very glad* to have you here. No, we're not frightened *at all*. You certainly don't look very scary, I'm afraid. You're not at all as frightening and horrible as you think sometimes."

He spoke gaily and warmly, but it was clear to Paulo that this was a very great man, and that he was simply trying to help Paulo feel more comfortable. He then said, more seriously, "And we're very glad that you finally made it here, Paulo. Let's sit down a while, shall we? Let's talk a little perhaps."

They settled comfortably on the soft grass under the great oak, and after a minute his magician-friend spoke. "It was a bit touch and go there for a minute, wasn't it… with that big stone, eh? You nearly decided not to come."

"But where are we?" the boy replied bewildered, though quite comfortable with his strange new acquaintance. "I don't understand – and where's everyone else?"

The wizard said, "This place has one simple name that seems to work very well for everyone who has the courage and perseverance to make it here. From now on, my dear friend," he said spreading his arms across the glorious vista before them, "you may call this place … *Home*."

Paulo gazed a long silent moment into the sun-filled land of warmth and beauty that lay before him, and felt a powerful emotion well up inside him. He nearly started to cry.

Zeph then said intently, without the slightest trace of laughter, "Paulo, my lad, this is where you come from … and this is where you belong. You left from here a long time ago, though you don't remember anything, I know. And you woke up one day in the dim and obscure place they call the Domain, the other side of the Wall back there, without knowing how you got there, or even who you really are."

"But how? How's all this possible?" Paulo couldn't even begin to ask all his questions.

"Lots of questions, yes, I know you have many questions, and we'll get to them all in good time. That's what I'm here to help you with. And to help you get to the Golden City, of course, if that's your wish. And where is everyone? You have many brothers and sisters who are waiting patiently for you…" the magician pointed towards the horizon and the glowing city on the distant mountaintop, "…over there."

Then he waved his hand in the opposite direction back toward the Domain Wall. "And you also have many brothers and sisters waiting for you back there, amongst the Townspeople."

Paulo now thought about his brother and his mother, then his customers and the other children selling in the market place. All of them were so busy with their lives and knew nothing about this extraordinary place right next door. It was so close; it was here all the time, and they didn't have the slightest idea of its existence.

"But that's terrible! They should be here. We should all be going together to the Golden City. What're they all waiting for?"

"Paulo, why did you wait? Weren't you afraid, too?"

"Yes, but now I see that it's all so unnecessary, it's all so ridiculous! Why're we waiting? We should all be leaving the Domain and walking to the City right now: that's our *real* home, *not* the Domain."

"You're entirely right, and it is very silly, indeed, as you say," the magician said. "But you know this now only because you are over the other side of the Wall in the sunshine and fresh air, and you see there is nothing really dangerous outside the Domain. But if you were still inside the Wall and didn't understand this, how would you find the courage to leave?"

Paulo listened thoughtfully.

"Paulo," the wizard looked kindly at the boy, "Do you remember why you had the courage to leave?"

He tried to think; something vague lay there in the back of his mind. He remembered something that happened long ago now, something that had changed everything for him. Then it returned, a memory from a time that seemed already an eternity ago…

"Yes, I remember now. It was one special day at the market."

"Tell me about it."

"I went to the market that day and I wasn't feeling very happy. Life wasn't fun at all. It wasn't long after my father had died – I missed him a lot, and I was also angry because mother had become so difficult and unhappy all the time. That day my wood was wet and people were complaining about it and sneering at me. Mother was going to be angry if I didn't sell well and bring back some money. Those days I was scared of the deep Forest and dry kindlin' was always hard to find. The Mayor came like he does sometimes and took a bundle and didn't pay – I started to get angry. But then I was really so tired with always being upset with my customers and my life, and I was wondering if there wasn't another way, if life couldn't somehow be better. I was thinking there just *had* to be a different way of being alive, of doing things and thinking about my customers and my mother.

"Then a man came to buy my wood and he wasn't a regular customer. He didn't look like he came from here, he looked strange and I did a terrible, bad thing to him. He gave me a silver ducat for the wood, which was a lot too much. I then gave him some coins in return. But I remember, I did an awful, terrible thing that I should've never done; I didn't give him back the right change. I… I… stole money from him."

Paulo looked at the ground in disgrace and the wizard looked at him patiently.

"But I didn't think he was looking and I was so upset with everything and I desperately thought that I needed the money. He walked away, and then I saw him start to count his money. I just wanted him to go away and started to get very nervous. I felt very uncomfortable because I'd never ever stolen before and knew it was extremely bad… If someone ever found out I'd get into fearsome trouble with the Guards and never be able to sell wood again.

"The man looked at his change and noticed something was wrong – then he turned around toward me. I don't know what happened, but before I knew it I panicked and started running. I left my wood stand and I ran and ran, as fast as I could through the streets to escape, but I heard footsteps behind me and knew he was right there. I kept running but he was too fast and his footsteps got louder and louder… And I came to a dead end, and I was trapped, so I just stopped running. I gave up and stood there, waiting for him to hit me.

"He came up to me and grabbed me by the shoulders – I was so afraid. He turned me around and looked at me and the first thing I saw was his eyes. He looked at me really strongly, like directly in the eyes and, then, suddenly *everything* was completely different for me – they were the loveliest, nicest eyes I'd ever seen in my life. They were peaceful, and calm. And warm. I felt that he didn't hate me, not at all, but that he really liked me instead… I was so surprised, I didn't understand anything. He didn't seem upset with me at all, like I thought he'd be, but I was still ashamed and afraid. He was a very powerful man, I could tell, the most powerful person I'd ever met. I'd never seen anyone like that before."

The magician asked in a low voice, "Do you remember what he said to you?"

"Yes," Paulo said after a minute, thinking.

"He asked me a funny question, I remember. He asked me if I wanted to know the Truth, *the truth of all things*. I didn't know what to say because I didn't understand. Then he asked me another question, he asked me if I wanted to be happy, and said it was the same thing. He asked me if I finally wanted to be *really* happy, and peaceful, too… happy and free above *all* other things in the world.

"I thought about it because the way he said it, it seemed to be a really serious question, and then after a moment I finally said, yes, I did. He said he could see this was true in me.

"Then he told me that I didn't have to sell the best, driest wood to be happy. This wasn't happiness. I didn't have to make a lot of money to be really happy, or to please other people, he said. This wasn't happiness, either. I could be really happy and peaceful anytime I wanted, wherever I wanted, even in the market place. He said this was so because the real Happiness and Peace I sought were here in my heart and my mind all the time… I remember this well.

"All I had to do was start knowing I wasn't the horrible, shameful thing I thought deep within me, he told me. No matter what happened to me, no matter what anyone said, and no matter what I thought about myself, I wasn't the rotten thing that a dark voice in my mind would keep telling me. He told me that the greatest, most remarkable gift I would ever find was inside me, and not in dry wood or in satisfied customers or in my mama being happy.

"And he said that I could one day learn to be like him, if I wanted. I was so impressed I started to cry, because I thought I was so small and terrible, and here was this great man telling me I could be extraordinary and magical, like him. I couldn't see how it would ever be possible. But he told me it was possible, so it had to be true. I believed everything he said.

"I told him I'd like that very much. And he said that I would just have to start looking into the quiet of my heart and my mind to find the truth and the happiness I was really looking for. I was supposed to learn to listen inside, so I could be less afraid, and to start by telling myself that I wasn't the terribly evil thing I most deeply felt inside."

"Then what happened?" the magician asked, coming down closer to Paulo's level.

"He didn't really care about the money at all, I was so surprised. He didn't want his money back, it didn't matter to him, and he just walked quietly away and left me there. But I remember his eyes. They were so bright and calm. I don't think he was afraid of anything, not like the people I see all the time. He wasn't worried or concerned about anything at all, almost as if he wasn't even there. It was very strange."

Paulo returned from his memories to the waving grass in the field and the bright day around him and now looked back at the magician. He stared curiously at the great man who looked across at him kindly. Then he noticed something different in the face, the depth of those warm, peaceful eyes behind the white beard. Clear, happy, sparkling and powerful eyes, that invited him to remember. And suddenly it was clear to him.

"That's you! It's *you!* You're the man from the market place. I can see you now!"

He rushed into the magician's arms who folded him in a warm embrace. Zeph chuckled, delighted that his young friend had remembered their first encounter.

"Yes, indeed. We first met over a year ago now, Paulo. But you listened to me, didn't you? You saw, you read my eyes, and you listened well. Now, here you are together with me in the land of Freedom and Joy. Who would ever have thought? After we met, that's when you decided to be less afraid, to listen less to what everyone told you, and to spend more time in the woods.

"Over time you learned to go deeper and farther than everyone told you, right? You learned how to spend time with yourself and how to listen, and how to trust. You learned that the scary things inside you weren't so real, despite what everyone thought."

"Yes," said Paulo. "Then I wanted to start listening to my heart, like you said. My heart seemed to be quieter in the forest, and the deeper I went, the quieter it got. That made it much easier to be in the crowds of the market place afterward. I also wasn't so worried when people didn't give me the right money or when they weren't happy. I knew that I could still be peaceful and calm inside."

"Isn't that what eventually gave you the courage to go up to the Domain Wall," Zeph asked, "where you heard me calling you? And isn't that what gave you the courage to trust your heart when you were afraid that maybe I was lying and was really laying a trap for you?"

Paulo replied, "Yes, exactly! I learned to trust my heart more and more. That helped me to find drier wood and to stay out of trouble. Things then started to look better because I was feeling happier inside. And I guess this helped me find the courage to really want to see what was on the other side of the Wall.

"But, Zeph, why don't other people listen to their hearts, too? They could have heard your voice, too, if they'd been willing to trust a little. They're just all so scared, like my brother, or … or, I don't know what, but they're not listening to their heart, that's for sure.

"No, you're quite right. They're not listening to their hearts, but they could: all the Townspeople can learn to feel what is right and good for them, and this will bring them to a place where they can hear what will help them. But most people don't. Would you like to know why now? Would you like to know why the Townspeople live afraid and imprisoned on the other side of the Wall? This is something important that you will have to learn about at some stage."

Paulo wondered what could be preventing everyone from hearing something so lovely as the Silver Voice and coming to the Outside.

Zeph spoke gravely, "It's because of a spell, Paulo… the evil *Spell of Banishment*."

CHAPTER TEN

The Magician's Fabulous Tale

The wizard studied the boy intently, and after a moment drew a deep breath. "I must ask you a question, Paulo," he said, "for you are on the edge of a path, as you see: the way to the Golden City. But it is a path that is *very* difficult, and will require that you confront the most terrifying demons and dragons, and the most invisible, subtle traps along the way.

"To know if you are ready now to discover all there is to know and all that the Townspeople have been hiding from you, you must answer a vital question for yourself, and it is this: In your heart of hearts, do you sincerely wish to come with me back to the Golden City?"

He looked at the boy who was suddenly lost in deep thought.

The magician continued, "You must answer this before I can continue to teach you. There is much to learn to follow this path, and you are only now taking your first serious steps. If you continue, the way will grow dark at times, exceedingly dark; and terror will surely assail you before the dawn's light finally comes. Only your heart's deepest desire will save you then, and bring you back to the Path. And so I ask: *do you wish to continue?*"

For the second time in his life, the boy had to consider whether his desire was strong, powerful enough to take him to his goal. Some minutes later he looked up from the ground and directly met the magician's eyes. "Yes," he answered. "I'm willing to face the road ahead. Please, go on."

Zeph looked momentarily out over the magnificent day that stretched grandly before them, and then turned to begin the formal teaching of his yet youngest student.

"Yes, perhaps you're ready indeed for this passage. Time will only tell. You're just starting now the difficult part of the journey – and I have faith in you, though you're still very young. So let me begin, Paulo, by telling you a tale that's so remarkable, so incredible, you'll find it very hard to believe … and yet it's all quite true. It is the Tale of All Things, the story of the *origin of the Domain* and the *birth of the Townspeople*. Now, listen carefully…

"You see the beautiful City of Light over there on the hill? Let me tell you that at one time in the past we were all of us, all brothers and sisters, living together over there in the great Golden City of the Kingdom of Happiness. We were very happy, very content and very, *very* peaceful. We had everything we could imagine because the City was ruled by an extremely kind King. This beneficent ruler had ensured that in the splendid Kingdom of Happiness there would never be anything missing; that's what it's like in a place of the greatest Love – you don't wish anyone to lack for anything, and thus you give everything to everyone, continuously. In this miraculous place, it was indeed possible to give endlessly, and continue giving, because each one felt, each one *knew*, he possessed everything and wanted for nothing.

"There in the Golden City no one missed or wanted for anything he did not possess already in full and just measure, and everyone enjoyed all things perfectly. It's rather difficult to describe this state because it has nothing to do with anything you understand and feel now in the Domain. In the Domain, giving and receiving always revolve around things, and having and more and less, and each person contains a deep feeling of lack and a need to have and get things for himself. But in the Kingdom there are no such lacks or limitations; there is simply Joy, Fullness and Plenitude. The People understood this state of perfection deep within their hearts, and they naturally shared this knowledge with all their brothers and sisters.

"Life was different there, too – very different, indeed. Life was not a question of beginnings and endings, of cycles of birth and death, but of Presence, of Being and Extension. There was no question of time and the mortal things that pass with it, but a simple sense of Eternity, or Foreverness. Life was everything with no opposite, and always would be, without exception and without question of change or flux. This extraordinary sense of Freedom and Happiness was all there was, all there ever would be, extending through Love to all corners of the Kingdom, forever and forever.

"There in the Kingdom we knew *who* we were, and this was the gift we shared endlessly since it was the knowledge of perfection and love. We were the *One Great People* of the King: whole, complete and exceptional. We knew *Ourself*, and within Us there were no distinctions or separations, no special ones or some with more or less. We were *One*, and within this Oneness there were no trace of difference to be found.

"It's not at all easy to describe, but it was a state of exceptional and wonderful peace, in the knowledge of nothing fearful or dangerous ever, or anywhere. This Oneness you might call Love, but not the love you are familiar with in the Domain which is dependent on so many conditions. It is Love that is Life itself, that is entirely joyous and knows that no other state truly exists. And it displaces fear entirely when it is present."

Somewhere in Paulo's mind he knew all this was true, and he didn't question it. It was almost as if he was being reminded of something he knew, or had known once, but had since somehow forgotten. He asked, "So, why're we here now, and where does the Domain come from? What changed all this?"

Zeph continued, "Indeed, it should have continued in this way for all eternity. But something most strange happened, something too strange to even properly understand, but I'll try to explain it nevertheless.

"While we were very happy and content in the City, one day some of us heard a foreign, enchanting voice from somewhere outside the City's Gates. A peculiar creature began to whisper to us within the quiet space of our minds, one whose presence we'd never felt before.

"We listened, and it spoke of things completely unknown to us: gifts, it spoke of, but gifts we couldn't even begin to imagine, and we were very curious. It spoke of gifts we'd never seen or touched, yet it said that such things were wonderful and extraordinary to behold. These gifts were *more*, and *other*, and *different*, it said, from all we'd ever known in the Kingdom.

"We couldn't quite understand the creature's meaning: such ideas of difference were completely unknown and unnecessary in the City. But apparently there existed somewhere in the universe a special place of things even more magnificent, more magical than all the King had already bestowed upon us. It even spoke of something more than the *Everything* with which our loving Ruler had blessed us.

"We stared at one another, completely confused. A group of us thought it was simply impossible to imagine something *other* than the exceptional beauty of the Kingdom, or something *more* than Everything. Those were the ones among us who simply ignored this beguiling foreign voice, and walked away to continue merrily and happily within the wonders of the glorious Golden City. But some of us were still intrigued and couldn't imagine what this might possibly be, this remarkable *More* of which it spoke; and we chose to listen to this mysterious presence to discover its special offerings.

"And so it informed us that first we had to leave the City by the Gates, because what we were now looking for wasn't within the Kingdom. We had never had reason to leave the City before, knowing there was nowhere else to go, and nothing more beautiful than where we already were. Nevertheless, we marched out of the Golden City by the Gates, the gates that were eternally open, quite aware that there was no danger that could befall us, and started down the hill, all the while wondering what this peculiar creature might possibly be able to show us there that we couldn't have known before.

"Once outside, we found hanging from the branches of a nearby tree, thousands of dark little fruits, which were not really fruits at all but little sachets of black material, just like this one —" The magician stretched over and put his hand into Paulo's satchel, pulling out the little pouch of magical herbs that the boy always kept there. "And we were told that in order to attain the special knowledge of all that the King had secretly withheld from us, we had to grasp this little black purse in our hands and make a solemn wish."

"The wise ones among us listened to this mystifying creature's speeches, stared at the little black purse, and then gave a scoffing laugh. They quickly concluded that these stories were altogether too absurd, and smiled at the quaint and preposterous notions of 'something else and more'. They knew there could be no other such things outside the Kingdom that could conceivably interest them. And so, chuckling all the way, they walked calmly back through the Gates to rejoin their brothers within the brilliant City of Light.

"But for others of our group, our hunger for these unknown things wasn't yet satisfied, and we continued listening to the bewitching voice and its enticing suggestions. Thus, without further consideration, we each plucked a little black purse from the tree, and placed it in our pocket, and committed ourselves to this promise of something exceptionally special and different."

Zeph was calm but somehow far away, staring outward toward some distant place. Then he brought his attention back to Paulo's wide eyes. "For that group of us, my young friend, life has never since been the same…

"We had no idea of our act, but the bag contained a selection of bewitched herbs, impregnated with an extremely powerful spell that began immediately to alter our every thought and feeling. It was a terrible spell, with the most frightening consequences : it was the Spell of the *Judgment,* of the *Damnation,* and of the *Banishment.*

"As soon as we accepted that little black sachet, the Spell took control of our minds and filled our thoughts with the greatest obscurity and confusion. The dark voice increased ten-fold and then a hundred-fold in our ears, and it so effectively blocked out everything else that we could hear nothing but its sound and think nothing but its sinister thoughts – and we listened, completely hypnotized.

"Indeed, this nefarious creature had much to tell us. One singular desire burned in its mind, which was the need to maintain power over us, its prisoners, and to keep us at all costs from simply turning around and returning back along the path through the Gates and into the City, as our brothers had. *And how would it do this? How could it break our bond to our beloved Home…?"*

Paulo had no idea at all, and listened, riveted to every word.

"This is how," the magician continued: "It would now make us become intolerably scared and abhorrent of all that the Kingdom represented, and to want to leave by our own request. It would, in essence, change our feelings so that we would hate our King, fear his Kingdom, and flee of our own accord.

"And so it set into motion a most devious, treacherous, plan. A myth, it devised, a story that would at once dominate our thoughts and feelings, and manipulate us into following its every command. It puffed itself up, it spoke loudly, it adopted an air of righteous authority; and it declared that each one of us standing there outside the Gates had now been judged, had been condemned, and finally had been *damned* for his despicable action.

"The One People instantly cried, 'But for what possible reason?' We looked at each other utterly bewildered, not understanding in the least what this strange presence could conceivably be talking about; but yet we listened.

"And the evil voice continued, delighted with our attention. It proclaimed: 'You are no longer the beloved One Great People of the King, but henceforth you have become despicable creatures of the most intense misery and despair. From this state, there will be no possible reprieve, and your punishment will be fearful, cruel and ever-lasting…

"Again, thoroughly confused and unable to think clearly because of the bewitched herbs filling our senses, we asked, 'But what could possibly be our crime? We have done nothing!'

"And the voice proclaimed, 'Indeed, yes! *You have sought the destruction of the Kingdom and of your King…!'*

"We stared around us, wide-eyed and incredulous, and the dark voice continued:

"'You have left by the Gates, you have abandoned his City and all the King bestowed in his Love upon you. In your outrageous selfishness you have rejected all he has given you, and why? – Purely in order to seek something special and different, something other than his Gifts to you. This is your Crime, this is your Sin, an act of self-will that knows no comparison for its evil in any domain: You have rejected the Kingdom and willed its destruction in favor of what you believed you could seek and accomplish on your own.'

Paulo stared at the wizard, his mouth dry, feeling the memory of a strange, disturbing presence in his mind, one that always made him tense with terrible fear and self-condemnation.

The wizard continued. "This invisible monster spoke within our minds, 'Do not think your King is ignorant of your acts – no! He calls your behavior treason and betrayal of the highest order. At this very moment he is undertaking a plan for your punishment, a terrifying sentence you cannot even begin to imagine. Understand well, no matter how much he might have loved you before, now he has no choice but to hate you, to pursue you … and to *kill* you. You are evil – your sin must be punished, and your guilt shall be worn forevermore as a badge of the deepest shame.'

"Thus this foreign invader spoke with great command in our ears, and thus it wove a myth in our minds that would become the foundation for our every thought, our every feeling … our every breath. This was the myth of the Dark Lord, the Ruler who judges, who punishes and kills, and the fear of this evil sovereign and the death he promised would haunt us in all our waking and sleeping moments.

"We were lost, completely and profoundly lost, but why? – only because we *believed* this wicked specter, believing in the many evil ideas woven into its spell, in these frightening notions of guilt, sin and separation. It was like a heavy dark curtain had fallen in our minds confusing our senses and blinding us to all true sense and logic," the magician explained.

"Nevertheless, we whole-heartedly believed in these absurd ideas of abandonment and betrayal. We accepted as true this legend of the King's so-called hatred, and his need to punish us for our acts. And we were completely blind to all else. Yet everything this insane creature told us, absolutely everything, was completely and utterly *false*. There was no reality, no substance or truth whatsoever to its declarations; this frightful creature simply spoke more loudly and potently within our minds to make fast our belief. And still the magnificent Gates glimmered radiantly behind us, and the path shimmered under our feet inviting us back to the City. But we had been instructed not to look back, or death would immediately seize us; and so we did not look.

"For if we had lifted our heads, for even just an instant, we would have seen our brothers calling to us, beckoning to us, *beseeching* us through the open gates to return. Instead we turned our eyes shamefully and dutifully away, and saw no more the entrance to our beloved Home. Our brothers within the City looked upon us, aghast and helpless, as we retreated from the Gates, as we ultimately embarked upon a terrible self-imposed exile in the dark, unforgiving land of complete and utter ignorance."

Paulo's heart weighed like a heavy stone in his chest at the thought of the People's desperate plight, and he forced himself to breath deeply once, twice, before bringing his eyes back to the magician. His story was unfinished, and Paulo hung onto every word he uttered.

"We looked now upon our guilty selves, and found there cumbersome bodies, strange and foreign to us, in place of the beautiful raiments of light given to us by our King, and these bodies felt things completely unfamiliar to us. Our breath was short, and our muscles tense … we were filled with *fear*, a mortal experience we could never have imagined before. We looked at each other in our terrible distress, convinced that *escape* was now our only possible recourse. We would have to leave the Gates of the Kingdom in all haste if we wished to preserve our lives from the blood-thirsty Ruler coming to erase our loathsome, guilty existence.

"We were so pitifully, desperately unhappy and had no idea what to do, where to go, but we knew we had to do something. We could no longer turn toward our beloved King for help, for in our minds he had become the monstrous Dark Lord, an executioner, an angel of death. So in our extreme need we pleaded to the only presence we felt within our desecrated spirits:

"'Please, oh, do help us! We know not who or what you are, but you must now heed our call,' we cried to the voice of darkness. And in our utter distress this maleficent creation spoke to us with the greatest, most uncompromising authority…

"'You shall call me Maker!' it howled, '– and I will be your *Master*! Listen to me, and obey my commands. You have sinned, and your punishment shall be long till the end of your days. I, and only I, can save you from this terrible destiny now. You have been condemned and the Dark Lord commands your death, but *I* can help you in your terror and misery. Trust in me, for only my love and care for you are true. Though the Lord of this land rejects and despises you for your atrocious betrayal, I will love you and lead you to safety. If you learn to follow me, you shall be forever safe.'

"Then we cried, 'But to go where? There is *nowhere* other than the Kingdom, where else can we possibly go?'

"And the Maker replied, 'Fear not for this! Fear only the Dark Lord and his wrath and judgment, but never for my assistance. I have prepared for you another world, a domain, a hiding place where you can escape his punishment. There you will never be found. Come with me, and be safe at last from certain danger and terror that is real.'"

The boy stared at the wizard in wide-eyed astonishment, feeling every bit of the fear and guilt of the People and their desperate hope of finding a safe haven. Paulo believed, too, that the Dark Lord's anger was quite real and needed to be fled, and deeply understood the need for escape. That's the way he had always felt in his life, shadowed by a feeling of being watched and needing to explain and defend himself. That's what he had felt in the Forest before the big stone in the wall, and then he had run for safety to the village … and that was at the bottom of all his fears and thoughts of defense and escape.

Zeph continued his story, "We believed we had no choice, and so we began to follow where this pitiless jailer led, turning our backs obediently on the Golden City, and plodding with leaden feet and weighted hearts along the path away from our Home. And we damned and condemned ourselves with every step for our stupidity and hatefulness toward our King. The way became darker the further we traveled from the Gates, and the Maker told us this was necessary so the murderous Lord wouldn't find us. Darker and darker the way became, until the Golden Light was just a glimmer of its former power.

"After what seemed like a long, long journey, the Maker brought us to a place where arose before us out of the chill mists an enormous stone archway. This was *the Great Door*, and therein he told us to enter. Here we would be safe, and our sinister teacher showed us the massive stone wall that surrounded the entire Domain.

"We looked upon the dark wall before us and bewailed our dreadful fate. Some of our number wondered how it would be possible we could be happy in such a stone prison, but others reminded them of the even greater horrors *outside*, that we could only possibly feel safer within. We might live now in terror, they reasoned, but at least we would be protected by the great defensive Wall.

"Many of our host rushed blindly inside, grateful for the protection and safety offered for their lives. Some of us, however, hesitated a moment before the huge wooden doors that towered before us. We stood with our heads bowed, wondering how we could have arrived at this place, banished forever from the state of Loveliness. Just for a moment we remembered the beauty of the Golden City, the happiness of our brothers, the giving and sharing of all things wonderful and joyful. We lifted our heads, just an instant, and heard a happy, lovely sound, a song like that of angels singing…

"We listened and remembered the endless bright green fields filled with wild flowers and sunshine, warm and strong, that had no end. And then we remembered our loving King… Just for a moment we felt again the fullness of His Love, the never-ending wellness, peace and acceptance. We recalled the feeling that, *just as we were*, He loved us and accepted us, without hesitation and without proof of worthiness … and this we knew was true.

"Just for a moment we remembered again having no doubt as to our beauty and wholeness, and the knowledge of our joining with all things in the blessing of perfect purity and sameness. We recalled our absolute Oneness, dressed in garments of silver and gold, and not our separated and painful bodies. Slowly we turned ourselves away from the Door and back towards the fields of sunshine – and then the Maker descended upon us.

"'*Go no further!*' the creature shrieked pitilessly and furiously in our ears. 'This I command, that you now enter here, my world of protection and separation. Your way is *death!* The song you hear is the voice of the murderous Dark Lord disguised to entice you, and what you think is sunshine is a lure to ensnare you. Nothing remains for you there now, no love or hope or security – only punishment awaits you. Believe in *Me*, and only in my answers to your pain. There is one solution, and that is in the protection of these walls. Remain here with me in safety, and seek no longer what shall never again be yours.'

"We listened, we paid attention, and our greatest mistake, Paulo, we *believed*.

"We brought our eyes from the last traces of sunshine outside and looked upward to the tall gray stone walls. We felt a heavy pressure inside our chest, a crushing sensation that made a strange water come to our eyes that flowed down our cheeks and fell to the ground in heavy, silent drops. We were filled with a feeling we would never again be without inside the Domain, and this was *sadness*. It engulfed us, so deep, so dark, and without any conceivable hope of respite that standing there at the Door, for the first time in our existence, *we wept*.

"And one by one each of us turned our backs on the Kingdom of Light you see here, and entered into the realm of eternal illusion and ignorance: the mysterious prison that is the vicious, dark world of the *Domain*."

CHAPTER ELEVEN

The Maker's Secret Weapons

Paulo brushed the tears on his cheek with his sleeve. He felt his own sadness, the strange melancholy that he could never explain for something long ago that he couldn't remember, a sense of love that was now gone. He'd always been told it was something in his past that he missed, love that he hadn't received, that his parents couldn't give. But this response had never answered his pain.

The wise man continued. "Inside, it was dark and gray, our eyes half-closed, adjusting themselves to the dim light. It felt perpetually cold and wet there and we were weak, not the strong and vital beings of before. But the Maker reminded us that at least we were *alive*. The darkness and the wall of stone, he added, would prevent the vengeful Lord from ever finding us, and so we should be doubly content.

"We tried hard indeed to look content with our new surroundings, with the fact that we were safe, independent, and 'alive', but it wasn't easy. Every day was an effort to remember why we were supposed to be grateful. In the beginning, we still held a memory of the beauty, loveliness and wonder of our Home and the great Love of our King. But then as we adapted to the Spell and life in the Domain, as we convinced ourselves that Love had truly been transformed to hate, the memory of his Kindness became dimmer and dimmer. We busied ourselves with our lives and found many important things to do, running to and from the market place and work-fields, and eventually the remembrance of Oneness and Eternity, of Home and Peace, completely disappeared from sight…"

Paulo considered for some long minutes the remarkable tale of the One People's Fall and their arrival in the Domain.

"So, our going there and our leaving the Kingdom of Light was actually our own choice," the boy said, voicing his astonishment at the People's decision. Then after deep thought, he asked the only question which seemed now to make any sense to him: "But how on earth could we possibly think we could learn to be happy in such a miserable place?"

The magician met the boy's intense regard and a smile lit his face for just an instant. "We did indeed learn how to live within our adopted prison, Paulo; and the proof is that we are still there, and still believe we are happy there, and can yet be happier. We even learned to derive a morbid, eccentric pleasure in the idea of our new independence and 'freedom' from our heavenly Home. But it did take much time and effort learning to adjust to the perpetual insecurity and pain.

"You see, the sense of Crime in our hearts had made it impossible to escape from a terrible sense of injustice, a sense that some type of despicable act had been committed, and thoughts of pursuit and judgment constantly filled our dreams. Dominated by this belief in our guilt, we felt we rightly *deserved* punishment, and so always expected an attack or a painful event to come upon us by surprise. Despite the Maker's defensive wall, and despite the secluded hiding place of the Domain, we nevertheless felt a constant background danger, a perpetual anxiety and foreboding, which is the nature of those under the Spell of Damnation. It was the feeling that no matter how we might protect and defend ourselves, there would always be threat of attack."

Paulo asked, "And this is why everyone's always so worried, though they don't really know why? I see a lot of people in Towne like that. But why don't they see where the real problem comes from, from this exile from our Home, and from this big Judgment, like you say? They're always telling me about some problem or other in their lives. But always one problem seems to follow on another – it's never ending!"

"Yes, no one sees clearly anymore, Paulo. There's a good reason for this, and it would be good for you to know why. But be aware, the Maker has taken great pains to make sure we don't follow the trail of his planning and scheming too easily. His strategy has been one of total confusion, from beginning to end. What we're about to discuss here may seem complicated and long, but I'll attempt to make it as clear and brief as possible. Are you prepared for this long and difficult discussion? It's quite necessary."

The boy nodded his agreement, and the magician continued.

"And so, why don't we see his machinations clearly? Let me explain… After some time our pain within the desolate prison-home of the Domain became quite intolerable, you see, and the Maker realized in an instant the true fragility of his position. He reasoned – and he was correct – that if ever we started to look for a way to escape from our suffering, we would eventually come to question the truth of this Crime which bound us within his prison, to see that the whole thing was a charade, and then eventually return through the Door back to the Kingdom. To strengthen his position, he saw he would have to undertake further actions to stop us from clearly understanding the true state of affairs.

"So, insisting again that the Damnation was real and unalterable, the Maker informed us that there were nevertheless some practical solutions to our predicament. Firstly, he commanded us simply *not to think* about our situation, about all our tears and woe. Yes, imagine that, just not see it at all! In other words, to draw a thick curtain over it, to push it into some obscure corner of our minds and there forget about it and pretend that it wasn't even there. In this way, he schemed, we would take our hurt and loneliness, our guilt-feelings and misery, and wrap them altogether within a thick veil of mist and fog, and ultimately learn quite simply and naively how *not to dwell upon* them. This remarkable act of magic the Maker called *Veiling*.

"And he was quite right: for the most part we managed very well to hide our real feelings, pretending, as told, that all was well within ourselves and in our world. This was the first part of his strategy to strip away our reason."

Paulo thought about this a moment. "And so that's why no one knows about the real problem, because they've forgotten it and can't see it anymore," he said. "And that's all?"

"Not quite, there's still more," the magician continued. "You see, pain as acute as that caused by exile from our beloved Home could never be kept completely hidden from awareness by simply 'not seeing', as you can imagine; and the Maker also understood this. And so he came up with a second plan, so much more devious even than the first one.

"The Maker understood that if ever we managed to pierce his veil of forgetting and feel the full extent of our sadness and shame, we would eventually come to realize how untrue the whole Crime really was, and would then find a way to return back Homeward along the path. He figured he would have to make sure we never correctly understood the true nature of our thoughts and feelings, even when we felt them: he would need to *disguise* where they came from, and what they meant. And so he told to us yet another story, a second lie, that would cleverly keep the original myth of the Crime away from all proper grasp.

"The Maker instructed us that whenever we felt any of the morbid, painful aspects of the Crime, it was never as a result of some dreadful condition within ourselves, or because of something we had done – certainly not! It had nothing to do with us, because it was always because of some frightful circumstance *outside* of us, of course! Due always, in plain language, to *something* or *someone else*. And so all discussion of the Crime haunting our hearts would be avoided and be placed far, far away from any understanding.

"In the Maker's calculations, if we did exactly as he taught us, we would continue to be imprisoned by the imaginary Crime against the King and to wander homeless within his dark world, but we would never even begin to question the proper reason why. Quite simply, the reason for all our troubles and anxiety would no longer seem to be within the Exile which we had chosen of our own accord. Instead, it would appear within the outside events that occurred, and in the many people we encountered every day. It was an exceptionally clever, devious plan of the Maker's to take all power and reason away from his prisoners – and it worked!

"From that moment on, the Maker began his surreptitious whispering into our minds, instilling his new lies there; and suddenly, magically, all the distress and anxiety in our lives sprung now from the people we found around us. In fact, in little time we managed to learn many skilful ways to put the blame for our upsets onto all sorts of different events and circumstances occurring within the Domain. The Maker's name for this new masterpiece strategy was *Ridding*, since his prisoners would *rid* themselves of the condition that was really bothering them from inside, and cast it away onto people and events all around them."

Paulo continued to listen attentively, though he felt something inside made it extraordinarily difficult to grasp fully the wizard's strange concepts.

"Over time it became much simpler and easier to cast off our pain and irritation in all possible directions, rather than confront the real source of discomfort in our hearts. And this was *precisely* the Maker's intention. If ever we made it past the veil of non-seeing and forgetting, and felt the terrible absence of our Home in our hearts, the guilt of our so-called selfish deed would seize us with terror and self-disgust. We could persist beyond this state to find the comforting presence of Love that was still there, but we wouldn't. Instead we would begin to *rid* and cast off. So rather than appearing within our very own choices where we could do something about it, our pain would continually appear as coming from the situations and people around us where there wasn't much we could do.

"Any true comprehension of our predicament was therefore thoroughly removed from our grasp: the mythical Crime turned our harmless desire to leave the Kingdom into some terrible, heinous Sin; then the secret of *Veiling* prevented us from seeing the Exile and its consequences in our lives. Lastly, the special technique of *Ridding* guaranteed we would never understand the true nature of our pain and fear by always seeing their origin as somewhere else, and having nothing to do with us."

Paulo interrupted, "So, if I'm understanding right, then in this magical *Veiling* you're saying that I don't see what I'm really feeling or just ignore it. Then, in *Ridding* I'll always think it's someone else that's bothering me anyway, like my customers or the Mayor or the market place, 'sthat right?"

"Quite right, Paulo."

The boy continued, "So unless I managed one day to see there was actually something wrong with *me* and with everything going on inside, I'd always keep believing I was upset because of something else. Like I might look at other people and always think there was a problem with them, not with me. Not that I ever do that, 'course."

Zeph didn't seem to pick up on his little lie.

"Indeed, my wise young friend," the magician confirmed. "And to make it all work even more perfectly, our new and vicious Master incited us to practice this *Ridding* in a very precise way: we were to look at people now, and reveal as many of the differences between them as we could possibly find. He told us to go out and identify these many differences between people, and then to analyze them, and discuss them, and to do this *endlessly.*

"Strangely, back Home in our original state of Love, we had known all things as one and perfectly constant within Ourself. But now all we could see were divisions and differences around us, and countless outside situations that bothered us; and all these differences and conditions completely occupied our minds.

"It was a simple mistake, still only a simple error, to make all these differences between people and things so very heavy and significant; yet it was an important error. If only we had given these perceptions less importance, less weightiness, the way back to clear vision would have been guaranteed. We would easily have found the way back Home again. But of the many different people we saw around us, we noticed multitudes of brothers who now seemed inferior to us and unworthy of our respect. Then there were others who now seemed so superior to us, and we adored these people, though some of them we really regarded with a great deal of jealousy.

"Yes, our brothers, who at one time had been perfect equals with us, suddenly became total strangers – adversaries, competitors and enemies to be defended against, or, on the other hand, heroes to be worshipped. And we became suspicious of *everyone*, even of those people we claimed we loved and befriended."

The boy remarked, "It sounds like there was little chance then of really knowing what was going on. We just couldn't understand anything at all! We didn't even know where to start looking!"

"Quite so, indeed," the magician replied. "This was an essential part of the Maker's total plan – this endless search to understand our world, but by looking where no understanding really lay. From that time on, we would no longer occupy ourselves with any search for real understanding within the universe of our own hearts, because searching there would have led us straight to the remnants of the Kingdom of Light still buried deeply inside each one of us. But, hypnotized and blinded as we were, we would not find the timeless Presence of wisdom lying in wait inside us, lying just beyond the borders of our awareness, that marvelous Presence that would have instantly reminded us of the glorious, unified reality underlying the many divided appearances we imagined before us.

"No, we never thought again of actually looking within our hearts to discover the true cause of our feelings: we were too fiercely fixed on the outside world, and too furiously determined to forget our painful feelings. Indeed, we believed we *were* part of this new outside world, and that our reality *was* these infinitely small, fleshy and soft bodies our dark master had imposed upon us.

"This is where we are here and now, my boy. Believe it or not, the One Great People no longer clearly understand *anything* they see or feel. The Maker's many insidious disguises and defenses have entirely concealed the real problem that haunts them, and not seeing it and not understanding it, they cannot possibly solve it. In effect, the People have been rendered 'mindless'; they have no further awareness of the sacred place within their hearts far above the world and their tiny selves which sees all things clearly, and it is this mindlessness that ensures they will always stay completely unconscious."

Paulo stared back at the magician, eyes wide with astonishment and disbelief.

"Home..." the wizard finished, and a note of sadness entered his voice. "Home certainly seems a long, long way away. Most terrifying of all, we are not even aware that we are *no longer there*, and have left to reside in a foreign, inhospitable land. We cannot return because we have forgotten that a place that was Home actually exists, or even where it might possibly be. Above all, the Maker demands we remain resolutely convinced that the only place of reality and meaning is his phenomenal, earthly world of the Domain; and he commands we forget entirely that another life and place were our original state and condition.

"Today all problems and even existence itself appear to have their origin in events and conditions in the Domain. How strange, when seen from out here... Yet questioning that this might not actually be the way things really are is usually considered in Towne society as a sign of some serious confusion or illness rather than reason.

"But blinded by fear and guilt, the Townspeople are now no longer aware of where they are, how they arrived there, or what the real problem might even be with their lives. And of course a problem that is not seen, not recognized, and not understood, cannot possibly be resolved. Thus the separation from their true Home persists in time because it can no longer be seen; and for their pain, loneliness and shame they occupy themselves with endless solutions – but always to the *wrong problem*."

Chapter Twelve

False or True Mind?

Paulo was dumbstruck.

It was obvious to him now that no one would ever make it back Home – if he didn't even know he wasn't there! And that was precisely the way all the people in his life acted. To them, they *were* already where they belonged, although their dark and dangerous home had none of the deep feelings of safety and happiness that he had always imagined it should have.

The wizard's tone changed, his look extended over the hills and an intensity crept into his voice. "The Maker's work is truly diabolical, my boy. Yes… it is capable of changing the firmest, most deep-set convictions into their exact opposite. In the Kingdom, we cherished our brothers and sisters, yet now we only felt separation, suspicion and exclusion, and none of the warmth for them that filled our hearts before. Instead of gentle brothers and sisters, we found creatures of wickedness and disgrace around us, spawned merely from our own shamefulness and failings. In truth, of course, the wonderful Love and Light of our celestial Home were still there inside them, but we saw none of it."

"How can that really be?" the boy asked, bewildered. "Why don't we see our brothers like they really are today, if Love's really there?" It was clear even to him that the real view he had of his own customers was far from charitable.

"You can no longer understand others clearly, Paulo, because you no longer know *who you* really are yourself," Zeph instructed.

Don't know who I am…? the boy repeated inside quizzically.

"That's the simple answer. What you think yourself to be is the starting-point for all your feelings and perceptions, since you always first look inward inside yourself before looking outward. So, imagine if you felt condemned and deprived under the Spell, though these beliefs might be very hidden, you would always find signs of judgment and lack and so forth in the world around you and in the people you met every day. In fact, my young friend," Zeph reached over and tousled Paulo's hair roughly making Paulo scowl; "that's the only reason you see so many people in the market place who seem so obnoxious."

Paulo had a sudden flash of awareness. Maybe if he learned to understand himself differently, he thought, then perhaps he'd automatically come to see others differently as well. That would certainly help at home, he figured, not to mention at work.

The boy then said, "So it's like I don't know anymore what I really am, 'sthat it?" That seemed plausible enough to him now; he'd already seen many changes in himself, and hadn't the slightest idea as to what all these different aspects of himself could really mean.

"I'm some part of the nice King's Love, is that what you're saying?" he continued. "Then this very uncomfortable feeling of having done something really wrong but not knowing just what it is – this 'secret Guilt' you call it – was put there only to stop me from knowing what I really am. OK… I guess then if I allowed myself to really see something warm and kind within me, like this Love, even for just a moment, I'd know that Home wasn't so far away at all. That's probably why I can see the Kingdom right now, I guess. That'd then maybe make the Maker and all his guilt and stuff go away, at least for a minute, is that right? …The whole thing actually sounds really crazy to me."

"That's perfectly correct, Paulo." The wizard smiled widely, delighted with the boy's willingness to consider these many difficult ideas. "And, yes, it's all completely insane. That's why we say that everyone in the Domain is unwell – 'sick', you might say, unable to see or think clearly. No one feels well and whole, because no one is seeing clearly. No one understands who or what he is, or how he came to be; and no one knows where he really is, or even where he comes from. Thus we say that everyone in the Domain is in his *false mind*, and not in his *True Mind* at all."

The boy asked, "What's that, 'True Mind'?"

"That's the place in each of us where the truth is found, quite accessible and still perfectly intact; and it exists despite all the Maker's frantic attempts to erase its presence. In this most magical of all places, everything is clear and easily understood, everything is seen for what it is, and for what it could be. All is very peaceful and in perfect harmony. It's what you feel in the golden sunlight of the Kingdom with me, sitting here under a tree and talking quietly about the Quest of Understanding.

"But the false mind! There, the Maker dominates and all is confused and reversed in meaning and in sense. In that place there can be no clarity; there's no remembrance of the real problem, and only false problems preoccupy our minds though they seem of the greatest importance. In the True Mind there's real happiness, peace and understanding: in the false mind there's only fear, shame and turmoil, and only false, short-lived joy and denial.

Paulo, looking thoughtful, asked, "But we can still see more clearly if we want to, no? I mean, if we can get back to this 'True Mind' place."

"Of course, absolutely. Everyone can learn to understand their lives properly by entering their True Mind; in fact, that's your personal role while you're in the Domain, Paulo. By going to your True Mind more and more, you'll eventually come to notice what's really around you everywhere: you'll start to find the radiant Love that's still there within you, the Love that would teach you that no sin has ever separated you from your Home, or tarnished your holy spirit. You'll come to find the silver-white purity of your Self and of the One People, which is an especially beautiful and marvelous sight."

There was a pause then, a silent moment in which Paulo felt something deep and wonderful glowing within him.

"So, to finish our story," the sage continued after a minute, " in time the Spell of Damnation with all its many malevolent variations was complete. In the People's guilt-enshrouded hearts, only pain felt real because of something unknown but terribly evil they had done that could not be undone. Over the years they learned to concern themselves solely with their losses, using the world to find what comfort and safety they could. Happiness came, but only in those brief instants when danger felt more distant, the tiny self protected and validated because of some fleeting circumstance or pleasure. Lost in the false mind, blind to the existence of their true spirit, the People lost all remembrance of the gentle, enduring answer to their real problem: the unifying Love always present, always waiting there patiently in the quiet, holy Kingdom of their True Mind."

Zeph raised his arm and pointed with an open hand back toward the gray wall behind them. "Today when we look at the Domain from out here in the Kingdom, it all seems so strange…

"We see the People busy themselves with daily life, frantically buying and selling in the market place in an effort to make time go by as best and painlessly as they can. Imagine! They are actually completely unaware that they live within a prison, keeping their pain and fear as deeply hidden as possible from sight. The barrier of guilt and self-hate remains well-buried, since they believe it to be the reminder of the certain oblivion on the other side: the imminent wrath and fury of the Dark Lord.

"A thick Forest has since grown up all around the impenetrable defensive Wall, and to explain their origin the People have fabricated a story in which it was their King that *banished* them from his holy Realm, and not they that sought to leave. Still others claim that the King does not exist, and never has. A figment of the imagination! Remarkably frightened, they are, of the idea of another Home which is not their cherished and familiar Domain.

"Yes! The One Great People, sacred and magnificent, have completely lost sight and understanding of their divine origin, and now call themselves the 'Townspeople'. Whereas before they were perfect and identical in every respect, now they see each self as individually different and compete amongst each other for importance, value and safety."

The magician's eyes sparkled with intensity, and he continued:

"What's more, the King's People believe themselves limited and have forgotten their infinite greatness, and each one who goes there but faces an ultimately mortal end. Alas! Their lives are short-lived, filled with sadness and suffering, pride and self-inflation. The People have effectively fallen into a form of deep sleep; their nightmares continue still today, playing out terrible scenarios of attack and suffering and injustice. Their time on earth is no more than a bitter, wasted hope for happiness in a place of barren illusion, and never do they wonder if there might not yet be another way."

Zeph straightened himself a moment, lifting his chin, and filling his lungs with air. "And yet there is still hope, Paulo, *tremendous hope*. Because no plan of the Maker, no hypnosis or unconsciousness, no matter how cleverly designed and executed, could ever prevent the One People from remembering that resplendent Love they had once received, and that still awaits them.

"That's the decision you made, Paulo: to *remember*; to remember the King's Love beyond all the fanciful terror and guilt, and more and more of your brothers will do so as well. Yet more of your brothers will have the courage to look again, to face their fears and to doubt what they have always seen with their body's eyes. To begin to doubt what they have been seeing and thinking all these long years; and then we shall meet with them, right here, in the splendid land of freedom and understanding."

CHAPTER THIRTEEN

The King's Love Misunderstood

Paulo gazed far out across the broad rolling fields and hills toward the luminous glow straddling the distant mountain top. A day of brilliant sunshine bathed their spot in a comfortable warmth. The wizard, sitting next to him, a slight smile on his lips, closed his eyes in a moment of quiet. There was not a whisper, not the slightest trace of fear or danger anywhere to be seen. Paulo glanced back at the wall behind him, toward the hole he'd so easily made just that day, and shook his head, bewildered.

He suddenly cried, startling the magician out of his half-sleep, "But how's it possible we could really believe in all this stuff? In all this exile and guilt and separation stuff? That Love could just stop and no longer exist? I mean, look here now, there's something else here – I feel it! It's so clear I'm not what I always thought before. Over there in the City, I'm not this broken person I've always thought, I just know it. How could we really believe that these tiny people the Maker forced us to be could be our real life? It's just so, so… I don't know how to say it, but everything the Maker's told us to think and do, everything is just… wrong! It's ridiculous, and *completely* untrue."

Zeph grinned broadly, the lines of his weathered face framing two intense sparkling eyes.

"Yes, indeed *everything*, my boy. It's all so ridiculous – *silly*, you might even say. Starting with the Door. The true King is very, very kind, and wants his people to be eternally free. Our jailer, the Maker, *could not* ever close or lock the prison door because the King had guaranteed to all his people that they could leave his heavenly Realm, and *return,* any time they wished. The bright light above the Door is the magical force that prevents the gates from ever closing and blocking our return Home. The Maker knows this. That's why he had to make us *believe* the path back to the Kingdom was impossible to return on. And that's why he posted the squadron of guards at the door.

"The King's people are free. They can leave their prison any time they wish. The door is open, if only they would look, but this freedom is thoroughly hidden from their awareness. The dense barrier of Guilt still dominates their minds, even though there are now many cracks and holes in it, if only people really cared to find a way through. You see, the Maker, despite his cunning, was never powerful enough to make any defense that could last forever against the light and beauty of the Kingdom. All defenses, you must understand, have their limits and weaknesses."

The sage's regard pierced Paulo, and he said: "The One People *shall* remember once more who they are, despite the Maker's unrelenting efforts to the contrary. *That's* their deepest wish, beyond any promise of personal life and independence. Against this wish the Maker has only limited ability. His only remaining power now stems from our wish to continue to believe in his tales of evil and abandonment. Once this belief is undone, he is undone; he is completely gone from our minds, along with his grim world."

Paulo lost himself in thought a moment, evidently bothered by something. It was all so strange, so many new ideas; and the magician sounded just so sure of himself. How could it all be…?

Suddenly a stern look swept across his face and he declared authoritatively, "But I do think it was such a terribly inconsiderate thing to do, to leave the King. I mean, that must've hurt him a great deal. If we'd never left the Kingdom, none of this mess would've ever happened. Just look at it all now. What a disaster! The King had given us this lovely kingdom and then we went and said it just wasn't good enough. We should always be grateful for what's given us, and if not, well… I think that's *just not good.*"

"Dear friend," said the magician kindly, "I'm very glad to tell you that you need never worry about how the King feels about you. He knows only Love for you, for that is his very substance, and only that. In his eyes there was no such betrayal at all, for he undid the problem as soon as it appeared to bother us. For him, it's as if it never happened at all, and that's precisely how you must learn to think of it, too. Only the villagers take the idea of separation from the Kingdom seriously, and that's a mistake they must learn to undo."

Paulo listened skeptically, frowning.

"In all that has seemed to happen there is absolutely no judgment," Zeph continued. "You shall, in fact, have to remind yourself of this *many, many* times. The wicked Controller of your thoughts has convinced you quite thoroughly that your King has indeed judged you, *and* condemned you: that's the judgmental character we have given the imaginary Dark Lord. But the true, loving King is incapable of condemning his People: he knows that they contain his very own quality of innocence, and this cannot be undone by anything his People might do in the dream-world of the Domain."

He glanced at the boy who still seemed unconvinced.

"Know now, Paulo Vitali," the magician said soberly, "your King does not judge and criticize you, and you must learn not to condemn yourself in his place. Your King knows *love* for you, no matter what you might believe yourself to be, or believe you may have done. If you wish, if you find it easier, consider that he has already judged you and has found you to be perfectly and wholly worthy of love, and that's all you need to remember. The final judgment of the good King *was* his perfect acceptance of His holy People, for he alone knows their perfect quality. "

Paulo was thoroughly lost. The magician saw that it was difficult for the boy to understand the nature of pure acceptance and perfect innocence. In reality, Paulo found it nearly impossible to think that the King loved him so dearly that he didn't need to do anything – *couldn't do anything* – to prove himself, redeem himself or gain his favor.

"I know it's very hard to believe, Paulo," the wizard tried to explain, "but there's nothing you can do to improve yourself in your King's sight: he knows you *already* as perfect. Of course not your imperfect individuality that the Maker conceded to you and which is of no great significance – but your true Self. You must learn now to relax and to accept this state of perfection which is the nature of your true Self, and to stop worrying quite so much."

"Stop worrying so much…" Paulo repeated out loud to himself, trying to grasp the magician's intent.

"Yes, and please try to understand: our turning away from the King has not been important to him in any way except that it causes *us* pain – but certainly not him. He offered his Gifts to us in love and is glad when they are accepted; but he is not offended at all if we refuse them. Our thoughts and actions have caused him no disgrace or shame; he is very patient and knows that we will eventually accept his Love, once we realize there *is* nothing else that shall ever make us so happy and fulfilled.

"Yes, it's true, we rejected our King and Creator; and everyone in Towne continues to do so every day. But this is of no consequence because he understands. He guards our worthiness safely, and he harbors not the smallest, slightest unkind thought toward his People."

Pausing, he smiled toward the frustrated boy.

"Let me explain. Many years ago, our King confided us with free will and gave it gladly and without reserve: this will was the power to choose our destiny, and we could exercise it as we wished. We could use it to bring us closer to him, or to take us far away. He would miss us if we chose to leave, but he would never be angry with us if we did. Do you understand?"

Actually, Paulo was making very little progress with the magician's words; it was exceptionally difficult for the young boy to make head or tail of it all. And he wondered, *how's it possible that self-judgment and condemnation aren't important?* He had lived all his life with these beliefs, and now he was supposed to do precisely the opposite. It just seemed impossible...

He said now with just a little indignation, "But surely it must be bad that we turned away from the King. I... I just *know* it is," he insisted. "I feel it, here, inside of me." He felt within him a sense of wrong that seemed innate and undeniable, and he could only believe it was because of something he had once done.

A warmth of delight lit the magician's face.

"Now, Paulo, my good friend," he said patiently, "let me reassure you once again that there's nothing 'bad', as you call it, in what we appear to have done. There is nothing bad in you or in your past choices, nor in anyone else. This is only more of the Crime speaking within you. In fact, in all the entire living universe there is no evil thing..."

Paulo's eyes shot wide open in surprise.

"...Nevertheless, I understand that this is extremely difficult to accept, especially when we observe the gruesome events that take place in the Domain. There is nothing bad, anywhere, because the King did not include anything evil within his Kingdom; and you must understand that the Domain is not part of his Kingdom, but the Maker's."

The boy shook his head imperceptibly from side to side in bewilderment.

"In the Domain you can *think* things are evil, you can have the *perception* of things that are cruel and unjust, and in the Domain many horrendous things are done out of the belief in guilt, exclusion and condemnation. But if the Domain is not your real Home and if the King has guaranteed forever the well-being of your true existence, then how is it so important if things in the Domain are distressing? And what is not important hardly deserves being so upset about, no?"

The boy held not a trace of agreement in his regard. "It's just not possible, the way you say," he said boldly.

"You must come to learn in time, Paulo," the wizard replied, "that you can do nothing to make your imagined sin real, or to banish the love of your King or yourself from the Kingdom because of some fancied act. You will always be loved and accepted, no matter what you think or say or do, and this is the same for each lost member of the One People: there is not one who is excluded from this Love."

Now quite beside himself, Paulo shouted, "That's great reason for doing just whatever we wish then. Being hurtful or unkind, I mean!"

Zeph explained patiently to the boy who continued to scowl. "No, this doesn't mean that you can do whatever you want in the Domain. There are rules, and there are things there that we must do, and things there we must not do. If we go against the rules in the Domain, we'll have to face the consequences in the Domain. But it does mean that whatever you do, whatever mistakes you make along your path, your King still loves you and will always accept you back into his Home.

"Just look at this idea further, Paulo. People do irresponsible things in the Domain today only *because* they feel a gaping hole where Love once was. They are wicked and selfish *because* they are frightened and confused by the condemnation they feel within them. They aren't listening to the quiet Silver Voice that speaks of peace, and so it's natural they'll feel acute pain and loss. The rules in the Domain are established *because* people are now blind and dominated by guilt, cut off from all sanity and peace. If everyone felt original Love in the place of the Separation and the Crime, they would know only clarity and harmlessness in their hearts, and there would be no more reason for the many rules that people need today."

Paulo had to take a moment for himself. He was aware he had little real comprehension of the wizard's full meaning. Something important in his words still escaped him.

"It just seems so different, Zeph… different from the way everyone thinks. From the way *I* think. Everything I believe is completely the opposite of all you're saying."

"Let me perhaps try to explain it another way."

Zeph paused, cogitating. He realized the importance of reaching through to his young student at this early stage of his learning and sought earnestly to give him something more to hold on to, something he could grasp.

CHAPTER FOURTEEN

Dreams and Miracles

"The problem, dear Paulo, is really only one of *confusion*," the wizard continued after a minute. "Try to see, you aren't yet able to understand all of this clearly because your thoughts are simply too obstructed and confused. This is why your judgments and conclusions are misplaced, and why *everyone's* judgments and understanding are incorrect: everyone is plainly and simply confused. Not sinful, but confused, and that's the reason for the chaos and catastrophe you see in your world.

"Try to follow this idea, Paulo: Every day that we wake up in the mist-shrouded world of the Domain, we all face this tremendously black feeling that there is something terribly wrong in existence, with us, with our world. It is felt by everyone, though it is nearly always denied and forgotten. No one in the Domain today wakes and feels completely at ease and peaceful with his existence, serenely happy in the knowledge of the perfect Love contained within him and all others, and of the inviolability of Life. He has forgotten the truth, and sleeps. Every morning in fact he wakes up – still *asleep!* A sleep plagued by troubling doubts and by frightening images of punishment and sacrifice for some crime he does not even comprehend.

"He is thoroughly, alarmingly confused, but does not know it. And this confusion is a source of great pain, though none of this is necessary. There is a simple answer, a wonderfully simple answer, but it will not seem simple while we remain firmly committed to staying asleep. There is a reason for our dedication to sleeping, but we will have to get to that at a later time.

"It's enough to know for the present that the People sleep, and in this uneasy, fitful slumber we appear banished from our original Home, firmly convinced our King condemns us and demands sacrifice for our sin. But this is a mistake, that's all, Paulo. A mistake that leads to great confusion and distress, it's true; but nevertheless only just a mistake, and certainly not a crime. And for this reason, I'm glad to tell you, the King has confided us with a powerful tool for correcting the confusion in our hearts, for correcting the many mistaken beliefs and the sense of deadly sin lying there: he gave us the *Atonement,* as a means of healing this miserable mistake."

"Atonement?" Paulo asked, bemused, "What's that?"

"I'm glad we've already reached this point in our conversations, Paulo, because this is a very special and important thing that I'd like to share with you: The real meaning of the principle we call the Atonement is that the so-called deadly Sin of Betrayal and the mortifying Banishment from the Kingdom *never actually occurred at all,* and that Love is still the Life we share. Atonement, as we call it, is the perfect response to the perceived problem of exile from Home, because it is the simple remembrance of the truth as it is, the truth that sets all things aright in our minds."

Paulo stared toward the ground, his eyes unfocused, listening intently. "*Sets all things aright…*" he heard echoing in his mind.

"Yes, Atonement is simply a truth, a reality accepted, a wonderful knowledge remembered; certainly not something that must be worked for or merited. And neither is it something that requires suffering or sacrifice, being always offered freely and without price. Many Townspeople today are finally seeing it is no longer necessary to continue repeating the same errors of old, and are choosing the correct understanding of Atonement and the peaceful release it offers everyone. They are remembering that the Atonement – and the attending Miracles it offers – can finally replace all their fears, all their mistakes, and all their false ideas."

"*Miracles?*" the boy wondered out loud. "What're they?"

"One day, Paulo, your life will be filled with Miracles," the wizard spoke. "An endless stream. And what is a Miracle, you ask? It is simply a moment of remembering, that's all; a moment of truth in which you have let go your insistence on how you see things, your insistence on your unhappiness and ill-ease. It is a moment in which you ask with a truly open and welcoming mind, *What is the truth here*?

"This is the Miracle, a tiny moment of wanting the truth to be true, above all you have ever thought, believed and sought. And, wanting your thoughts and feelings to be corrected, they shall be: *this* is the healing.

"Your path Home shall eventually be paved with a multitude of these healing Miracles, my boy, tiny bright instants of remembering that join together to form the brilliant passageway leading back to the City of Light. And so in this sense your path could be said to be one of a course in Miracles, Paulo, a course in learning to replace your grievances and losses with healing and happiness; a course in learning simply to end all illusion and replace it with truth."

The sage paused, and after a moment returned to his fabulous story of the People's plight. "Yet all this time we have spent wandering lost in our dreams of hate and guilt, our King has never stopped loving us. As soon as we left, he immediately sought for us and started calling to us quietly across the Kingdom, calling to remember his Love and return to him. He waits for us even now, to hear and to know that he is not angry, and welcomes us still back Home."

Paulo appeared thoughtful and asked, "Is that the sound I hear? When I'm in the forest, when I'm quiet, there's a lovely sound sometimes. It reminds me of this place here."

"That, Paulo, is indeed the call of the King's Silver-Song. If you go to the Forest on a still day, if you quiet your heart full of feelings and your mind full of thoughts, if you really listen, you will hear it. The rich sound of the King will you certainly hear, blended in magnificent chorus with the love of the Kingdom, the holy song that he sings across all eternity. It binds all living things together in a melody of sweetness and safety that knows no comparison in any other world. This is the harmony of loveliness that *everyone* hears in the back of his mind, the loveliness and gentleness that puts all fears and doubts to rest, that reminds us that something else exists other than all the troubling and tragic things we perceive there in the Domain.

"But you see, when the Maker gained control of our minds, he forbade us to ever listen to this call, claiming it was evil, the lure of the wrathful Dark Lord tricking us to leave the protection of the Domain. So whenever we heard the beautiful melody, even faintly, we believed it to be the fore-calling of a vengeful hatred come to bring our death, and we ran back to the Domain in fear. This is the real reason people are scared to be in quiet places or to be alone, moments when they might hear the Silver Call. This is why no one listens to the Call – or nearly no one.

"There are those like you, and like others yet, those among the group who first hesitated at the Wall before entering through the Door. Some of you have chosen now to listen again to the golden song and remember it is the voice of Kindness and Love, not of death. This is what you have done, Paulo. And others as well, like you, are now looking away from the Domain for the answers to their questions, willing to confront their fear and cross the wall of ancient forgetting, to find the truth on the other side."

Paulo asked, "But, Zeph, why did you choose *me*, why did you call *me* of all people? I heard you calling clearly."

The magician responded gravely, correcting the boy, "It's not so much that you are specially chosen, Paulo. Understand, the Song of Remembering calls to everyone, because you *are* all One: the call is an inherent part of the essence of every person. But you, however, chose to listen and to hear what everyone can hear. Everyone is the same: everyone is called, but as yet few have chosen to listen. Perhaps that's changing now."

The wizard then asked the boy, "Why did you choose to listen, Paulo?"

Paulo thought a moment before answering.

"I was just really tired, that's all," he said. "Really, truly, fed up. I guess it was just because I was so tired of the same old problems. And the same fears and anger, too. I was tired of hating my customers and the Mayor, and getting upset with my mother, and irritated with my work. I saw that life wasn't ever really going to change and get better, not really. Not even if I had all the things I was looking for; and it hurt terribly to think there was no hope at all. I wanted so badly just to know there was something else, something better than the Domain and my stupid little life within it. I felt there *was* something else, though I didn't know what."

"And you were quite right," the sage responded. "Deep down, in the quiet of his heart, every villager realizes there's something better than the Domain and his tiny little life within it. Whenever a Townsperson allows himself to feel just that, he lets himself come a little closer to the Kingdom; he opens his ears just a little more to hear the gentle voice that speaks the truth within him. Because he is finally admitting that perhaps the Domain does *not* hold the real solution to his problem, but that a real solution does exist … *somewhere.*"

CHAPTER FIFTEEN

A Very Unwilling Return

Paulo considered the magician's beautiful words for a moment, and allowed his gaze to stretch far out over the fields and hills to the splendid glowing mountain-top in the distance. Then he exclaimed in a down-to-business sort of way, "Okay, so how do I get to the Golden City to meet my sisters and brothers there? It looks quite simple from here, really."

The boy turned to stare fixedly in the direction of the path gleaming brightly in the valley below. He couldn't wait to start.

"Ah… now that's a very good question," Zeph replied. "However I'm not so sure you're going to like the answer very much."

The wizard paused and looked like he was preparing for an important, even difficult, discussion. He turned himself to face the boy, and the tiny pinpoint stars on his velvet robe caught the light, flashing brightly. "Let me explain… The path Home is not straight, young Paulo. It is magical, and was made to protect you from unhappiness and to teach you the true nature of peace. Does that make sense?"

He waited a moment, surveying the boy intently. Paulo wore a most determined, uncompromising look.

"Paulo," the magician started again, somewhat hesitant, "if you try to walk along the Golden Path *without the correct preparation* it will always take you *back* to the Domain."

Paulo stared back at the magician, his mouth agape.

"*But why?* That makes no sense at all!"

Zeph paused to assess his young apprentice further, then explained solemnly, "Paulo, to know how to get to the Golden City, you must now return back to the Domain. It is only there that you can prepare yourself fully. It is there that you will find the *Knowing* that will allow you to return; the Knowing, and the *Key* that will unlock it."

Paulo swept his eyes from the luminous horizon to stare back at the dense gray wall of the Domain. He cried, unbelieving, "You mean I have to go *there?*" He repeated, pointing toward the Wall, *"Back there … to Towne?"*

"Paulo, it is most important that you return to the Domain, the world of the Spell, the world of guilt, and illusion. That is where your path Home really lies, and where you will ultimately find the happiness you seek. It is there. But *you* must find it."

This time Paulo stood up abruptly in disagreement, holding himself firmly on his two sturdy feet. "But it's dark and gray there and everyone is sad and angry," he refuted loudly. "They do nasty and stupid things. And all I hear about is their ridiculous problems. Why can't I just come Home now? Why do I have to go back to the market place and deal with my rotten customers? Why can't I just throw this silly black bag away and come with you?" He was already quite upset and was trying hard not to get even angrier.

"I would like that very much, Paulo," the magician said gently, "But I'm afraid you would be too frightened to come with me right now. Please try to understand, the black Spell Purse is still too important for you. You have kept it close to you all your life –"

"No! That's not true!" the boy protested.

"– And you have become more accustomed to the dark of your world than you think. You would find the bright Light of the Kingdom quite intolerable until you first became used to the light that is already present in the Domain."

"But *there is* no light there," Paulo exclaimed despairingly. "There it's dark and awful. And I *am* ready; I do want to see the light – *now!*"

"Paulo, please try to listen," Zeph said kindly but firmly.

Paulo sat down and tried to restrain himself.

The wizard continued. "A long time ago, Paulo, you closed your eyes and slept. More than anything you did not want to see anymore, to see the truth of who and what you were, to see the Light from which you came and the remarkable Love that was your Home. You willingly accepted the ideas of the Maker and thus they became a part of you – in essence you *became* the Maker. A part of you is now fully imbued with the spirit of the Maker, and you have absolutely no conscious awareness of the extent of his power over you. While you wish to return Home, the Maker within you still wants very much to remain separate and distinct from the Kingdom.

"Since the initial forgetting, the secret Maker part of you has covered over your True Mind with many layers of self-judgment and hatred to ensure that you would never find your way back to that place of truth and freedom. Now you're trying once more to remember; but you must believe me, you're still very afraid of your great Self. You're not at all what you think you are – oh, no – and you can't even begin to imagine the brilliance of your true Self, and that's why you need time for more learning in the Domain."

Paulo tried hard to understand the sage's meanings, but it was especially difficult. He couldn't seriously imagine being anything other than what he thought he already was. And he was starting to wonder just how much effort and time it would possibly still take him in the Domain. He now had to go back there in order to salvage the memory of his Self, a memory supposedly still lying somewhere in his mind out of sight. But where? And how was he possibly to find it? It was all so discouraging.

"Paulo, you must now learn to open your eyes, but *slowly*," the wizard reassured. "Even though you realize that the bewitched herb purse and your little Maker-self are just part of the Spell, you still have a big interest in pretending the Domain is your true home. You must, over time, learn to understand the nature of this decision you made to banish yourself from your Home. And you are still too afraid to look frankly at the real cost of this choice for separation. You know that it was ultimately the choice for unhappiness and a desperate state of loneliness and insecurity, and that's understandably a very fearful act to face. Nevertheless, you still believe there must be some good reason to remain in exile from your Home and your true Self, since that's the choice you still keep making each and every day."

"So what on earth am I really supposed to do? How'm I supposed to undo all this mess?" the boy asked impatiently.

"The way you undo the problem," Zeph said, "is by beginning with first steps. Firstly, you have to look for the traces of the Maker's surreptitious work in your life, which means following the path of your many daily decisions to turn away from Home. You turn your back on Love and Truth – a decision you still repeat every day – every time you allow condemnation and fear to dominate your thoughts.

"So, begin by searching for these many moments of separation instead of keeping them from your awareness. Find them, seek them out. Then, slowly, over time, practice choosing otherwise; practice choosing against this desire to remain under the Spell of the Crime. You *can* turn back to the Light and away from the paths of Exile: you *do* have the power: it all begins with wanting to be once more in the quiet, peaceful halls of your Home."

"That's all I have to do?" Paulo asked, doubtful.

"Look, search, find those moments in your life of reinforcing the Crime. They're there, the signs are all around you; don't hide them any longer. That's indeed a first step.

"Then you must learn to admit that everything you despise in the world isn't actually there in others around you. No! What's making you so desperately reluctant to return back to your daily life is what you're terrified to discover … about *yourself* – not what you fear to face in others in the market place! The evil and horror you so abhor are *within* you. That's what you've most feared all along; that's why you've refused to walk the path Home till now."

"Huh, it's *in me*, you say, all that bad stuff? Right."

"It's not in others," the magician answered, "it's nowhere out there in the world: the Desolation you feel is within you, and that's precisely why you are so powerful. It is *your* choice, hence it is within *your power* to undo it."

"My power?" the boy repeated, uncomprehending.

"Find the unhappy consequences in your life of the Banishment you have imposed upon yourself these many long years," the sage continued, "then realize this is no longer what you really want. Exile has no further attraction for you anymore; its promises no longer sparkle and gleam in quite the same way as before. It hasn't brought the rewards you sought; but neither has it had any real or lasting consequences and effects, not on you, nor on anyone else. Your joyous, peaceful Reality has been kept quite safe all this time; and you will naturally feel this, a profound sense of wellness and joy in the place of despair and anger, whenever you manage to put aside your self-judgment, each instant you touch again that love and quiet kindness still present for you."

"So, I just learn to look?"

"Yes, begin now to look at the darkness and evil you once accepted into your heart, but no longer want, and this shall make it disappear. Learn to look carefully at yourself, but do it now with kindness and understanding, with charity and compassion. When the shadows within you begin to fade, then I promise, Paulo, you will clearly see before you the golden path Home to the City of Light."

– CHAPTER SIXTEEN –

A Particularly Useful Place

Paulo looked from the magician to the woods, staring absently, then turned his sight out toward the horizon.

The magician followed the boy's eyes. He wondered, in fact, if his willingness was really up to the challenge at hand. It was certain the boy didn't really understand the true difficulty of the road he had chosen to take, Zeph pondered. *Would he actually continue if he really knew?* Only time will tell. He is still very young, though I'm quite sure he does have the ability and will-power. I will have to follow him closely.

Then the boy asked, "But why, Zeph? Why does that mean I have to return to the Domain of all places?"

"The Domain is a very useful place for you right now, Paulo, I assure you," the magician replied. "It has one very powerful, unexpected use: Within its shadowy shapes and scenes, it has the ability to reflect back to you quite perfectly the real contents of your mind, somewhat like a mirror, you might say; and that's essential for you right at this time, since you aren't even aware of the thoughts and choices that your mind presently contains. The Domain can, in this way, help to undo this veil of intense secrecy the Maker has cast over your thoughts, so you can discover what you have been hiding there in their depths.

"You don't like the Domain, Paulo, I understand. But you'll learn that the things you most dislike about it, your heavy grievances, regrets and frustrations, are only the reflection of your own tenebrous thoughts, and nothing more. So I'm asking you now to return to the market place in order to look honestly at your feelings about people, about all the many faces that come and go in your life as wood-seller. If you pay close attention, you'll start to see the judgment and irritation, the sadness and blame that are there, lying unsuspected in your mind. These are the thoughts and feelings that are most damaging to your search for peace, because they are born from your on-going desire for separation and exile.

"Then, if you wish to be happier, you can listen and you'll hear a pure, clear Voice singing, reminding you in the midst of your aches and worries … *nothing is really happening*. Nothing ever really happened! Love is there, not gone at all, and never departed to leave you sad and shamed and fearful. Listen, and you'll find that there is no banishment from Home, for Love is still a part of you. Listen, and remember you are not this insignificant, vulnerable creature searching vainly for comfort and validation from an uncaring, uncertain world. For you are still as you once were: healed, whole and entirely loved, a beautiful and exceptional part of the One Great People."

Paulo's thoughts fell entirely still for a moment.

The boy spoke slowly now, apparently troubled. "So, Towne is just some kind of a mirror, is that it? And I only have to look at everything that's going on around me to see what's really going on in my mind."

After a moment he expressed his worry, "I got to be honest, Zeph, I don't reckon I want to know what I actually think about everyone in the market square. There're things I'd really prefer not to know at all, as a matter of fact."

"I see what you mean, Paulo," the magician replied; "and I understand. It takes a good deal of courage to admit one's true feelings, and it's no laughing matter to confront one's real opinions of others.

"I know it sounds difficult, but you must learn this step – it's imperative. You have to learn now how to observe the voice of judgment in yourself as it speaks in all the problems and situations you encounter. Only in this way will you learn that what it declares is false, and quite entirely silly, really."

"And this is supposed to help me?" the boy asked, somewhat doubtful.

"If you practice now exactly as I say, you'll begin to feel the darkness lessen its grip on your heart, this is a promise; and to feel a soothing calm and quiet begin to appear behind the grim appearances of pain. But for this you must first raise your courage, and be willing to let the hate and judgment within you be found. Yes, *first* let them be seen honestly, and only *then* may they be replaced by peace and comfort.

"I promise, if you practice as I'm teaching you, in time you'll find that the Maker will have no more power over you or your mind. *You* will have all power and mastery over the Maker. In this way, all sadness and powerlessness will start to disappear entirely from your life; and then you'll easily be able to find the special *Key* and *Knowing* that you will need to walk the path all the way Home."

CHAPTER SEVENTEEN

The Winding Path to Happiness

"So I've got to find some type of Key and some special Knowledge, s'that right? And this'll set me on the right track Home?" Paulo asked, quite dubious about the magician's many lofty promises.

"That's right," the magician answered. "The Key is what you shall use to find the Knowing. This secret understanding then dissolves the Spell and unveils the passage Home." He gave the boy a wise, caring look from behind two gray, bushy brows. "Don't worry, Paulo. You'll discover all these things for yourself in due time."

The boy, however, was looking quite lost; his shoulders hung low, his eyes turned away. He was trying not to feel completely disconsolate, finding it hard to believe the daunting task that his teacher had laid before him. Zeph could see Paulo was confused and upset.

"I still think the Domain is the last of all places I ought to have to learn my lessons," the young wood seller said somberly. "There just has to be a better way than that!"

"Try to think of it another way, Paulo," the magician proposed gently. "While you haven't yet dissolved all the Maker's craziness within your mind, you'll naturally be drawn back to the Domain. That's normal, that's because you'll still be tempted to think that the Maker's Domain could offer you certain things that don't exist in the Golden City. Just imagine, if you arrived at the Golden City still wanting any of these things from the dark world of the Domain, you simply wouldn't be happy there, would you? And so if you started along the Path Home and felt any regret for the things you still wanted in the Domain, or felt afraid for what you might lose by arriving Home, then the Path would simply return you to the place where you believed you could still find them. So, you see, you *have* to go back there. It's inevitable, until you've learned how to undo the influence of the Maker in your thoughts."

Paulo gave absolutely no reaction.

"The Golden Path is just the road to happiness, that's all," Zeph explained. "Wherever you believe your happiness is, the Path will take you there. If you end up back in the Domain, it will be because that's where you still believed happiness lay. Do you understand? Regret and fear will always take you back to the Domain so you can find what it is you're still looking for there. It's *you* that determines where your path leads you: you only ever end up where *you* have chosen to be."

Paulo didn't look any better for hearing these clearly spoken words, and he avoided meeting the magician's eye. He had, in fact, a growing suspicion of something insidious in the wizard's arguments, and was desperately hoping his fears wouldn't come true.

Zeph continued determinedly: "This path is only one of kindness and certainly not one of punishment or sacrifice, Paulo, despite everything you might be thinking. There's no question that the King wants you to find all that you seek, and to sacrifice nothing. He knows there is nothing in the Domain that will ever make you really happy, because nothing there is real enough to possibly satisfy you; but while *you* still think you can be happy there, the Path will guide you back there – that's all."

The boy grit his teeth in a fiercely sullen look. It had now become all too evident that not only did he need to return to that miserable place the other side of the Wall, but, in addition, he wasn't even guaranteed any happiness there as he saw it. "This isn't sounding like any fun at all," he moaned loudly. "What's the purpose of going back if I can't even look forward to my little dreams? You say I'll never be really happy there."

"Please make an effort to understand, Paulo," Zeph implored; "if you return to the Domain now, it's only to learn the true nature of happiness – not to live in despair. In this way, when you do finally arrive at the Golden Gates with me, you'll know that you're there because you truly wish to be there more than anywhere else. In the meantime you can pursue as many dreams for happiness in the Domain as you wish – this is a promise. We ask you simply to begin looking carefully at where you have been striving for happiness and safety all this time, and to be very honest with yourself about the results of your efforts."

Paulo was now trying desperately hard not to look thoroughly disheartened; the magician's well-chosen words of comfort had not improved the boy's outlook on the future one bit.

Zeph offered, "You see, my young friend, you can stay in the Domain as long as you want and the King will still love you and wait for you. The Gates shall never close, and he shall never, ever grow impatient with you. Time is yours to decide when you wish to return. That is the extraordinary gentleness that the King placed in Eternity –"

"But that means I'll never be happy!" the boy cried, thinking about how long and difficult it would be to overcome the Spell.

"Oh, no, quite the opposite!" the wizard replied. "Firstly, you can come back anytime you wish to this place on the hill to meet with me, and I'll help you and we can talk again together. Even just an instant of time spent here in your day will make you feel very much better.

"But most importantly, Paulo, you can feel just as happy and free there in the rainy gray of the Domain as here. Starting today, if you wish, you can learn to feel in the market place exactly as you do here in the Golden Kingdom – I assure you this is true. The peace and happiness you most desire, you can indeed claim them there in the Domain for yourself."

"Really? Are you *sure*?" the boy said, finally finding just the smallest trace of encouragement in the situation. "You say that I can learn to be just as happy and free there as I feel here? That just doesn't seem possible."

Zeph responded, "Maybe it seems unlikely. But even the market place can become a place of wonderful happiness and freedom, if you wish. Yes, even your customers can become a source of happiness – imagine that! You can learn to see their problems differently, in a way that'll bring you peace and joy instead of frustration; and they'll become your *reminders*, your guides. In fact, that's precisely where you'll find the Light you're looking for, Paulo: in your brothers and sisters in Towne. Seeing the Townspeople differently, given what you shall be learning with me over time, is precisely *the way* you begin to turn back to your True Mind where light and understanding are naturally present."

Paulo asked warily, quite disbelieving, "And you reckon I'll be able to learn all this just by looking at the Townspeople differently?"

"Indeed, quite so," the magician replied confidently. "When you observe just one other person as beloved of your King, *despite his burdens and anger,* you will begin to see all people that way – because you are all One. Do you understand?

"Listen to me now: The Spell claims you are all separated and imprisoned within the tiny, vulnerable lives the Maker has bestowed upon you, banished far from the love of your King, exiled forever to the battlefield of the Domain. Your job, Paulo, is to fight the temptation to see this way, and to remember otherwise. By the power of your mind, you *shall* undo this dreadful Spell, I promise.

"And just imagine, Paulo: you need never again see the Townspeople as trapped in their mundane lives and problems. The peace and happiness they seek are still really there, glowing brilliantly before them; and you can help find it for them. You can uncover the light and strength present within them, no matter what is happening, no matter how gruesome and frightening their circumstances appear.

"This is the way you'll eradicate the darkness you accepted so very long ago into your own mind, my young friend. This is how you will help yourself see that *you* are free of the imprisonment the illusory Exile would proclaim. You learn how to smile and laugh at all the things that once made you so sad and angry, and so terribly afraid. You learn to laugh, just as our brothers in the Golden City did so long ago, at all the preposterous, amusing notions of the Maker. Whereas we forgot to laugh before, now we remember. It's not too late. And then you share this new breath of delight and freedom with everyone else. Do you understand?"

"I think so. But you're *sure* that I can come back here to see you?" the boy asked, apprehensive at the idea of returning alone.

"Anytime you wish!" the magician answered, and his face lit with a broad smile. "You've made your own personal door in the Wall and now can return anytime you want. Even better…" Zeph smiled tenderly and his eyes twinkled, "…I promise that if you call to me inside your thoughts, my voice will come to you whenever you need me, whenever you are sad or confused, no matter where you are." He spoke softly, his face bright and cheerful. "If you want, Paulo, we need never be apart again. In fact, I think we could make quite a team, what do you think?"

"Yes! That already happened – twice I heard your voice!" Paulo was far happier, now that he started to understand how he could return, and still keep one foot in the Kingdom. "Oh, I think this is going to be much more fun now. Wait till I tell everyone. Francesca – just imagine what she'll think! And Fredo, he'll be *so* impressed."

Zeph hesitated, and looked slightly stern. "I don't think you should tell anyone right away, Paulo. I don't think you should talk about this very much yet. These thoughts are all still very new to you, and I'm afraid you will be quite confused about their real meaning for some time yet: you might in fact frighten people with these ideas. You know, people are *very* scared, and they might think you're dangerous to them. But don't worry, you won't need to tell them anything; they will *know* something is different, because they will *feel* it in you.

"You don't need to say anything to people at all, and yet you can give them a great gift, just like I did with you in the market place when you took my money – remember? That's the way you can also be with others: you'll tell them through *your eyes* that something else exists, something other than the sorrowful grayness of the Domain. In fact, that's your primary work while you're still within the Domain: to learn to look past the darkness, and to return your thoughts to your True Mind."

The magician now stood up and the gold and silver stars sparkled radiantly all over his robe. He waved his hand and made a motion for Paulo to stand; he put his hands on the boy's shoulders and looked him directly in the eye.

"Paulo, my friend, I make this request of you."

The boy gazed into the magician's face and wondered what this important task might be.

Zeph spoke solemnly: "Learn now to smile and laugh, and learn that you are free."

Paulo grinned broadly, surprised by the unexpected, simple demand his mentor made of him.

"No matter where you are," the magician continued, "no matter what is happening to you, learn that you are free and loved, and then mirror these lessons to others. Teach them through your kindness and your peace that the ancient decision for damnation and imprisonment has had no consequence, and that there is a real reason now to be happy once more…

"Does that sound too difficult for you?" the wizard asked with a trace of laughter in his voice. "Teach happiness to my beloved brothers and sisters who still believe the sad prison of the Domain is their only home, so they too can be free. Then you can come with me to the Golden City, I promise. The road you undertake now is the path of the greatest learning and teaching, and this path leads you back through the Domain: I *know* you shall succeed.

"Now – go back through the wall and wake tomorrow happy to spend time with your brothers and sisters in the market place. Take a last look here, and remember it well. Remember that wherever you are and whatever is occurring, happiness is true. Just try a little, despite the great temptation to be irritated and sad, to remember that misery is maybe not as powerful as you think, nor the only thing around you. And then share this vision with your brothers."

Paulo took a last look at the exquisite day around him, a day he had been able to spend in the extraordinary Kingdom of his true Home, a day that he would remember for the rest of his life.

"Some time soon I'll get there," he said determinedly, gazing out toward the Golden City in the distance.

The young wood seller then turned and left the field, strolling back through the forest, and climbed back through the breach in the wall to the Domain, into the archaic prison of the Maker, to begin the search for the hidden path Home. And to remember to laugh, and smile…

Part 2

CHAPTER EIGHTEEN

Market Place Strife

Paulo was silent at the dinner table that night. He had so much to think about and everything around him seemed utterly too busy. Mama had asked him to bring in the goats, then help prepare dinner, then set the table, then wash himself, then… There was such a long list of things to do, and he couldn't find time just to sit quietly and think about all the amazing things that had happened to him in the Kingdom that day.

Fredo looked at him curiously, and Paulo continued to dry the dishes after the evening meal and ignored his brother's inquisitive stares.

"Are you okay?" Fredo asked. "You were really quiet at dinner…" Then he drew a breath and his eyes shot open wide with fright. "You didn't go out to the Beyonde today, like you said you would, did you? Promise me you didn't!"

Paulo replied sharply, "Why don't you just stop bothering me with all your questions. I've just got things on my mind, that's all," he said, but without telling his brother what he wanted to know, and Fredo turned back to his tasks. He felt frustrated, not being able to say anything about the Kingdom, but didn't want to lie. In fact, since he wasn't permitted to stay out in the beautiful sun-lit field with the magician, he had been invaded by a poignant feeling of injustice.

Then Zeph's voice came quietly to him. "If you want to be happy like in the field, Paulo, then learn to be patient with the way you're still seeing things there before you. There's no injustice in your circumstance, it's only the Maker whispering to you of imprisonment again."

Paulo answered sullenly inside, "What would you know? You're not the one sitting here and dealing with this. It's miserable here, not like there where you are."

Zeph replied kindly, "Only *you* say that because that's what the feeling of Damnation provokes within you. The Maker doesn't want you to approach joyfulness, so he'll make you see everything as dismal as possible. As in a prison. The beauty and happiness you seek *do* exist – they're present even now. Find them there, find them now in Fredo. Remember who Fredo is."

Paulo continued grudgingly doing the dishes, thinking.

What on earth's he talking about? *Remember who your brother is.* What could that mean?

He stared at his brother and he looked the same as always: large eyes with thick eyebrows, short frizzy brown hair and snub nose. He looked again and noticed that his brother was curious about the Wall and the Outside. *Of course he's curious*, Paulo mused. Indeed, he should be! It's a marvelous, remarkable place. Surely he'd like to go there too so he can learn about happiness and freedom.

"Fredo," Paulo ventured timidly, "Can I ask you a question? Do you want to be happy in life, I mean *really* happy?"

Fredo looked at his brother strangely, and leaned against the kitchen bench. "I guess so. What a weird question. Everyone wants to be happy… don't they?"

"But I mean *really happy*, Fredo, like there were no more problems ever, anywhere. Like you just knew there was *such* a good reason to be happy."

"I don't really know. I've never thought about it like that. It's not really possible to be happy *all* the time – is it?"

"You know what, Fredo, I'm starting to think that maybe it *is* possible. Don't tell anyone, but I've *seen* the reason to be really happy." He didn't want to say anything directly about the Kingdom. "There *is* a real reason to be happy. So we can finally stop being so upset about everything. Wouldn't that be great?!"

"I don't think I understand. What's the real reason to be happy, exactly?" Fredo was quite confused.

Paulo tried to find the right words. "Well, what if the only reason we were unhappy was because we were under some kind of a spell that said that we *had* to be miserable all the time? Like it said there was no reason ever to be happy because of some huge feeling of judgment and disappointment inside of us that made us feel as if in some kind of a prison." He paused, hoping he was sounding convincing. "But, you see, there's also another but a nice and kind presence inside us that helps us remember that we're not hated at all and can be happy if we want to. Then, all we have to do is listen to this gentle voice when it speaks. It'll say that we were unhappy only because some wicked creature was telling us to feel guilty and afraid and to have a problem with this and that."

Paulo looked at his brother to see if he was following. The young boy continued determinedly, "You can be happy, because, because–" He wanted to say, *'because that's what the kind King created for us, and he wants more than anything for us just to be happy again,'* but Fredo would never have believed him anyway.

"– because that's what you want and that's what you want more than anything and it's possible and that's good enough reason. *That's why!*"

His brother looked quite bewildered and after a moment Paulo insisted further. "There's no reason why not. We don't have to wait forever to feel exactly the way we want, isn't that right? We don't have to wait for everything outside to look perfect. Why can't I be really happy right now, just doing the dishes?" He was in fact trying to convince himself, and believed this is what the magician wanted him to do, to understand that happiness was actually already present and not a question of being in another place at all.

Fredo looked at him and didn't say anything about Paulo's thoughts, but he was thinking about them. He started to do the dishes again, reflecting.

"But Paulo, I can't just be happy all the time," he declared after some minutes. "Sometimes I'm scared of things and they don't go away. Like the blacksmith. He gets furious sometimes and bangs this huge hammer down on a piece of burning iron that makes sparks fly all over the place and it frightens me a lot. Then he glares at me with these giant black eyes of his as if I've done something terribly wrong, even though I don't know what. I think I must be very bad because he's gets so angry."

Paulo didn't know quite what to say because he often felt the same way when his mother got angry or a customer was upset. He also felt that there must be something very wrong with him and didn't know where the feeling came from. He was starting to feel that this must be another part of the Spell of Damnation.

"I know what you mean, Fredo," Paulo said sincerely. "I'm not sure what to say, but I just *know* there's a way of feeling better about it, about everything," he offered. "After all, it's not really *us* they're angry at – *is it?*"

Paulo went to the market the next day and threw his wood down in a messy heap on the wet cobbles next to Benito, the fish-seller. Benito looked at the boy warily and Paulo glared back, forcing himself to give a short, gruff 'hello'. Francesca waved gaily from the far side of the square and he raised his hand half-heartedly and tried to smile back at her.

He was making a rather poor effort at looking happy and he knew it too, which didn't make him feel any better. But he found it impossible to feel good inside. Questions turned over and over in his mind, and he felt trapped in a prison with no exit.

How'll I ever find the Key and the secret Knowledge to return to the Golden City while I'm stuck in this stupid, rotten market square all day?

How can I possibly walk the path of learning here of all places? he asked, looking sulkily around the busy town square.

He put his hand in his satchel and found the little black herb purse. *All because of you!* he said to himself. *If I weren't under the Spell, I could get out of here and run Home right away. How'm I ever going to get out of this stupid Spell if I can't even move from here?*

All that morning while collecting wood in the Forest a burning, angry sensation had filled his mind: he just couldn't understand why he deserved to be treated so badly. He had tried to calm down and feel that everything was alright just as it was, but the burning sentiment of being badly treated seemed to return without any effort at all. And now he was stuck again in the market place which seemed today more like a jail than anything else.

He looked around, thoroughly irritated. Benito's fish smelled absolutely revolting that morning – they must be *months* old, he figured – and the smoke from the soldiers' brazier fire was making his eyes burn. 'I'd better get another spot on the other side of the market if Benito is going to insist on selling rotten fish, he said to himself. Maybe closer to the fire, then at least I could keep warm – why do the soldiers have all the privileges here anyway?'

Then he looked over at the other side of the square and saw there were more people than normal at Francesca's stand buying eggs. 'And where are *my* customers when I need them?' he demanded angrily.

At last Mr Salvatori came by. Paulo said rudely, without thinking: "Yes – *I know!* It's a bit wet today, isn't it, sir? And perhaps you're not feeling so strong, as well. Oh, dear, I'm *so* sorry."

Mr Salvatori blinked and looked at him curiously. "You're not the same today, Paulo. What's wrong, is everything okay?"

Paulo reddened furiously with embarrassment, all the more ashamed because Mr Salvatori hadn't become upset with his rudeness.

When his customer left he wondered what could be happening to him. Unexpectedly Zeph's quiet voice filled his ears. "A small warning, Paulo – today will be quite different from other days at the market place. Remember, the Spell is extremely powerful and above all the Maker doesn't want you to undo it. He feels now that you're on to him, that you're more aware of him, he *senses* it; so he'll disguise the Spell and make you see your problems as everywhere *other* than where they really are. This is what your eyes will surely show you.

"But the only real problem is *inside* you, Paulo: remember this. And it already has a perfect answer. My boy, *you have no more problems*, just remember Home, just remember Kindness. You have no more problems because you know the Golden City exists. Yes, you've seen it, and you know your King loves you. Remember this now today."

Paulo thought to himself: *I have no problems...*

That seems pretty stupid actually – it looks like I've got quite a number right here. There're the fish that stink, my customers that hate me and complain endlessly, and there's no time to find that stupid Key... and the Golden City is still a long, long way away, no thanks to you! he said, thinking of the wizard.

Mrs Belladonna came by to pick up her bundle of kindlin' as usual. He tried to get rid of her as quickly as possible, hoping she wouldn't stay to talk. She finally departed and Paulo heaved a sigh of relief, but too soon. A minute later he saw her disappearing figure turn around and come stomping straight back toward him.

Holy Maker, no! he said under his breath. *What now?*

She returned to his stand and her round face was patchy red and sweaty: she was evidently very angry about something. Her hand shot out menacingly and in it were a few coins. "Paulo Vitali! What *on earth* is the meaning of this? Are you playing games with me?" Her face screwed into a grimace of disbelief and disgust.

Paulo was completely confused. Mrs Belladonna didn't leave him time to wonder.

"Paulo, *just* because the shoemaker is a lousy cheat and a thief doesn't mean you can start to give me the wrong change, too. *Humpf!* You can be sure it's going to be a *long time* before you see me again as a customer, my boy."

She stamped away leaving him standing there totally perplexed.

When she left, Paulo looked upward to the sky and implored, exasperated, "What on earth have I done to deserve all this? Why is this happening to *me? I* haven't done anything bad."

The magician's voice returned to his mind. "Remember, Paulo, you have now officially begun the real work of walking the path Home. As such, the Maker will make every effort to ensure you continue to believe in his darkened world, and you'll do and say some very silly things unless you're quite careful. You run the risk of creating problems for yourself precisely *in order* to keep your thoughts based in his world, and away from the pure, inner reaches of your mind.

"You're only now starting to become aware of the contents of your mind, to undo the sleepiness there, the forgetfulness that is the first of the Maker's plans to prevent you from realizing the truth. You're simply learning now to pay attention to what's really there in your mind. But you may yet provoke some dramatic, unfortunate events outside yourself in order to avoid this work. Pay attention, be very vigilant, and above all, listen – *Listen to the Spell in your mind!"*

Paulo pondered.

Right. Listen to the Spell. That must mean that horrid little voice. What was it telling me just a moment ago? Let's be honest. Oh, yes … Mrs Belladonna. Well, we all know how truly horrible she can be, don't we? She can cope with a little misery in her life, since she makes everyone else's lives so miserable –

Mr Bravuro arrived in a hurry, dressed in his long fur-trim black coat, his arms full of various parcels. Paulo paid particular attention to be quick and accurate for the gentleman, knowing Mrs Bravuro was waiting for him at home.

He was about to give him his change when something made him hesitate. A loud and pernicious voice jumped into his ear – 'Why *on earth* do I have to rush like this. It's not my problem if he can't take two blessed minutes at my stand. Why can't he just tell his stupid wife she can wait? I have half a mind just to take my time – *that'll* teach him.'

Paulo looked sheepishly at Mr Bravuro, hoping desperately the customer couldn't hear the ill-mannered litany running through his mind.

"Is everything all right, Paulo?" he asked.

"Quite fine, sir. Thank you," he replied under his breath.

CHAPTER NINETEEN

Benito's Rotten Fish

When Mr Bravuro left, Paulo dug his hand into his satchel and pulled out the Spell Pouch. It seemed heavier in his hand, and somehow hot, too. It was working extra hard, Paulo thought. I better be real careful: there's lots of extra mean stuff coming from its magic today.

He looked carefully around the market square wondering what other spells might be filling his mind that he wasn't aware of, as Zeph had said, trying to listen purposively to the obscure dark voice in his thoughts.

There he was, Benito, fortunately busy, selecting and wrapping produce for shoppers. Look at him. Hmm.

Okay, the fish smelled terribly, Paulo thought. But maybe it was really only because the dark voice said so, telling him it was the fish seller's fault. In fact, now that he listened, the dark presence was clearly telling him that Benito had been doing it to him – on purpose – making his foul odors blow toward Paulo, just to bother him!

So, Benito's attacking me with his stinky rotten fish, 'sthat right?

It was now clear to Paulo that the fish stank more than usual this morning *only* because a malicious instinct told him they did; otherwise the market place smelled exactly as it did every other day. The voice was telling him that he was being attacked, and that it was the fish and the rude, inconsiderate fish-monger that were the cause. *But yesterday was fine; I wasn't bothered yesterday by any odors.*

And what about all the many people buying eggs and chickens? Were there really more people than usual? – *I don't think so.* It just looked like it was a problem that there were people at Francesca's stand today. *But only because some strange voice is telling me this is a problem, probably because I'm worried about today's sales.*

He, Paulo, was still the same, and life was still the same. But the noisy sound in his ears was undeniably stronger. Or was it? *Maybe it's always been there, but now it's just become louder and more obvious.*

He looked around again.

Yes, life's still just the same.

The scenes in the market square jostled and bustled before his eyes like a series of fast-moving pictures.

'Something inside me will keep on giving me messages about the images before my eyes,' he concluded. 'Sometimes it'll see good things that are happening, and sometimes it'll find bad things: that'll never change.'

Again his eyes darted about at the rapidly shifting and moving scenes and suddenly an amazing thought occurred to him:

These images don't really mean anything! At least they don't mean much till something inside me tells me what they mean. It's all just a bunch of images with no real sense that something, somewhere, is giving meanings to all the time. How totally bizarre!

And the message is the same all the time. Listen: Here there're good things that would make me happy, and over there, there're bad things that I'll have to steer away from. Good things to get, bad things to avoid. Bad things and good things; but everything that's happening here isn't really good or bad at all, it's just what it is. It's all pretty neutral, just images and pictures really, that's all.

It was permanently there, that strange, mean voice, Paulo noticed, telling him always how to feel. He would listen and it would instruct him to feel a certain way as a result of looking at the scenes before his eyes. He would feel deprived because other market stalls were selling more than him, and this meant of course that he was a failure; or he would feel infuriated when a customer cheated a merchant – how incredibly unjust! – because the merchant was obviously injured by this, so the malicious secret voice told him.

Then when a poor stallholder finally won an argument with the unscrupulous Mayor he would naturally feel delighted – but only because some strange creature was informing him this was a good thing. Why was this such a good thing anyway? Paulo didn't honestly know, since it didn't really change anything in life, neither for the Mayor nor for the merchant, especially considering that the Love of the King was supposed to be present there for both of them. Then no matter what happened, it wasn't actually that important.

The whole game seemed so incredibly odd.

What could the funny dark presence be saying all the time that could possibly be so important, he wondered. He focused on the background muttering in his mind, and then it slowly became clearer:

'There's a problem, Paulo, look! Just look around you – there's a problem over there…'

He cocked his head to the side, then suddenly he heard a series of further messages, astoundingly disjointed and incoherent:

'It's really serious, Paulo, you should realize that now. You've got to judge everything that's going on here – that's the only way you'll be able to get by and defend yourself. So just look with me at what I'm seeing. Right here in front of you there's a tremendous injustice being done – find it there; just look! You're in desperate lack and need, didn't you know that? And it's *their* fault.'

Now that he'd scratched the surface of the dark spell-voice's veneer, there came an outpouring of seemingly unstoppable messages:

'They could give you what you want – they just don't want to, so you're just going to have to take whatever you can, whichever way you can. It's not your fault, that's just the way it is: you're vulnerable and unsafe here, just make sure you defend and prepare yourself, get what you need, make yourself stronger. Yes, yes! Always get what you need for yourself.'

Paulo shook his head in utter bafflement. He had no idea his mind contained so much outrageous spiteful and selfish babbling. And he was astonished to find that it was so fixed on his personal condition and that it saw the world as such a harsh and unjust place.

He listened further, spying now on the sinister presence lurking within his thoughts, and he heard: 'You're such a weary, pitiful victim, Paulo. You've *got* to be suspicious – yes, of everyone! That's the only sure way to avoid any unpleasant surprises. There are victims everywhere: just look at them over there, look at those poor, poor people; you sure don't want to end up like them, do you? It's just that everyone and everything's against you, so that's why it's normal to be aggressive and constantly angry. It's not your fault after all…'

He wrenched his thoughts away from the pernicious howling there and sought for a tiny space of calm. How could he possibly feel this way, he wondered, so victimized and subject to so much unfairness. It couldn't be real, there wasn't that much injustice and danger there in his world… Maybe, what if it was just him after all, what if it was just all in his mind –

'What a ridiculous, *preposterous*, notion!' the malicious voice reacted suddenly and violently in his ear; 'You don't think for a single second that all this attack, deprivation and injustice come from *you*? You really *are* stupid! You don't think *you're* the source of all these feelings? Not in the least – *they are*!'

But who on earth are 'they'? Paulo asked, mystified.

'Other people, of course!' the answer came back immediately; 'Everything outside of you! Danger and injustice and lack are everywhere, and it has absolutely nothing to do with you. *Life* is the problem – life's responsible. No, listen to me now: it's really the evil Lord, that's who, Paulo: it's because of the evil Dark Lord that you're stuck here and you're no longer safe and provided for. After all, you didn't choose to come here, did you? You were kicked out, so it *has* to be his fault. When ever did you make the choice to come here? It couldn't be clearer, it's got nothing to do with you...'

Paulo listened in disbelief to the malevolent presence spinning around in his mind and then tried to take a step back from its insistent crazy jabbering.

Where could these thoughts be coming from, he wondered. In all honesty, he couldn't believe that they were really coming from the world he saw before him; after all, the outside hadn't even changed that much from just yesterday. His feelings about life and himself seemed to change constantly, literally *all the time*, yet the world never changed that much. It had to be something inside, he concluded. Yes, it must be something inside that keeps changing its story from day to day.

He pursed his lips tightly, then asked aloud: "But then why do I always believe it's the world that's the problem if it's not really responsible for the way I'm feeling?"

A quiet warmth now surrounded him and the sound of the magician's voice gently filled his mind: "Because of the Maker part of you, that's why. What you feel is the little 'you' and is under the Spell utilizes the outside world as a barrier to prevent you from uncovering the truth. That's what I taught you is called *ridding* – the attempt to hide a problem by not seeing it where it is, but as somewhere else. You think the problem is out there in the world, because if you looked honestly within your own thoughts you would discover the terror that's sitting there. So to avoid looking directly at this horrible sight, you see the problem as everywhere *except* where it actually is."

Paulo responded, frustrated with what seemed to be the magician's impractical explanations, "But how on earth am I supposed to fix all that? It's exhausting! And I never even knew that stupid old voice was there before – you've got to make it stop!"

"It's a *process*, Paulo, one that you'll learn to apply at first slowly, then more and more," the wizard said patiently. "Peace and happiness will finally come, but not before you pass through what seems like a lot of distress. And what you are starting to do here in the market square is a very important first step.

"Over time you'll learn to use the outside conditions of your life in order to turn your attention inside and work with what you find there. This will help you already to stop blaming the outside scenes in your life so much. Only, in the beginning, what you find there won't please you one bit because you haven't yet learned to look inside yourself without judgment and fear. The fear and criticism will slowly diminish, but only when you see that Kindness is there to support you every step of the way."

Paulo sighed heavily. He found it quite disheartening to think that the Path to Happiness would require confronting so much anger and hatred and general craziness.

Why can't it be simpler?

"I know it's difficult, Paulo, but it's the only way," the magician said calmly. "If you don't look within yourself you'll just be pretending these feelings aren't there – pulling a thick curtain back over them; this is what we spoke of yesterday as the *veiling* of your thoughts, remember? While you remain terrified of your deepest inner nature, you won't be able to resolve your questions about yourself and approach your real identity and your Home."

"Fine! So what do I do, practically speaking?" the boy demanded. "– If that's not too much to ask!"

"You look straight at the crazy voice of anger and hate, without fear and without judgment, and that will begin to make it disappear. And you no longer make believe these unpleasant feelings don't exist or see their cause as elsewhere. Look at their foundation calmly, with my help, and the pain and fear melt away."

"And that's where I start?" Paulo asked, still unconvinced.

The wizard continued talking placidly within his mind: "You start by looking where the general problem really *is*, which isn't as you've always believed in the worries of your life, or in other horrid people. That's really *not* where it is. The Maker is always insisting that the only way to feel better is to fix the world; yet now you're being told that the solution to everything in your life is always within your heart and mind.

"No matter what type of problem is facing you, the ability to change things for the better always lies within your power, because what you ultimately need to change is always within your mind, and hence within your grasp. No circumstance can imprison one of the Great People who has decided to claim his..."

But Zeph's voice was drifting slowly away as Paulo became lost in his thoughts... It was hard to make sense of it all. He could only see a multitude of irritating and upsetting things around him, and certainly no trace of Love anywhere. So many problems, worries and disturbing things to think about; so many things he still wanted to change in order to feel better, in order to get his life going in the right direction, and to make his world still more satisfying and fulfilling.

And everyone else seemed to be thinking the same way! Everywhere he looked in the market place people were hard at work listening to the same miserable voice: the stallholders were now furious with the town officials in the square who intended to raise the cost of levies; Mrs Belladonna was ranting at the bread man who was busy telling her in no uncertain language to go harass another merchant; worried, anxious people grimaced upwards at the sky, wondering if the clouds would break and let through a little of the sun's light and warmth.

Paulo knew when he returned home his mother would have found a long list of such 'essential' things that had to be done. Why? ... simply in order for her to feel better. Everyone was feeling miserable with something around them, no one was considering for a second that the real problem and the real solution might be entirely inside them. No one, in fact, was really happy at all, and everyone was still convinced it was because of something on the outside that had to be fixed. Not one person was looking inside: *everyone was ridding and veiling*, and everyone was ignoring the real problem just sitting there in front of them.

Paulo shook his head slowly from side to side, totally confounded. It was only yesterday he'd broken through the Wall and been touched by such an exceptional experience of happiness. He'd discovered there was finally something other than the prison of the market place, something extraordinary and wonderful. And all this time, he thought, while all of us here are feeling so awfully deprived and attacked, so depressed and irritated, the sun was still shining … brilliantly and peacefully, just the other side of the Wall, the barricade of powerful, secret self-damnation and fear.

Truly, it must all be some kind of crazy joke, he thought. Real happiness and sunshine were indeed right there all the time. *It's just there*, he thought. *But where? Why's it so terribly hard to keep things straight?*

And Zeph spoke a gentle reply, "We'll get to that, Paulo. There is indeed a reason. But one step at a time now…"

The rest of the morning Paulo tried to remember that – *somewhere* – all his problems were already gone and a lovely light was shining for everyone, even if no one saw it and even if their hearts were weighed heavy with black thoughts. He tried also to remember that the outside was really quite a neutral place and not the actual cause of his feelings. Thinking this way seemed to be a good way to pass the time, and it helped avoid making any more silly mistakes.

At market-end, Paulo picked up the empty canvas roll and bid farewell to the last of his customers. Most people were making their way back home as the church bells struck twelve, but he had no desire to return to the cottage quite yet. Not really knowing in which direction to go, he left the square by a side-street and wandered aimlessly for some time through the twisting narrow lanes of the town. Pigeons cooed from the eaves and a few heavy lead-glazed windows were opened to let in the warmer afternoon air. A man he knew as the cobbler passed him and nodded a greeting before disappearing into the dark inner space of his house. The door closed behind him. Paulo sighed.

Quite by accident he found himself once again behind the Town Hall in the former merchant's district. Without reflecting, he made his way between the tall half-timbered houses that straddled the dark street like sentinels, and came within sight of the heavily guarded square in the distance. He tucked himself behind a stone pillar well away from being seen and just watched. The guards were sleeping peacefully again, just as the other days. In fact, it didn't look like they would ever wake up unless someone passed by.

How bizarre…

– CHAPTER TWENTY –

A Painful Mistake

That evening, when Paulo returned to the cottage after his chores, he found Fredo sitting on his bed, his arms wrapped around his legs, staring vacantly toward the ceiling. Something wasn't right.

Paulo approached silently, then sat next to him on the edge of the bed. He waited a minute before speaking.

"What's wrong? Did anything happen?"

"The blacksmith got angry today – again," he replied in a subdued voice.

Paulo looked closer at Fredo and saw that his cheek was puffed and bruised. He wasn't sure if he should say anything. "Did you do something to upset him?" Paulo asked.

Fredo lowered his eyes. "I did something dumb."

"You wanna tell me about it?"

Fredo heaved a breath. In his thoughts he brought back the event exactly as it had happened that day…

It was morning and the workshop had been filled with a suffocating heavy smoke and sparks were flying in all directions; the blacksmith was hammering furiously at several pieces of iron at the same time that he was turning into tools he said were for urgent collection later that day. Then a farmer had marched in with a badly damaged plough-head and he outright insisted that it be repaired for that afternoon and no later: he had to finish tilling before another rain-fall made it impossible, he said.

The blacksmith just glared down at the farmer who stood his ground. The sweat was pouring off him, running down in streams from his heavy leather jerkin, and Fredo could see his jaw tighten till the tendons were popping out; but he only just grunted an agreement.

The giant man threw the plough-head into the fiery coals along with the other tools waiting to be fixed, and turned it several times impatiently, waiting for it to heat. He pulled hard at the bellows and sent fumes and sparks billowing into the darkness above. Some time later, when it was fully heated, he took it to the anvil where he worked it fully once, hammering and smashing the iron piece back together with another section of metal. When it needed to be reheated he whistled at Fredo who was busy at the other end of the workshop, jabbed a finger at the fire and nodded at the tool.

Fredo reached out and grabbed the plough-head with the long-handled tongs and made his way carefully toward the coal pit. But for a reason that still escaped him – he knew what he was supposed to do, he just got confused – he didn't shove it in the blazing flames to reheat but instead placed the still smoldering iron into the water trough used for tempering knives and blades.

A searing hiss erupted from the trough, and through a column of steam the blacksmith came pounding over the cobble-floor and wrenched the tongs from the boy; but it was too late. The tool had already cooled, and it would a long time again to bring it back to proper working heat.

Before he knew what happened, Fredo felt himself sprawling on the floor among the straw and workshop debris, grasping his burning cheek. He looked up and the dark figure loomed over him. The blacksmith growled, "Be very careful now, boy. Another mistake like that will cost you a hell of a lot more next time..."

"He told me if I ever did such a thing again I'd have to find other work," Fredo explained to his brother.

Paulo could understand perfectly because he'd also done an unexplainably stupid thing that day, thinking of Mrs Belladonna. "Yes! It's weird isn't it!" he said brightly.

Fredo looked at him, raising his head, and his spirits lifted a little. "That happens to you, too?"

"Yes! Today I did a really ridiculous thing, too. A really *stupid* thing. And then afterwards you think you're so horrible and pathetic, no?"

Paulo went on gaily, "I wonder where it all comes from. Do you hear it, that strange little creature that tells you outrageous things? Today it told me all sorts of bizarre things. I felt angry and irritated, then annoyed and sad, just because it told me to. But I'm starting to think, you know what I'm starting to think?"

Fredo couldn't guess at all.

"I'm starting to think…" He paused wondering how he could talk about the powerful curse of the Damnation.

"I'm starting to think that maybe we all feel really upset inside, even though we think everything's fine – then we actually see problems *outside* us. Like it's more that there's a serious problem with the way we're *seeing* things, rather than with the way things actually *are*. Maybe everything outside is really just the way it's supposed to be, but something inside us keeps changing the way we feel about what we see. What d'you think? Maybe that then makes us do ridiculous things in our lives because we're secretly hurting inside, and we aren't even aware we're doing them. When we're not paying attention, our secret feelings just take over and we find ourselves doing dumb things without even knowing it!"

Fredo was thoughtful. "But I was really trying to be happy today, like you said, not miserable. It's just that, well, it wasn't so easy."

Paulo lit with excitement. "Yeah, we have to learn to be *extremely* careful and to listen very closely. Just imagine if we were all under some type of evil spell that fills us with an absolutely horrendous feeling we just can't stand to keep inside. Maybe we try to see there's no reason to be unhappy, but the spell's actually much stronger than we think and talks to us in the secret part of our minds where we're not looking. We feel bad because we're listening to the curse and don't even know it, and we see problems around us and do lots of silly things. Then we get punished, and then we even say it's got nothing to do with us!"

"An *evil spell*, you say?" Fredo asked, pondering Paulo's bizarre ideas.

"Well, isn't that what it feels like sometimes?" replied Paulo.

Fredo had no answer and just thought about what his brother had said.

CHAPTER TWENTY-ONE

The Two Teachers

The following day Paulo made his way to market, determining all the while that he was going to be particularly careful and not make the same outrageous mistakes as the day before.

He dumped his wood at his feet in an untidy pile and looked warily over at Benito, sniffing loudly, trying to figure out the direction the wind might be coming from. There it was again. He heaved a sigh, totally discouraged: there was no doubt about it, the air was redolent with the odor of smelly fish. The fish merchant cocked his head toward the wood seller, glaring back at Paulo with his two black eyes, and hissed in a low voice, "Hey, kid! If you don't like it, look over there, you see it – it's a free space. Make yourself at home!" and he pointed a fat smelly finger in the direction of the far side of the square.

Paulo turned away from Benito's aggressive stares and tried to get down to work. He edged his stand a little further away from the surly fish-man and began crying out, "Dry kindlin'! Excellent dry wood to start your fires!"

While he waited for customers, he looked around the busy square trying to see it as a kind of classroom instead of the usual prison, but before long he was preoccupied by a terrific noise in his head. That morning while collecting wood in the Forest he had tried to remember what he had learned with Zeph the day before, but it was really difficult. Now, behind his stand, the dark thoughts returned to his mind only too easily, and he felt trapped in the market place where he thought he'd have to stay imprisoned for the rest of his life. For him, that seemed like hell.

He thought automatically about trying to fix his situation: another job, another place, more money, less injustice, more consideration and respect, some type of warm companionship – but then tried to see that the problem wasn't really there in the outside world at all, as Zeph had suggested. He sincerely tried to observe his thoughts and feelings lightly, without judging them, and to be willing to see the silliness of his serious mood; he even thought about trying to laugh and smile at himself for a while. But his thoughts were just too busy and insistent. And morbidly dark.

Two tall gentlemen now strolled in front of his stand, dressed in smart wool-felt coats. *Just look at them – they think they're so incredibly superior. Look at me, do I need fancy clothes to feel good? I think not!*

Paulo startled at this sudden thought entering his mind. He didn't really think there was anything wrong with the town gentlemen. Elegant Mr Bravuro was often dressed smartly, he reminded himself, and he certainly wasn't arrogant or haughty.

Then another thought raced through his mind uncontrollably: *Look over there – the gaunt women with pale faces are so unbelievably cold and unfriendly. They can't even be bothered to look in the direction of someone like me.*

But Mrs Belladonna, he reasoned with himself to the contrary, has chubby red cheeks and isn't pleasant at all, so it's not just thin, pallid people. She certainly pays attention to me – I can't even get rid of her from my stall! He shook his head from side to side in disbelief. There was no sense whatsoever to these thoughts.

"Why would the dark voice insist today on so many differences and judgments, and ones that don't even make any sense?" he inquired, curious.

A now familiar presence replied within his mind. "Yesterday, Paulo, you learned that the secret voice always instructs that there's a serious problem you must pay attention to in the outside world; and for the first time in your life you began to question whether this was actually true. As a result the dark voice is even more firmly dedicated to winning you over today, to convince you that the world around you is, indeed, the fundamental cause of your experience. Remember: *be very vigilant today!*"

Paulo looked inside his thoughts and indeed heard the dark sneaky voice, as yesterday, crying shrilly, '*Pay attention!* Look now at everything I'm showing you – that's the only thing that matters here. There's so much to judge here, look with me – *now!*'

Paulo turned his attention back to Zeph.

"Judging differences," he heard the gentle voice of the magician continue to explain, "is the particular technique the Maker uses to make the outside world appear especially real and important in your personal view, to make the scenes before you appear to be the source of your feelings.

"To the Maker, there are thousands and thousands of judgments to make every day. Nothing is ever exactly the same and perfectly equal in his world. Perfect sameness is the quality of the Kingdom, but not of the Maker's domain. So you compare all things, making them better or worse, good or bad, in an attempt to break up the inherent Oneness behind everything. That way the separation and fragmentation remain very real and significant to you.

"As you perceived for an instant yesterday, the world is just a series of images that have *no real meaning*, images that are perfectly the same in content and in quality. But then the dark voice will come and insist that you pay close attention to all the nuances and differences between the images, making them very serious, *as if* they had important meaning, and as if they were affecting you."

"To be honest, Zeph," Paulo said genuinely, "this doesn't make much sense to me."

"Then just try to tell yourself that despite what your eyes are showing you right now, in reality there are no significant differences within the scenes you see around you. This is the first step in unifying your perception, so you can learn to see once more the fundamental, inherent Oneness that you knew before.

"Of course there are differences in the *form* of what you see, notably in the appearance and activities of people, but that is not of great importance. When you begin to understand the nature of the truth you will see that the *content*, or the *inner meaning*, of all things is perfectly and exactly the same. And it is this content, and not the different forms, which you must seek to understand."

Paulo declared, still perplexed, "I'm sorry, but I still think what you're saying doesn't really make much sense. Things just do look different to me."

The magician persevered, "Let me try to explain it this way. If all things are just neutral images without any inborn meaning, as you've already seen, then we must wait for something inside our minds to give them sense and purpose. There are only ever two voices, or teachers, who can explain the meaning of things to us, and we are always listening to one or the other. When we listen to the Maker, the dark voice of our individual, separated life, the scenes and events in the world will mean one thing. But when seen from the point of view of the Kingdom, they mean something quite different.

"In the Maker's view the world represents danger, deprivation and injustice. It stands for one desperate hope, of avoiding these traps and of satisfying the self so it might feel a little better, a little safer or more acknowledged. And its devious, unspoken goal is always to make you and your little life seem significant, to make this world seem very real, and to make you completely forget the existence of the other, holy presence that abides in you.

"On the other hand, when looked at through the eyes of Kindness, everything around you has a different role and purpose. In its sight the world is a place where you will learn to let go of all your problems and fears in order to perceive what is all the same and quite peaceful. The goal of this Teacher is to help you remember your *Self*, and your Origin, and the means he uses is the changing, the *healing*, of your perceptions of your daily world. When your perception is finally healed, you will be fully capable of remembering your Home and of seeing the Truth."

"What's this got to do with the differences I still see everywhere?" the boy inquired bluntly.

"Well, the Teacher of Oneness has a special way of explaining that there are no important differences – *anywhere* – because he knows that the reality above all appearances and situations is always the same. Yes, even there before you in the market square.

"In his true vision, each seemingly distinct situation is used for one unique purpose which is to bring your perceptions around to find the innate Sameness in everything. All situations *are* the same: each one presents you with the opportunity to see the true nature of all things, the perfect safety and continuity of reality, of Love. And all people are the same: each person presents you with the opportunity to remember a brother with whom you once shared one perfect life, and with whom you still do.

"In fact, Paulo, it might surprise you but there are no important differences between *you* and the many people you see there in the market place. In terms of everything real and important, you're still exactly the same as all your brothers, as you were in the beginning, despite the many appearances you perceive now.

"The Maker says precisely the opposite, of course, that there are vital, critical differences between you and others. You might see yourself as especially better than others or as worse off, as more or less fortunate, but never as perfectly one and equal; never as one exact same Life simply with different appearances. It's the distinctions that the dark voice notices and makes significant in order to have your individual life seem special, separate…"

But Paulo was no longer paying attention. Preoccupied with his own tumultuous thoughts, he was lost in a kind of fierce indignation and Zeph's voice simply faded away. '*What? Since when aren't I special and different? How's it possible I could be exactly the same as all these people, and one with them? He's got to be wrong. I certainly hope I'm not the same as everyone here – just look at them!*'

He looked around again at the people coming and going in the market place, trying to see what might possibly, *conceivably*, be the same in everyone in front of him. He looked again, harder, but started to lose heart. His mind was extremely undisciplined and filled with all kinds of raucous, clamoring thoughts competing for attention:

The Mayor doesn't give a care in the world about the market people. Just look at him – he thinks he's so terribly important… It's going to rain again, what a crummy day… How's the baker selling? Of course you do well if you sell cakes and bread… inherited the business from his father… doesn't know how lucky he is… should have become a baker… didn't have the money, never will…

What did Zeph say again? – I'm supposed to tell myself that these thoughts of difference and judgment aren't so important. Hmm. They sure *feel* important. Does he know what he's talking about anyway?

Try. Just try a little, that's all Zeph said he wants.

A few moments passed, then –

…The wind's blowing the wrong way…

What does that really matter, since that's not where true happiness lies?

– It means the smoke's in my eyes, that's why it matters. If only they'd put out that stupid fire. Do I have a fire to keep me warm? What an injustice, just like all the rest.

Just try to be quiet a moment…

What's that unholy stink? Benito's fish are still reeking!

Does that really mean you are suffering?

I don't bother him with rotten, reeking wood. Why can't he sell fish that don't stink? Lord, that Benito can sure be exasperating!

Not only did the fish smell, he noticed, but even Francesca's chickens from all the way over on the other side of the square! He started to think that perhaps he was the only reasonable and responsible merchant in the entire market square who wasn't poisoning the air.

It was much more difficult in fact than he thought telling himself that the little dark voice was unimportant. It certainly sounded real *and* important, and he certainly felt less fortunate than others, and also decidedly superior and capable of judging everyone else for their failings. The secret malicious voice had something to say about absolutely everyone and everything. No one cared at all about him and his problems and suffering, and it was clear that it was all everyone else's fault. If only everyone and everything else changed, he'd feel that much better. *So* much better…

"*That's not true, Paulo.* They're not the cause of the way you're feeling." Zeph's voice spoke softly in his mind, and somehow, despite himself, he knew that this was true.

So he stood at his stand and tried to listen more…

Patience.

No customers yet.

That's okay. You can be peaceful while you wait.

But they're not coming.

That's not what's really important. Peace is here.

How can I possibly be peaceful? My customers aren't faithful to me, they'll buy from anyone!

It doesn't really matter. That's not stealing away the peace you seek.

No, my customers like me and they'll come back because I have the best wood in this whole ridiculous market square – in the whole of blessed Towne itself. I'm special, I'm important to them. They can't do without me, simple as that.

He listened some more, astonished by the innumerable things he could think were a problem or a situation to remark upon. On and on the voice would comment, criticize and find reason to explain why Paulo felt uncomfortable, was set apart, and why somehow things just weren't right.

Casting his eyes around, it was becoming only too obvious to Paulo that the problem wasn't really the fish or the Mayor or his customers. It wasn't any of these things, nor the soldiers or the rain or the smoke, or even the lack of coins in his pocket.

Even if all these things were fixed, even if no one was bothering me, even if the sun were shining and I had lots of customers and money, that stupid old voice would still be there telling me outrageous and upsetting things.

The problem was that mean old voice inside.

It constantly filled his mind with the darkest thoughts and feelings, and he didn't have nearly as much control over it as he hoped. It was just there, *all the time*. Just days ago he had never even heard of the Maker's presence within him, and now he couldn't stop it!

It was tiring listening to the secret dark voice and it made him feel utterly depressed. The wizard had also told him that he would feel miserable listening to it but that was *not* because of the depressing things it said. He said Paulo would feel wretched only because he *believed* the things it said.

But it was so hard not believing it! It had so much authority and power, as he had told his teacher; how could you not believe all the terrible things it was saying all the time?

"But who is the one giving the dark voice so much authority?" the wizard asked.

And Paulo felt truly exasperated.

CHAPTER TWENTY-TWO

Creeping Blackness

That day Paulo's customers came and went as usual. He made an extra effort to be smiling and friendly, trying especially hard to be responsible for the way he was feeling; and despite all his doubts, the day went well with everyone: they were happy that the good old Paulo had returned. Mrs Belladonna did, after all, come back to buy her wood from him and Mr Salvatori had forgotten about his rudeness the day before. Even Francesca had come over to say hello, and that certainly made a difference; but inside things were still far from calm.

He had tried to keep his mind off of the blackness that he felt was creeping back into his thoughts, but the effort thoroughly wore him out. His self-pitying feelings still seemed to be there despite his best efforts, blacker and darker than ever. Yes, it was clear that it wasn't anyone else that was the real problem. No, it wasn't them and what they said and did. They had their problems, and they were afraid and defensive for their reasons, and doing the best they could. Just like him. No matter how hard other people might try with him, he wasn't necessarily going to feel much better. There was a problem, indeed, but it wasn't other people.

It was *him*.

He reviewed his thoughts: his life would never change or be better, he felt, and it wasn't satisfactory at all that he remain a poor wood seller all his life. His mother wanted him to make more money at market, hoping for the day when he could contribute more ever since papa had died. He felt he wasn't helping his family enough and that his ridiculous ideas about happiness had got his brother into trouble. The villagers didn't offer him the respect he deserved as a good and worthy wood collector, and his poor upbringing would imprison him in menial jobs for the rest of his life. All sorts of dark and shameful thoughts came into his mind, and he felt he'd never be able to do the job the magician asked of him.

It was obvious that he was failing and disappointing everyone, and suffering from injustices far beyond his control. He felt sad, sick, and a long, long way from Home, unable to ever possibly get back: the gray sky had come inside and filled his life with hopelessness and disgrace. Everywhere it was black, like there was a dense shadow inside of him that made him see darkness all around. It was clear that the evil voice in his mind was no longer bothering to call all the market people wicked names…

No, it had another far more important mission in mind.

The church bells rang loudly clanging twelve times, and the stall people started to pack up their stands. It had been a good business day on the whole and all Paulo's kindlin' had been sold, so he folded up his heavy oil-cloth, tied it down with rope, and slung the roll over his shoulder. The coins from the morning's sales jingled in his pocket, and he thought quietly to himself – *I should be happy*. But still there was no real feeling of happiness or satisfaction in him. Yes, business was doing fine. Then why, he wondered, was there still that terrible feeling of something not right?

He turned in the direction of the river to leave the market square and was about to head for the bridge and home; then he stopped. He thought a moment, then quickly changed direction, picking up his pace and breaking into a trot. Down two short streets and the Town Hall appeared before him. He slowed an instant just to slip his head over his shoulder – no one was looking – and ducked around the back.

Within minutes he arrived at the broken 'Off Limits' sign posted before the narrow passage in the old merchant's district. The little street became darker and gloomier the further Paulo progressed down the lane but he hardly noticed. His spirit was determined and these things such as the lonely, abandoned quarter didn't bother him: he knew where he was going, and there, it was heavenly … And now he knew how to get there safely.

Quite unlike his previous forays to the Great Door, he walked boldly down the center of the dirty cobbled street and made his way to the end filled with a bright and happy confidence. He didn't need to hide behind pillars, or to plan escape routes, or to seek out door recesses for protection: he strolled calmly and directly right into the middle of the square where he found the giant guards sleeping peacefully, as usual, in their tall straight-backed chairs in front of the passage to the Door.

He approached the dozing soldiers and stood some moments in front of them. He gazed at their huge armored figures and at the glinting steel of their swords and spears that had so terrified him before: none of the soldiers moved so much as an inch; and Paulo continued past them in the direction of the tall stone arch that was the Great Door into the land of Beyonde. He passed smoothly by under the magnificent vault of stone lit by the golden force that kept the doors from closing, and looked deep into the land of freedom and happiness.

Soon sunshine, green fields and bright wild flowers were all around him. His feet picked up speed and he danced along the Golden Path till he found a nice tree under which he could sit and just think for a while. It felt good to be back in the peaceful land of freedom, and he wondered why he didn't come there more often.

– CHAPTER TWENTY-THREE –

Smokescreens and Camouflage

It wasn't long before Paulo saw a familiar white-bearded figure ambling up the stone-laid path. From a distance he could already see the miniscule stars flashing brilliantly on Zeph's dark blue cloak.

The magician came up to him and placed a hand on the boy's shoulder. "And how are we doing today, my fine young friend?" he asked warmly and sat down without ceremony on the ground next to Paulo.

"I'm sure glad to see you, Zeph," Paulo said despondently. "I was doing fine until not long ago. Then there seemed to be darkness all around me and I couldn't escape, it felt like I was in a hopeless prison: everywhere I looked there were absolutely miserable things about me. Yesterday all the bad stuff was outside and I thought everyone else was stupid and doing mean things to me, but today the evil seemed to be coming from inside, like it was *me*. Whichever way I turned I was damned: I couldn't do good or be good – nothing! That thing there just wanted me to give up and die, there was no escape at all. It's *awful*!"

"I agree, it's not very nice inside there, is it? And you know, that's the way everyone feels although they most often hide it. That's why we want you to follow this path as quickly as possible, just so you can start to be happier, Paulo. Now, what do you think is the matter?" the magician asked.

"I really don't know – let me think a minute."

Paulo had managed to stop believing he was unhappy because of other people and the village. He had ceased insisting the problem was everything outside and the market place; and he had started to pay attention to his real, hidden thoughts and upsets. But that hadn't really made the problem disappear. That was just a first step.

"I know!" he exclaimed excitedly. "The dark voice is now talking about *me*, isn't it? It wants me now to think that *I'm* horrible and evil and not other people. The voice doesn't really care about condemning them anymore – it wants me to believe there's no hope because of *me*."

"Very good, Paulo. Yes, the voice above all wants you to believe that you are, indeed, the evil, despicable and shameful thing it declares."

Paulo said sadly, "So then it's true."

The wizard couldn't help from chuckling. "No, not in the least," he said cheerfully; "I'm glad to say. The Maker wants you to *believe* it's true, that's all; that's your only mistake. You've begun to listen very well and to avoid the first of the Maker's traps which is to make you blind, to make you forget there's a problem; and you've started to undo the *ridding* which would state the problem is always elsewhere.

"But now you must learn to listen … and *not to judge*. You must learn to look and listen, but now from your True Mind where you feel a calm and loving presence. When you observe the Maker, as you've begun to do, and forget there is another, quiet and clear presence that accompanies you, then you will indeed believe him and get yourself quite stuck in all that mess."

"But what can you do about it then?" the boy asked, quite frustrated about the whole thing.

"Do you really wish to know?"

Paulo was taken aback by the question an instant, then nodded.

"Because if you really wish to know, Paulo, then we must begin a more important, a more intensive step in your learning, and I just wonder if you are really ready. There is still much to learn, and I can assure you the going will be quite tough at times. So, again I must ask you, are you up to the challenge? Do you think you really wish to continue?"

As at the other times Zeph had asked, Paulo reflected a minute, then solemnly agreed.

The wizard acknowledged with a tilt of his head and silently remarked: *He's so new to this learning, and yet so hungry for more!*

"Then I must begin by explaining to you a number of things," the sage said. "We'll start with the origin of your feelings, your perceptions and many motivations. We shall also have to discuss your relationships to others, and, of course, what you can do about all your upsetting experiences.

"We must cover all this because it's the only way you'll be able to progress further now. It may be a rather long teaching session, I warn you, since by your own wish you'll now be entering a more advanced stage of learning normally reserved for those much older than you. And the subjects we cover may not always leave you feeling comfortable. But I promise that by the end, you shall not be quite the same young man as when you arrived here this morning; you shall return far better equipped to make sense of your world and life, and to find more peace. Are you sure you are ready and wish for this?"

The boy looked somewhat warily at his mentor, then nodded a second time.

"Then let's set forth! On we go!" the magician exclaimed. "Remember, our story always returns back to the Maker and all you believe that has ever happened in the past, starting with the Great Exile…

"Having listened to the wrong counsel and chosen this terrible path of exile from the Kingdom, the Maker claims you actually managed to create a new identity for yourself, as one of his own ill-begotten children. He claims there is no choice in the matter of your existence now: you are abandoned by your King who seeks retribution for your treason, and your only hope lies in building a more protected life for yourself inside the Maker's prison-world. Surrounded by his Domain, your mind is now thoroughly under the sway of the Maker, and in his eyes, you are indeed a despicable creature of the utmost shame; and *that* is the origin of these terribly dark and insistent thoughts in your mind. That's where you have stopped – at the Maker's condemnation of you. This is where he would leave you, loveless and fearful.

"Above all he forbids you to go back to the very beginning, to look past all this horror and find out what's really going on – the truth behind this entire insane masquerade. Because if you did you would eventually see quite simply: *it is not so – it is all make-believe.* You are not abandoned, you are not alone, you are certainly not the loathsome thing of which he speaks, and you *do* have a choice with respect to the world in which you live. But you are confused about all this."

That's for sure! Paulo whispered to himself.

"The Maker uses these dangerously dark feelings of shame and damnation in order to prevent you from understanding who and what you really are. They are a disguise, a *smoke-screen.* The closer you look inside and the more you try to understand the truth behind the appearances around you, the harsher his damnation will appear; the thicker become the blackened coverings."

They sure are black! Paulo stared back attentively at the sage and kept his thoughts to himself.

"In this way the Maker would have you believe that your only reality *is* his damnation because it is his only way of destroying your vision. For if ever you saw clearly again from your True Mind, you would find you are loved, and loveable. You would find a Presence beyond the shame – kind and gentle and entirely unlike the Maker – and you would follow this Teacher where he leads, which is back Home toward your Self. And then the Maker would be lost.

"That's why most people stop before reaching this place of calm and peace inside their minds. They're confronted by what they believe is *real* shame and self-disgust, and the mortifying fear of some cruel punishment as a result. This is the barrier that so terrifies the Townspeople, the Great Wall of crushing self-hate and fear, though as you have started to learn, this is no real obstacle at all.

"You're doing well, Paulo," Zeph reassured. "Don't worry, and don't stop now. You've begun to work through the Maker's first lines of defense, which is the *veiling* and *ridding* of the problem. Now you're approaching a more difficult defense, the fundamental part of his arsenal of protection – the deep conviction in your own guilt and evil. You'll work through this one as well and find a lot of happiness on the other side, but you must spend a little time learning about it in order to master it fully."

The boy was struggling. He was still convinced he was doing absolutely everything wrong. "Well, I was doing the best I could," he said sourly. It's just not that easy, you know. Especially when you're stuck in that stupid market place all day long."

"I do indeed understand, Paulo. *Of course* you will feel this way. As the Maker proclaims, why even bother looking within yourself to explain your feelings of upset when you can find so many 'reasonable' explanations in your surroundings for your difficulties? You were doing precisely that yesterday in the market place: you were looking outside and finding problems with everything around you. Remember, this casting off – this *ridding* – is one of the Maker's all time *favorite* games."

"No! I was looking at what was *really there*, that's all." Paulo defied the magician with a deeply sullen look. "I just don't think you understand very well what my life's like. That's pretty obvious."

Zeph continued despite Paulo's obstinacy. "Why don't we try looking at it another way then … Okay, how about trying to see that the whole village and everything that happens there are sort of like – a camouflage; yes, that's the word. They are a camouflage that the Maker uses to disguise itself, making sure that you never discover what's truly happening in your life and mind," he explained.

"In this way the entire Domain becomes a means he uses for getting you to focus on what is *not* the real problem, so it can't be found and thus certainly can't be resolved. Now, you're just slowly learning to draw back the curtain, and you see that your feelings are actually coming from somewhere else, from somewhere inside yourself and not really from what's happening in the world around you.

"It's just that when you begin looking *something* prevents you from going further to get to the bottom of it all – that's where you're now getting stuck; this is what causes you to insist that the problem isn't within you, but within your surroundings. This terrible 'something' is what you are *imagining* is the truth about yourself. And it looks so frightening, so real; but just persist, and you'll see. Take courage and know that we are there to look with you. Remember you are safe and loved no matter what gruesome things you might see. You're on the right track – just try to stick with it instead of running back to blame the outside world."

A distinct look of angry fuming crossed Paulo's face, and the magician wondered for just an instant if he had not gone a bit too far, a bit too fast, in their discussions.

CHAPTER TWENTY-FOUR

Damnation's Extraordinary Hidden Purpose

Paulo objected vociferously, "I still don't think you understand anything I'm saying. When I look around me in town, I'm seeing things that *are* a problem. There *are* unpleasant people, and there *are* difficult situations. That's just the way it is. And that's the way the world is – *I do have eyes!*"

Despite the risk, Zeph attempted to reach past the boy's resistance and confronted him head on. "But looking isn't always seeing what's actually there, Paulo, nor is it necessarily understanding what you see. What you call looking is still for the moment only more *ridding*: you've first chosen what you want to see there in your world, and then you've looked around yourself in order to see that it is so."

Paulo now rolled his eyes in his head as if to say, *You don't even think I know what I'm looking at?*

The wizard continued his explanation patiently, "You could say that what you call seeing is actually for the moment like a self-fulfilling prophecy: you look outside in order to prove that what you already believe is, in fact, true. That's why on the path Home our job is to take a step back and to spend time looking carefully at what we *think* we see before us – our perceptions – to understand exactly what judgments and beliefs we hold in our minds.

"You'll get there if you try as I say, I promise. You'll be able to turn the Maker's diabolical strategy of ridding *against him* by observing – not by judging – but by *observing* what you believe is going on around you, and then by undoing your conviction in its truth. When we practice in this way, every single feeling of upset and anger becomes a stepping stone we follow back toward truth, instead of remaining stunned by appearances and judgment."

Paulo heaved a weary sigh and dropped his shoulders heavily. He pleaded, "But that's just the way I understand and see things, Zeph. It feels like there's nothing I can do with these dark thoughts – they're so powerful. The Maker sits inside me and just damns and judges all the time."

"There is something beyond the hate and the desire to condemn, Paulo," the wizard said gently. "There is a peace which comes when you learn that you can no longer do battle with this voice of hate … and then you let it go. You just let it go, that's all. You no longer fight it by trying to convince yourself that you're indeed good in the face of its terrible accusations: that's a losing battle and very discouraging.

"You accept simply that this presence will always believe you are a hated, evil thing and deserve only punishment and death, and you shrug your shoulders and leave it at that. You don't believe it, you don't disguise it, and you certainly don't fight it or try to change it. You just say to it, 'You can think what you want, it really doesn't matter. You're not the voice of truth or reality, so it doesn't really matter what you say. You're a hateful shadow with no substance, and that's all, there's nothing to you whatsoever. You want me to die and you believe I deserve nothing good – but so what. There is Truth, and you're just disguising it.'

"So you don't fight this evil voice, and you don't make it your enemy – that would just be giving it more power and belief. You simply observe it, and learn over time to give it less importance and less belief."

"But it's really not that easy!" Paulo cried sharply.

"Well, actually, it *is* that easy," Zeph persisted. "But only if that's what *you want*. Only if you *want* to begin to release your intimate and tight hold on this dark and independent presence within you."

Paulo stared blankly back at the magician, out of ideas for the moment.

The wizard measured the boy a moment, hesitating, then decided to continue. "You see, Paulo, the feelings of self-hate and damnation you contain have a mission and are really quite purposive: they serve as a *defense,* a barricade, and they are secretly desired and even cherished for what they accomplish. This is the same for all your feelings of frustration and conflict and sadness: you use them and keep them for a *secret* and *powerful* reason, and that's why it seems so difficult to let them go…"

Will I be pushing him too far if I continue with this? the wizard wondered, then made up his mind.

"If you didn't value the purpose of these feelings of self-hate anymore, you wouldn't use them and they would disappear. They're not there by accident, but by *choice* because of what you believe they accomplish. Understand that self-hate is not bad in and of itself: it is just a tool, a way you believe you can protect yourself –"

"*What?*" Paulo cried flabbergasted. "Use *hate* to protect myself – against what? I must be really *stupid* if I keep choosing self-hate."

The magician replied with infinite kindness, "No, not stupid, my boy, but scared. You're just trying to protect yourself against something you fear even more than your own self-condemnation and conflict."

"Wha… what on earth could I possibly fear more than such hate and spite?"

"*Love,* Paulo. You are just afraid of Love."

Paulo had to stop for a moment. His head was swimming.

Finally he exclaimed, "Against Love? You're crazy! That's not possible, you're not being serious. I *want* Love and Kindness – more than anything!"

"Indeed, Paulo, it's not only possible that you prefer self-hate, but it's also the most powerful defense against Love you possess."

Paulo refuted loudly, "But that makes no sense at all!"

"You see, your fear of the Truth of Love is in fact so great that you will be willing to suffer much pain and sickness, and even die, if you are not careful," Zeph explained. "You are afraid of Love because you have spent many, many years pushing away from It. Now you deeply believe that *Love* has become the enemy because you think that by pushing away from It, you have actually been able to forge for yourself an alternative identity that is separate from Love and opposes It. You believe that Love is the presence that would now suffocate you and take away your self-made, independent existence. If you're not adequately prepared, the Love of the King will feel oppressive, all-consuming – *terrifying*."

Paulo was totally bewildered.

"Let me try to explain," the magician continued, persevering. "To your little mind, the mind that has thoroughly absorbed the presence of the Maker, the absence of that constant hateful, fearful voice does not signify peace, but *death*. That's because the presence of the Maker now feels like life within you – like *your* life. Since the Maker's substance is hate and guilt, you believe that while you're still feeling hate and conflict and guilt you must be alive; and likewise you believe that the *absence* of hate and conflict, *which is Love*, would be your death and annihilation.

"You are in essence deeply attracted to feelings of hate, injustice, sadness and guilt, despite your conscious desires to the contrary, since these feelings represent the life you're still most familiar with, and for the most part still most desire. Thus unconsciously you hold on to hate, sickness and sadness and make them stronger every time you believe that Love and Peace – that extraordinary space of calm above the small self – are at your doorstep and have come to erase your private world."

Paulo felt he was going mad. "Why on earth would I feel fear like that? Love's supposed to be nice, not awful."

"Love *is* nice," the wizard explained. "It is the most remarkable and peaceful thing you could ever experience in your entire existence. This is true; but that's *not* what your Maker-self, your individuality, your self-importance, believes. Love feels threatening because you're still very attached to your ego smallness, and not yet close enough to your real identity as the One Great People.

"When you approach divine Kindness, your Maker-self will take fright and react violently against your efforts to advance any further. It behaves this way because it knows that it will disappear in the presence of Love – fade into complete insignificance, back into the emptiness from which it was born; and that's why you're afraid of Love. That's also why you must take this path *very slowly*: in order to get accustomed to the idea that you're perhaps not some idea of separated smallness at all; you're not what you've always believed, but an inherent and vital, magnificent part of the One Great People.

"Listen, Paulo: anytime you feel self-hate and depression or do something unpleasant to yourself such as get sick or have an accident, you can be sure it's because underneath you've become afraid of your inherent oneness with Love. You've felt the threat of real Peace, that extraordinary quiet space in which the mournful, hateful cries of the Maker are no longer heard, and you've simply become afraid. This isn't bad, of course. Being afraid of Love is just a mistake, that's all."

Paulo was overcome by a feeling of something great and remarkable that he couldn't quite fathom. "I don't... I don't think I can even imagine it, something so big, so all-encompassing – it seems so... *overwhelming*."

Zeph answered, "And that's precisely why you're still scared. It is true, Love is much greater than you can even imagine, and for the moment this scares you a little. However, you must remember that Love is not any *bigger* than your Reality. It's infinitely bigger than the dark little identity you're currently familiar with, and this is why it still seems quite frightening; but that's not a reason to be afraid of it, Paulo."

The boy listened, rapt.

"You *belong* to that great presence of Love, my friend... That is what You are, in truth. Strangely, your tiny, impermanent self is just afraid of your great and true Self, and that's all. So when you feel any dislike or depression, any loneliness or sadness, you can softly reassure yourself that you need no longer be afraid of Love, and that it's quite alright to approach the presence of Kindness, the presence that will only ever take you gently by the hand and lead you back into the quiet fields of peace."

Paulo was silent. Just for a moment nothing moved within his mind. All was completely still.

CHAPTER TWENTY-FIVE

Mastery of Experience

After some moments of contemplation, the magician turned back toward his apprentice and continued his lessons. "Try to listen just a little further, my young friend, and in time it will all become clearer, I promise.

"Now, returning to your experiences in the market square, we have just a few more important thoughts to cover. Paulo, you need to know that the Townspeople are *not* the despicable creatures you have always so firmly believed in the back of your mind. You have spent many years now judging and condemning them for the many hurts and insults you have actually been levying upon *yourself,* by listening to false ideas. As you continue further on the path now, you will finally begin to free all these people from your judgments and condemnations: because you will realize that they are not really responsible for how you are feeling at any time of the day."

Paulo's eyebrows rose in puzzlement. *This doesn't make much sense...* he said quietly to himself.

"Remember, this is so since your mind is perpetually embraced by Love, that remarkable, transcending Love that heals and soothes, no matter what troubling situation might present itself to your eyes."

No matter what disaster hits me? Paulo asked inside dubiously.

"Okay, it's true – we might not all feel this Love in times of great distress or sorrow, I understand. But that doesn't mean it's not there; and if we choose not to know kindness and comfort during these difficult times, it's certainly not because the Love is absent or unavailable. It can be quite helpful at these upsetting times to ask yourself why you might still be insisting that Love isn't there for you. Inevitably you'll find there's still some active hidden *desire* to retain a sense of conflict or injury, instead of letting go; a desire to prove something about your existence, perhaps a condition of abandonment or vulnerability or injustice, rather than accept your true Life as it is."

The wizard looked at the boy questioningly, but Paulo had decided not to respond to this last point. He had indeed been feeling that it was Love's fault for not being there when he most needed it, but he wouldn't admit it.

"Try to understand this following point now," Zeph continued; "this is important in your learning: It is only when we better understand our personal need to reject healing that we can begin to release the criminals in our lives, release them from the blame we have attributed to them over time for the hurts we *believed* they had perpetrated upon us. We naturally release them from our accusations when we understand that these people never committed any real act against us capable of removing the magnificent healing presence of Love from our minds and hearts, something that would be quite impossible.

"This special act of healing and faith has a name: it is what we call *True Forgiveness*. It is *true* because it is complete and does not accept any aspect whatsoever of hurt or attack. It absolves, releases and blesses completely merely because it understands completely. It understands that only our own minds could ever refuse Kindness or remove Love from our experience and replace it with pain. Ultimately we release and forgive others for what they *did not* do to us; we release them only from our own mistaken perceptions and judgments, from our insistence on using pain as a shield to Love; from our own mistaken self-identity."

"It's a nice idea, Zeph," Paulo interrupted, "but I don't see how it could really work in my life. I mean, just look at all the wicked things people can do to me. And to others, too." For Paulo it all seemed so clear. "People are truly sinful," he added succinctly.

The wizard went further to explain his last thought. "Of course, this isn't to deny that people might sometimes have the power to change circumstances and conditions in our lives, to attack or belittle us. But – and this is extremely important – they will *never* have the power to remove the active presence of Love and Kindness from our minds. They can never replace It with an experience of pain, to shut and bar the gates and cut off our access to the Kingdom, unless we are willing for this to happen. In all situations of pain and discomfort, Love – that remarkable, healing experience that is not of this world – is always present."

Paulo was still quite unconvinced about this 'True Forgiveness'. "I still don't get it. When someone does something to me that I don't like, it hurts and I get angry. It's that simple."

"I know it's difficult to imagine, Paulo, but you should try to remember that whenever you feel hurt or angry, it's simply because at some moment you have really first attacked yourself, by compromising the integrity of your own true being. It's not actually because of what another has done to you that you feel damaged, but because of what *you have done to yourself,* by accepting the Maker's concepts of individuality, self-hate and weakness in the place of inherent Greatness."

"It sounds totally crazy!" the wood seller claimed bluntly.

"Only *we* have the power to hurt ourselves," Zeph went on; "no one else has any such power to take away our peace. And we do this to ourselves whenever we listen to the Maker's command to feel divorced from Love, feeling enmeshed within the small, victimized self, instead of listening to the quiet truth of safety and wholeness."

Zeph looked compassionately at the boy, aware of the enormous challenges he was presenting to his young student.

Something nagged now at Paulo's mind and begged another question. He seemed to find yet another objection to the sage's bewildering thoughts, and he asked, incredulous, "Zeph, I really want to learn these lessons and to walk this path with you, but I don't possibly see how. What you're saying about Forgiveness just *can't* be really true. What about the customers who steal from me when they take my wood without paying? Am I just supposed to feel peaceful about that?"

He stared at the magician, unblinking.

"And the bullies in the village who make fun of me? Sometimes they even throw my wood in the river and beat me up. How can you possibly feel peaceful at times like this?" He threw his words out in challenge at the wizard. "There are truly wicked things that happen here, and peace just doesn't come at times like that!"

Zeph paused, a weathered finger stroked his long white beard, and then he replied, "Indeed, Paulo, people in the Domain are often evil, manipulative, and violent, and willing to inflict great pain on others – of this there is absolutely no question. Whenever anyone listens to the Damnation inside, he will feel confused and in acute pain at a very profound level. He will systematically go projecting this hate and anger onto others, to use them as the source of his suffering instead of taking the responsibility on himself. He will then attack other people for what he mistakenly thinks is their attack on him, even if it is quite clear he has not been aggressed.

"But, let me tell you that despite all their hate, Paulo, this doesn't mean that *your experience* of their assaults must be one of pain and victimization…" Zeph eyed the boy carefully. "And this doesn't mean that your behavior in return must be vengeful or suffering. In fact, you don't necessarily have to feel their attack at all–"

Paulo's jaw dropped at this and he gaped blankly back at the wizard.

"You heard me correctly," the magician continued soberly. "Your experience of any situation is always a choice within you, no matter what others may be doing to you. You can indeed feel peace and strength if that's what you prefer, rather than resentment, hate and pain: the great Love that exists deep within you is *always* available. You can always say to yourself when faced with a situation that provokes you to be angry or sad, '*I can see peace and calm instead of this attack. True and lasting Peace is also present here, no matter what I'm feeling and perceiving at this moment. Let me now feel Peace instead of this hate. Let me now feel strength instead of weakness.'"*

The boy still looked quite dumbfounded.

"Paulo, you *can* be free of your anger and condemnation, if you want. But only *you* can choose to change your mind."

The boy asked, extremely annoyed now, "Oh, so I'm just supposed to feel happy inside when the village bullies throw my good dry wood in the river?"

Zeph smiled at the boy's obvious challenge. "Once you feel more peaceful, Paulo, once you've released some of the sense of attack you obviously will feel, you'll know best what to do. This world will always challenge us to feel we are attacked: that's the temptation to which events here will always lead us, to believe we have been personally attacked, or our group has been threatened; to believe that our judgment and condemnation are always *justified*.

"Your personal job, Paulo, is precisely to choose against this sense of injustice and blame directly in the face of all these temptations. You must realize that it is simply the face of the ego-Maker, the face of fear, projection and illusion, and nothing more. You must know that not one person need be condemned and attacked simply because he has been afraid and has acted irrationally. No, he just needs to be understood."

A quiet peace hung in the air as the magician finished his thoughts. A peace, however, that Paulo found absolutely impossible to share.

CHAPTER TWENTY-SIX

The Problem with Ruffians

The wood seller shook his head mechanically from side to side, wondering how on earth he was ever going to be able to achieve this special calm in the face of the many daily unjustified attacks the world waged on him.

As if sensing the boy's inner challenges, the magician offered some further advice. "If you find it difficult to find this all-encompassing Peace, Paulo, then simply be honest and acknowledge that you've become scared once more of Love. That's all."

I do what? Okay, see that I've become afraid again of Love…

"You've become scared once more of your reality within Love, above the physical world, and *that's* the reason you retreat back into resentment and hate. You're perhaps still using pain as protection and defense; nevertheless, try not to reinforce even more what appear to be the outside causes of your upset. You might have become attracted again to conflict and injustice, but only because of your fear of the great peace within you, this special peace which represents an identity you don't want to acknowledge for the moment.

"And so you may say to yourself at these times of confusion: *'These feelings of anger and resentment are just a shield I'm using against Love. They're just a barrier I'm holding against the calm peace that is here all around me right now. I could feel this great peacefulness here and now, but I've chosen instead to experience this upset and distress. Yes, I've become afraid again of Love, that's all, and need do so no more.'"*

Paulo wanted to roll his eyes in exasperation but unfortunately he found the magician's thoughts very wise, even if he didn't like them one bit. So he kept his comments to himself for the moment, and tried to let the words just work themselves into his mind past his reluctance.

"Try to comprehend clearly your real motivations for feeling upset," the sage continued determinedly, sensing the boy's resistance. "Try to become aware whenever you're feeling upset, and then try to uncover the secret motivation behind it – the fierce need to keep peace and Love banished from your senses."

"But I'll never be able to do that!"

"Well, then try not to come down hard on yourself when you find yourself failing. Don't judge yourself for your unwillingness and your fear. Just relax and accept where you are."

"I just don't see how…"

"In your learning, try always to come back to that place of gentle, non-judgmental observation of yourself, of your own thoughts and feelings. That's all. This will bring you already very far along the path Home. In the Domain it's impossible not to judge, and so this path you're on doesn't ask you not to judge. But you can begin to *become aware* of your judging, and then suggest to yourself that you've perhaps *been wrong* in your judgments and assessments."

The boy countered, "But sometimes my judgments aren't altogether wrong."

The magician replied, "If you are truly at peace, and if your judgment asserts the inherent perfect and tranquil identity of each person, and the capacity for everyone to be confused, then you can be sure that your judgment was correct. Otherwise you might suggest to yourself that there's perhaps another explanation for what you've been looking at.

"Just try not to accept unthinkingly the first response which comes into your mind which is always to assume that others and certain situations are the obvious cause of your feelings. Look inside to see what's going on, then ask yourself: '*What have I honestly been trying to find here in this situation? What have I honestly been looking for here: for peace or conflict…? Where am I still hesitating before accepting that there might be real peace right here somewhere?'"*

Paulo finally exclaimed, no longer able to contain himself, "But there're people in the village who really *are* terribly offensive and unkind. Are you supposed to love them, too?"

"No, not love them as you would think of it – but *understand* them. We all contain the impulses of the Maker, Paulo. *Everyone.* No one can judge without condemning himself. Again, we are not many, but One, and all exactly the same. All things that happen in the Domain are a reflection of what is happening in our minds – together as one. Aggression is simply the inherent way of the Domain, so you needn't be surprised by all the hate and viciousness you find there, and in yourself."

Paulo could find no words, but Zeph did not let up.

"In fact, aggression should come as no surprise to anyone, given the dark, disturbing principles on which your world was founded. But *you* can do something about that. The way you contribute individually to the undoing of hostility in your world is by undoing your own personal choice to feel attacked and victimized in your daily life.

"And just how would I go about doing this?" the boy demanded.

"How do I do this? I remember that my personal suffering cannot be justified because of the unsuffering Peace that is still very present in the recesses of my mind, even if I don't yet feel it. Then I allow my judgment of others to be undone because their behavior is only an *error.* Their attack is not a sin, but an error – a mistake. You remember where their hate comes from and then–"

Paulo, thoroughly indignant, blurted out, "I have absolutely no idea where their hate and aggression come from, thank you very much. It's different for each person."

Zeph, quite unsurprised by Paulo's reaction, continued his explanation. "Of course you know where their hateful actions come from, my boy, because you contain exactly the same hateful impulses and destructive fears yourself – *don't you?* Perhaps you express them differently, but they are after all quite the same feelings at heart. That's how you understand others. That's why you can be truly compassionate."

The boy stared belligerently back at the sage.

"Or, of course, on the other hand you can pretend you don't know anything about your own tendencies to *rid* and your own capacity to see others as your personal problem. You can pretend you don't know anything about your own selfish desires to get others to act for your own personal benefit, even when those actions might be against their will or their best interest.

"You can even pretend that you are holier and superior, acting as if others are more evil than you, and put on a pretty and self-righteous face of innocence… Then your attack on others and your judgments of them will certainly appear justified, I'm sure; and your attitude of disapproval and condemnation will seem quite sanctified and proper. It's always your choice, my boy: to hate, blame, and present a façade of innocence; or to understand, forgive and release. Peace or anger, it's always your choice."

"But the boys who throw my wood in the water…" Paulo interjected, quite distraught with what the magician seemed to be claiming. "I'm just not going to stand by anymore and let them do it – I won't!"

"But no one said you should!" the wizard answered matter-of-factly. "How you act in response to the violence in others is always your choice. What is important is your *attitude*, not your actions."

So, it's my attitude and what I'm thinking, not what I actually do, that's important? Paulo queried inside.

"There are many different actions you can choose from when faced with the aggressiveness in others, but the result for you will always depend on your *intent*," the sage explained. "Faced with the hostility in others, you are free to do whatever you feel is most appropriate; and you will naturally feel what is appropriate to do in any situation once you have clearly brought to mind the universal source of aggression. This means once you first establish that *you are exactly like your enemies*, doted with precisely the same hostile, vulnerable thoughts and feelings…"

That was the sticking point for Paulo. He found it hardly possible to imagine being understanding and compassionate because he saw himself like his aggressors, and they as the same as himself.

Zeph continued, "As your brothers – granted, very confused and certainly not acting in a very brotherly way – these people always deserve your utmost comprehension. Thus you first remember that you too contain exactly the same tendency to use hate and upset as a form of personal protection against Love, and to cast off this hatred and anger onto others. Then you remind yourself that this is merely an error, in yourself and in them similarly, and certainly not a sin deserving of condemnation. It's only a mistake and thus you can withdraw your judgment which would, quite undoubtedly, only lead to self-righteousness and mindless counter-attack."

"It all sounds a bit much really. Pretty impossible, actually," the boy said, airing his true feelings.

The wizard cast an earnest regard upon the young wood seller. He knew the boy was bothered by his hateful feelings towards the other village boys, and deep down wanted a real solution. He continued:

"Try to respect others for who and what they really are above their misguided selves, recognizing *your* own misguided self in the process. Do you see? Remember to acknowledge your own personal tendency to think and behave in *exactly* the same unconscious way as those you dislike. And most importantly, try to appreciate the tremendous cost of your hate to your own sense of peace. Finally, you calmly release your judgment of these people, seeking to replace your anger with an appreciation of the difficulty that this confusing classroom presents to all brothers."

Paulo looked stunned. "And that's all?" he cried. "They're about to throw my super special dry wood in the river and I just…

What… I just *appreciate* them?" He couldn't even find the words to express his frustration.

"No, my young man, that's not all." Zeph was imperturbable faced with Paulo's insistence on attack.

"Once you've clearly seen your unspoken desire to prove injustice and moral superiority, once you've recognized your personal attraction to hostility and victimization, and once you've ultimately remembered this is definitely *not* what you wish for yourself, you will know what to do.

"Once you've clearly seen precisely the same violent and hateful impulses as much alive within yourself as in your brother, and have said, 'I make the choice instead for peace', you will know how to act – this I promise. When you've stopped taking attack personally, in order to reinforce your philosophy about an unjust world, you'll feel very calm, and you'll know exactly what to do. And the actions you undertake will make you feel especially peaceful."

Paulo was hardly convinced.

"Listen and try to remember now," the wizard insisted once more. "The other boys are not fighting with *you*, but only with the *image* they hold of you as an ego-entity – not with your *reality*. That's how you learn not to take anything in this insane world personally."

"Not with me? That sounds bizarre."

"*You* choose to remember your splendid Reality that can't be attacked personally, above your image of your damaged self. This then helps you see *their* true being, above the darkened picture you have made of them; and this in turn gives them the chance to see you differently, because all minds are One… They will *feel* your decision."

"And then they'll stop, right?"

"How they respond is then their choice," the wizard said lightly, leaning back and placing his hands on the ground behind him. "Perhaps they'll let go of their desire to attack, and perhaps not. Just know that once you've done your part and let go, you're not responsible for their decisions or for their choice to stay with anger and pain, and you'll choose the actions that are necessary for you. Even if your choices and actions upset them, which may well happen, if you remain detached and respectful then you'll not be a true source of provocation."

Paulo then cut to the heart of the subject, as far as he saw it. "So do I fight back or not?"

"That's entirely up to you, Paulo!" The magician held the boy's willful look firmly. "Remember, all actions in the Domain have their consequence, and everyone is there to learn. There are many different ways to learn there, and many different actions which will teach. But your actions are one thing, and your attitude is another. No matter how you respond, you must know that *how* you feel is your choice, and deciding *what* you want to feel is your greatest, your singular priority."

Paulo screwed his face into a grimace, trying to work out if the magician had answered his question. "I don't get it. It's not clear to me yet whether I should give in or fight."

"Well, everyone in the Domain must come to understand at times that there's no harm or damaged pride in conceding or retreating. And everyone must *also* learn, when necessary, how to respond determinedly and forcefully to control the confusion in others that leads to harm and excess. But we must above all learn to undertake both actions in peace and with understanding and respect for others, and for self. This means with no sense of self-sacrifice or resentment, and no sense of vengeance or superiority or of righting injustices."

The magician let the boy think on this. Then after a moment the sage asked what appeared to Paulo to be an essential, vital question.

CHAPTER TWENTY-SEVEN

A Slippery Question

"What you really need to start asking yourself now, my boy, is 'How do you *want* to feel with respect to the attacks waged on you by others?'"

Paulo tossed the words around his mind – 'How do I *want* to feel?' He was baffled because he had never thought there was a choice in the matter; his feelings had always seemed to just be there.

The magician then added enigmatically, "The answer to the question is not nearly as obvious as you might think."

Zeph waited a moment before pursuing his line of thought. "You asked me a moment ago if you should fight. Now I'm going to counter that with a further, very important question: Isn't there in all honesty something within you that secretly *wants* to suffer at the hands of other people ... in order to demonstrate something?"

Paulo was totally lost.

'...that wishes to suffer *to demonstrate something?*' he repeated to himself.

The wizard explained, "Whenever you're in pain or feeling belittled, isn't there behind this some secret, joyful proclamation to the world? Does it not say in one dramatic form or another: '*Look upon me, my brothers, in my outrageous mortal suffering. I am wounded by no hand of mine, but by yours alone – Yes, you I condemn!*' Isn't there in fact a type of burning importance you give to your feelings of suffering and of being a victim? A sense of power you gain from your ability to be in pain, and then to uncover and accuse the evil-doers in your misery?"

Paulo felt a damp sweat break out on his brow. He was visibly shocked.

"I know this will seem strange, Paulo," the wizard continued insistently, "but each moment that is not one of perfect peace in your life is actually an act of blame, of projection. Something other than myself – I whisper in my moments of pain – something in this world has caused my accursed, painful condition and needs to be corrected. Something in this tangible, deceitful universe has removed the peace and gentle happiness of the Kingdom from my mind and replaced it with anger and sadness, and is to blame. More to the point, it is a way of saying that if only something outside me were changed, I would be restored – all would be well, all would be returned to balance… A way of constantly insisting that peace or deliverance is not my personal matter but one of outside factors over which I have desperately insufficient control."

Paulo placed his head in his hands and closed his eyes, deeply shaken by Zeph's penetrating words.

He couldn't deny that every time he felt upset he was focusing on some outside causes of pain, causes that seemed to be infinite and ever-changing. He had never thought that his peace, his salvation, his perfect self-fulfillment, could be entirely and completely a matter of his own decision, and acceptance. But Zeph seemed to be saying precisely that, that it wasn't really an outside condition at all, and more like a state within his own heart and thoughts. *Could that be possible?*

The magician continued his thinking, "Or would you like to know a perfect confidence now, above all the provocations of the world, and to know that Love is real *despite* the slanders and attacks perpetrated upon you?

"This is a very important decision you must make, Paulo. And so I ask you: what do you truly *wish* now to communicate to all your customers and the boys in the village? That you are indeed in pain and victimized at the hands of brutal and stupid people? Or that you are cared for and safe, no matter what transpires in the world of shadows, despite the efforts of others to destabilize you?"

Paulo stared wide-eyed back at the magician. No words came at all.

"Do you *want* now to demonstrate that the ruffian boys are innocent in your understanding – certainly mistaken and confused, and perhaps filled with harmful intent, but not truly sinful, and not capable of causing any real harm, not to your greater Self…? Or do you still seek to demonstrate that they are despicable, evil and worthless, capable of real attack and injustice, and it is your unfortunate but necessary role to demonstrate their wrong-doings and failures?"

The boy sat there with his head in his hands once more. He felt a burning pain erupt in the pit of his stomach, which didn't help matters a bit.

"You have a real choice here, Paulo. You can remind these people now of their own strong and unsuffering Reality which has no need to attack or to be afraid … Or you can condemn them to their hateful and vulnerable ego identities, which you know will only continue down the spiral of condemnation and counter-attack. It's all up to you."

Paulo was silent. He was much more affected by the magician's powerful words than he was openly willing to admit at that moment.

After a moment Zeph finished his thoughts, "Once you are clear that you prefer freedom and happiness rather than hate and anger, ask yourself simply, what is it now appropriate to do? How is it appropriate to respond to this situation? Who knows, perhaps you'll feel it best to walk away and not to respond directly to their provocations, and to find another way to work with their confused behavior.

"Or on the other hand, perhaps you'll feel it best to respond in an active, forceful way to contain their hurtful behavior. But if you *do* respond with forceful actions, you don't have to feel righteousness, nor vengeance or defensiveness in order to control the situation. You can feel true consideration and understanding, even as you use powerful restraining or defensive actions. You will know that, in the quiet of your mind, this is the best response to deal with the confusion and misperceptions of others."

Paulo looked backed at the magician intensely, a gleam of understanding now flickering in his eye.

"You enter the battle but now in peace and with respect, not in anger and righteousness," the magician concluded. "Even if momentarily you do become angry, as will happen, you can always try to remind yourself of the perfect moral equality you share with your adversary who is still nevertheless, and unchangingly, your brother."

Some minutes went by and Paulo had grown unusually quiet. He had been thinking about the enormous life-altering changes the wizard seemed to be asking him to make. It all seemed far too much to conceive of at that moment.

A heavy breath escaped between his half-open lips. "I'm really stuck, aren't I? I'm not as nice as I thought at all, I haven't even *begun* to deal with this stupid Spell, have I?" He threw down a stick he'd been toying with. "At this rate I don't think I'll be getting Home any time soon…"

Zeph reached over and before Paulo could shed a tear, tweaked the boy's ear sharply so he would turn to face him. "Who's the one saying 'You'll never understand this, you stupid creature! You'll never, *ever* get Home?' Is that you, or is that the Maker's voice again?"

Paulo tried to focus on the question. "That's not me? So that's that crazy old voice, trying to get me to feel bad again. But I'm in *such* a hurry, Zeph, I want so much–"

The sage interrupted, "Remember the big stone?

"Everything will come away in its own time," he explained. "There's no reason to rush or to make demands on yourself. Remember, you're only stopped by your fear of all-encompassing Love and of your true Self. And the best way to deal with this fear is to be accepting with yourself and not believe the mean old voice in your head when it chants so gloomily –"

Suddenly Zeph jumped to his feet, holding out his arms like wings with elbows bent; he flapped his arms and rocked from one foot to the other looking like some very crazy bird, and chirruped in a high, screechy voice:

'You're not doing very well, my little boy, now are you! Oh, no, not well at all!'"

The magician cocked his head to one side and stared at the boy out of one flaring eye. "Look at you, you lazy slug, you must not be trying hard enough if you can't see Home yet. Get up now and get straight to work!"

Paulo roared with laughter, and lay backwards on the ground holding his stomach. "I'm not *that* silly!" he said, between guffaws.

"Oh, indeed you are, my boy! If only you knew!" The magician's cheeks were flushed with the exertion from his little show, and the light twinkled brilliantly in his eye.

Zeph continued, his calm returned and his voice even and warm, "That's all the Maker and the Spell are, Paulo, a series of very strange and truly ridiculous ideas. Imagine, trying to convince the One Great People of Light that they could be divided into little broken fragments of nothingness, filled with secret darkness and evil, destined to end in dust, in unending and frantic competition with each other for importance and survival. *How ridiculous!* How could we ever have possibly believed it? Yet we did, and still do every day.

"Try to remember that this dark, deceiving presence is not you at all. It is just a voice, a presence, and it is utterly incorrect. It is an interpretation, a story giving rise to vague and ultimately very untrustworthy images, and nothing more. If you remind yourself of this every time you have a self-critical thought, you'll start to remember what you really are, which is very different from all you've ever believed about yourself. It's so entirely different from all you've ever imagined that you're just a little scared to remember now, that's all."

Paulo gazed far over the sun-lit meadows.

"Trust me, Paulo. What you really are is exceedingly different from what you currently think of as yourself, as you will find out shortly, I promise. It is infinitely bigger, and infinitely more beautiful. This seems all just a little frightening for the moment, that's all."

CHAPTER TWENTY-EIGHT

The Moment of Always

For some moments Paulo pondered the magician's outlandish ideas in a tense silence. A soft wind whispered, a few stray clouds wandered overhead without disturbing the perfect, sunlit day. But yet again in considering his life, Paulo was quite unable to fathom how the wizard's lessons might really function.

"But what you say about being attacked, Zeph – it can't be possible," the young boy said, his voice rising anxiously. "I mean, when my mother punished me because I did something she didn't like, it really hurt. She could get me really angry, and still does. And then when my papa died, I was very upset and hurt. I loved him and lot and he left me and it wasn't fair, and now mama expects Fredo and me to do everything that papa did.

"Zeph, I'm sincere, I really do want to return to the Golden City. But I can't see how it's possible to do what you want."

The magician looked kindly at Paulo, hesitating a moment before speaking. "Then let me explain a little more. Yes, I know it's confusing because what I've been saying seems so contrary to everything you've ever learned in the Domain, and to the way everyone thinks and acts every day.

"In fact, one of the most potent ideas in the delusionary thought system of your world, Paulo, is that you are not entirely responsible for the way you feel, but that the world is. It seems as if it is everything else *other* than yourself that causes your experiences and feelings of life: other people, the weather, your home or work situation, the Town Hall and the Mayor, the market place, your body and sicknesses, and 'life' in general. But this is just not the truth."

Paulo's eyebrows knitted even more tightly.

"No one and nothing outside of you can really be the cause of your personal experience. I'm sorry if this is not comfortable news, but you *are* master of everything inside of you. And that is all that really counts, because only your inner world is real."

"But they *did hurt me* – you can't take that away!" Paulo's severe expression left no doubt as to his sentiment on the matter.

"I know that's the way it feels, Paulo. It feels like the hurt is in a place in your body, in its heart and feelings, and that it is quite, quite real and important. But what happens to your little self is not really what causes your feelings and experiences, as strange as this may seem. Seriously, the place of your experience, the source of your feelings, is always within your upper Mind outside your body, and not within your smaller self at all."

Paulo shot out a sharp breath, aghast. He truly couldn't fathom what the magician seemed to be saying.

"This is exceptionally difficult to accept, I know," Zeph continued. "It doesn't seem like this at all, I understand. But only because we have all spent countless years now identifying with this tiny individual self and placing our experience within the body, its life and its circumstances. But this is just a choice. It is only a choice we have made to place our identity and experiences within the body and its physical, emotional conditions."

Paulo stared blankly back at the wizard. No further demonstrations of objection came: he was out of energy.

"Yes, this all-inclusive idea of personal responsibility seems to go against everything you think and feel. It goes against everything that the Towne and the market place teach. This doesn't mean that you should hide what you are really feeling or pretend; it just means that it would be wise to think again whenever you find yourself getting upset and blaming your experience on the things around you," Zeph advised gently. "It is wise because it is the only way that you can begin to feel better, and ultimately to understand the truth."

"But I'm *always* going to feel that way," Paulo cried now. A note of acute desperation edged the boy's voice. "It's always going to feel like things are punishing me, back home."

The wise man spoke reassuringly as he answered.

"Paulo, my friend, you can now return to the village and have an entirely different experience there. Deep happiness and real peace can replace all your sadness and pain: you no longer have to feel like a victim or lacking freedom in any situation. If you wish, your everyday life in the Domain can have a totally new and important meaning. Going about your daily activities can actually be a way of *resolving* the painful experiences in your life, and then freeing your mind from its prison."

They stared at each other for one tense moment.

"Paulo – your prison *is* your path to freedom."

Paulo turned his eyes away and stared vaguely into the distance.

"In this way," the magician persisted, "learning that you are the sole cause of your experience can indeed become a great blessing, and not a curse as you now feel. It brings peace and it also helps you remove all your judgments, all the condemnations you have placed on the people in your memories whom you have blamed for all your hardships and failures. These judgments have caused you much more pain and limitation than you think, and you'll find tremendous relief when you begin now to release these people from your unjustified condemnations. *This* is your path to freedom. This is the true nature of Forgiveness, and its results are real healing, and joy."

The wizard interrogated Paulo with an intense regard, but the boy was still staring away.

"Trust me, just try."

After some time Paulo brought his gaze back to the magician. His thoughts returned persistently to all the unhappiness he had felt at home, and he spoke insistently, "But it can't really be true that what I feel is my choice. I just don't see how…"

"It's not really so difficult to understand how this idea might be true," the magician replied to his unfinished question, feeling he had found an answer to the problem. "Try thinking of it this way, look at yourself at this precise instant: here you are in this place of glorious sunshine, Happiness and Light, and you know that right now, listening to me and learning these things, all is well. If you closed your eyes you could in fact be anywhere: you are well, and that's all that counts. The outside disappears, you need nothing else, nothing else really exists. This moment of peace is every moment of your life, Paulo, *no matter* what is going on.

"This instant, this exceptional holy moment of time and peace, is *Always*. That is the nature of the Eternity the good King placed in his Kingdom; and nothing that ever happens in the scenes and images of the Domain can ever change this…

"Now, in order to be *unhappy* you must make a decision to leave this tranquil place and to look into your past for a remembrance of a painful situation. Or you look into the world and find something distressing there. You establish perceptions and interpretations of suffering about the situations you find around you in the world, and then you conclude that pain is real and true. Unhappiness is specific and follows from specific perceived situations of misery; and the deep-rooted desire to remain separated from the Kingdom will always produce these perceptions of unmerciful situations. But they nevertheless remain just that: simply perceptions and interpretations – not reality."

"But my unhappy thoughts are just there and come unwanted," Paulo argued defensively.

The wizard explained further. "It might sometimes appear that these observations and memories come involuntarily, but it's just the mind that has the habit of finding them automatically… because you're actually *looking* for them, without consciously being aware of it."

Paulo's brows shot up.

"Something inside *wants* us to find upsetting situations and painful memories," the wizard continued, "and this something is the Maker and the Spell, the ego and individuality. This something is your desire to remain an adopted, separated self instead of embracing your true and perfect abstract state. And these painful memories and thoughts are simply the stuff of which this divided identity is fabricated. Their purpose is to keep you away from your true Identity. However, you can, if you wish, refuse to follow these interpretations and stay instead in that place of great calm, in this present, holy instant. If that is your wish."

Paulo interjected, "But when my father died, that *did* hurt. I was very sad and upset. I didn't just imagine it all, you know!"

His eyes sparked with a dark light and his square jaw defied the magician to answer him.

The wizard softly replied, "Yes, in the Domain many terribly bitter and painful things happen – the world of darkness is indeed a place of tremendous grief and solitude. And it's very important to know when you feel pain, and not to hide or disguise it. It's also important to know, however, that your experience of any situation can also be your choice, Paulo, and that Peace and Comfort are always available to you, if that is your wish. Understanding this will give you great power, over all situations in the future."

"But... *how?* How can you find peace at horrible times like these?" Paulo asked, bewildered.

"What I say is true, Paulo, because Love and eternal Gentleness are always, *always*, present, even in the most difficult, trying circumstances. This is the absolute promise that the good King made His beloved People even in their self-imposed exile. Sometimes it seems impossible to think that one could feel this Love in certain dangerous or distressing situations. But then you can try to remember that it is only a circumstance, only painful-looking images, and that Love is still true no matter what is appearing before you – even if you're still just a little unwilling to feel the kind and gentle presence of Love in that particular situation."

Paulo interjected, "But sometimes Love just really doesn't seem to be there."

"I understand. The great temptation of this world is always to think that Love and Peace are gone as a result of some painful situation, but this is not actually true. In fact, the Maker within us all provokes disastrous and punishing situations *in order* to prove that the King's Love is absent, and to prove that our vengeance and sadness are justified. But His Love has not departed, and it is not unreal.

"This magnificent Love is always present for those who wish to remember it and make it present within their minds, despite everything that might be going on. You can always try to remind yourself in the face of all stressful circumstances, 'Despite what I see and feel here, peace is truly present. All is truly well.'"

CHAPTER TWENTY-NINE

The Healing Perception

Paulo thought intensely about his own personal situation, at a loss, and then tried to answer his own question.

"So what you're saying really is that when papa died, Love and Peace were also there at the same time, is that right? Even though I couldn't see them at the time, they were still there nevertheless."

Zeph nodded.

Paulo went on. "And so instead of feeling this horrible pain of having lost my father and everything he meant to me, I could've felt this calm and quiet inside instead. Like somehow everything was still really okay, despite all the upset I was feeling.

The boy's sight turned deeper inside. "So it wasn't actually what was happening in my family that made me feel so bad; it was because I was still thinking I was alone and weak and had lost something important. And that's only because I wasn't thinking anymore about the wonderful warm Love that was still really there together with me right by my side."

He returned back into the silence of his thoughts. Then he continued, more focused: "It was only the King's Love I was missing, even though I thought it was my father. His warm Love would've made me feel better right away if I'd thought about it. And maybe I was also feeling bad because I believed I'd done something terrible for love to have disappeared…"

The magician waited patiently, then after a long moment the boy spoke further, the words coming quite naturally and smoothly from some clear place inside him.

"But the important thing wasn't in fact gone; the kind Love I wanted wasn't really gone at all. I felt terrible only because I was somehow pushing away the wonderful calm that was already there around me, despite all the chaos… And you're saying this was the same with all the times in my life when I felt alone and hurt?"

"Indeed, that's all quite correct," the wizard responded. "Your inner listening is teaching you well. Yes, this splendid, generous, healing Love was indeed always there waiting for you. And remembering this will bring you great peace and comfort in the future, Paulo. Many years of pain and sorrow will melt away like snow before a rising sun when you remember that Love was always there for you, even in your most difficult and trying situations."

The boys eyes cast far into the distance as he let the sage's words quietly settle into his heart.

"Sadness and grief of every nature will fall away when you see that such painful feelings were simply a mistaken choice on your part, and not the result of a cruel world or some wicked ruler. You simply are *not* the vulnerable, abandoned and ill-treated thing you have always thought. No – you are part of that great Love itself, such Love and Strength you can now learn to feel within you all the time. And you no longer need to be nearly so defensive or sensitive about what happens to you in this life anymore. You will instead feel calm and understanding the moment you start to let go of your old perceptions and emotions, and fully accept Love for yourself."

"I think I understand this better," the boy now said, "but I still don't know how all this might really be possible. It seems just so *impossible* – or impossible *to do*. How can I really feel my father wasn't so important to my happiness?"

Zeph replied sympathetically, "I do indeed understand the difficulty, Paulo. It is difficult, but simply because of everything you currently think you are, and everything you think others represent for you within the Domain. When someone is gone, it's like something extremely important has died and left. It's like a part of you has disappeared, leaving a deep empty hole, as if existence is now unstable, unsafe, and missing something vital."

"That's exactly it, yes!" the boy exclaimed. "Like it was because of them that life was safe and normal, and then suddenly they're gone!"

"Of course this isn't true, as you're starting to see," continued the magician. "Your existence is never lacking in anything; and your existence can never be truly unstable and unsafe. However, in the Domain that's certainly the way it can appear and feel. The people of Towne live today confined within the beliefs of their tiny Maker-selves, insecure and frightened, within the narrow limits of their own separate and individual existence. They have forgotten their stable and complete life as the One Great People of the King.

"In their greater Identity, the One People need nothing and no one else in order to feel whole, happy and utterly peaceful, because all is one and joined … all is complete and safe. But the mind locked within the separated Maker-self will always feel abandoned and insecure, constantly looking for outside support and reassurance."

Paulo spoke, "Then a person should just look within his own heart and mind to find the comfort he needs, no?"

"He certainly might do so, if he were not too afraid to look there," Zeph explained. "But most Townsepeople will instead seek another, more convoluted solution. Whenever a person mistakes himself for a separated, isolated villager instead of an integral part of the One Great People, he will naturally feel very fragile and very vulnerable. Unless he decides to listen to the presence of the whole Love within him, he will fall into a trap, the trap of trying to find another special, isolated person to help him feel safer, more complete, and somehow more whole.

"These special individuals become suddenly very purposeful in his life and serve an important role: he will begin to *use* them to feel better in his life, as if he could extract something from them for his own well-being and stability. He will blind himself to their resplendent and perfect Identity – a real disservice to those he considers his loved ones – and will see them as valuable only for what they can offer his little Maker-personality. These chosen individuals will be enticed and lured and even snared into his private world, and at that moment they become a key part of the way he sees himself and his mortal life.

"When these people we've woven into our lives leave us, as sometimes they must do, we will feel somehow quite disturbed. All of the things that we sought and extracted from the other person are suddenly gone – the sense of being someone special, of having a source of support, of having a certain role to play, of seeing ourselves in a certain way, of not being alone and abandoned: all the roles this person played for our Maker-self are revealed. The hidden shame and dormant fear are laid bear; and the pain of this stripping away can be extremely acute."

The boy said, "So again you're saying that none of the pain I felt at my papa's death was really because he was actually gone. In fact it had nothing really to do with him. It was still something else, 'sthat right?"

"Quite so," said Zeph. "It's not at all because someone has departed that we feel upset, as contrary to our experience as this seems. If I feel sad and distressed in life because of someone leaving, it's still because of the gaping hole between Love and myself I have imagined is there, and have not healed. And though for a time it feels like finding another person will help with this pain and loneliness, the only thing that can truly heal my need, of course, is not another person who will cover over my searing shame and fear. Rather, it is remembering the presence of the vivid and real Love and Comfort that are there, present for us all, in every moment of our lives."

CHAPTER THIRTY

A Lesson in Humility

All of this was terribly new and strange to the boy, and it was becoming obvious to him now that it would surely take a long, long time yet to fully understand all the magician's perplexing thoughts.

"Yes, it's all a lot to take in, isn't it, my boy?" The sage grinned cheerfully. "And we're not yet over for the day! In fact, we're only about half way through what we set out to cover this afternoon. But I promise, when you return, you won't regret the heavy work we've done here – I do promise!"

Paulo blew out a long, slow breath and let his vision stretch far out over the fields and hills.

The world before his eyes could not possibly have been more beautiful: enormous billowing white clouds lay off to the east set against a clear azure-blue sky, and toward the west, bright wispy clouds were trailing in some far distant wind. Looking across the gentle rolling hills before him he now noticed a small lake in the valley below. A shaft of sunlight had caught it and the water shone for an instant like a bright silver dewdrop nestling between two broad green hills. All this beauty Paulo saw from his resting place on the hill, and he wondered if all this peacefulness could really, possibly exist within him.

He stretched his hands behind him on the thick fragrant grass and breathed deeply a few times. Warm odors of fields and flowers carried up the hillside to his place under the tree and he tried to draw them inside. Plucking a tall stalk of wild grass, he chewed its juicy end.

Okay…

He wanted just to remain there always, and to remember that this loveliness was true no matter what was happening in his life. The scene before him was one of such peace that he positively *knew* that happiness was true. It was easy to listen to the magician when he was this calm, even if what the wise man said did turn his whole world upside down. It was just a matter of looking around and seeing there was no real danger.

Now that he had a moment to think about all the outlandish ideas the magician had presented to him, something else entered his mind and begged a new question.

"But that doesn't mean I'm really like them, does it?" Paulo asked.

Zeph turned a questioning eye toward the boy.

"Like the Mayor and the others in the market place…? You said we're all the same. But I'm not really hateful or arrogant and critical like they are, so how can it possibly be true that we're the same? What were you really meaning to say?"

"We are all the same," Zeph answered quite matter-of-fact, "because, strange as this may seem, we are still only One Self, with our original identity as the One People of the King intact, and not many separate people like you might think and as it appears. No difference of behavior or shape, of character or belief system can ever change this."

Paulo countered boisterously, "But that can't be right! I just know it isn't!"

"Of course, on the surface there are many *apparent* differences," Zeph clarified, "like those between yourself and the Mayor, as you say. But these have no great significance. Such differences would only be important to your tiny Maker-self which would use them to demonstrate some type of superiority or inferiority, or some aspect of right and wrong, good or bad.

"This narrow perception makes the separation from your reality and from each other seem particularly valid. But there are no *real* differences that can separate you from one another: you *are* all One, and this is an immutable condition. You are all filled with the Maker; *and* you are all filled with the Light of your King. You are all the Same, and there are absolutely no exceptions."

"But that's certainly *not* what it looks like," Paulo declared obstinately. "You must've become confused, or something. Because that's really not the way it is!"

'The magician smiled knowingly. "Do you remember the story I told you on the first day we met?" he asked. "In the beginning we were all One People – holy, whole, and perfect. When we accepted the Spell, the illusion and its powerful message of culpability, we adopted separate bodies in order to disguise the true problem. As such we *appeared* to be separate and different from each other. This division into little independent selves was the physical expression of our original desire to know something different, something better and other than the Oneness of the Kingdom. And this little self became the object we henceforth learned to dote with an enormous and exaggerated sense of importance and difference.

"Each judgment we make today based on this sense of difference with others is simply a reflection of that original desire to separate from the Kingdom. We use this poignant feeling of difference along with our judgments to perpetuate and qualify our new sense of individuality, our 'specialness'. Whenever you attempt to remain different from your brothers – as you do whenever you judge the Mayor – you simply maintain your unconscious wish to remain banished from the Kingdom. To stay 'you', at the cost of remembering your origin."

Paulo rose to a sitting position, thoroughly irritated now. "But I do *not* go around making myself more important than others like the Mayor. Or being angry and hateful like Mrs Belladonna. I'm just not like that … I'm *nice* to people!"

"Paulo," Zeph looked at him laughingly and widened his eyes in provocation, "– would it upset you to know that you resemble these people you dislike much more than you think? You, too, contain the Maker, and thus you too are filled with exactly the same intentions as the Mayor and Mrs Belladonna – You *are* one."

Paulo didn't look pleased at all.

The wizard continued. "Perhaps you don't behave in the same way, I agree; but you certainly contain the same *intentions* and *attitudes* as them. Maybe your feelings of arrogance and superiority take a different, more socially acceptable expression, but they are nevertheless exactly the same feelings. They are still the same feelings because we are only One Mind, and there is only *one* Spell that we all share, that moves and motivates us.

"The Spell is not different in the Mayor. He just expresses it differently. And, I might add, it certainly makes no sense to judge someone for a different expression of exactly the same condition that's within you – *right*?"

"Well…!"

Paulo had no good answer.

"But how can you possibly say we're all the same? *Just look at us*," he cried, exasperated. "You couldn't be looking at what's really there if you just see the same thing everywhere – We *are* different!"

"But my young apprentice, perhaps *you* are the one who is not seeing what's really there. I grant that maybe you don't go around wearing ribbons and medals like the Mayor," Zeph answered pointedly, "telling everyone what they can and can't do and claiming special privileges. But maybe your way of trying to show you are special and superior takes another form."

Paulo stared uncomprehendingly at the magician.

"Let's see, perhaps your specialness looks like doing something in a particular way that makes you slightly better than others, *cleverer*… even if that's just collecting especially good wood or knowing how to tie a good strong knot. Or maybe it's by having special problems and a difficult family that no one else can possibly understand, by suffering in your own personal, unique way; or perhaps by having some special knowledge, by understanding something others don't. Maybe even things about the Maker and everything else we discuss."

The wizard looked carefully at Paulo: the boy was trying desperately hard not to show what he was feeling.

Zeph continued, "In fact, maybe you are 'trapped' selling wood in the market place, as you say, *only* because this still gives you a particular and unique identity as the poor little wood seller that everyone knows so well; the wood seller whom everyone is so fond of and feels so sorry for, who is so nice and humble despite his difficult situation and troublesome family. Maybe your whole identity as 'Paulo' is, in fact, based on simple arrogance, specialness and aggression, the same desire to remain within the confines of the life you know, the exact same nature as that of the Mayor and Mrs Belladonna –"

"But… *no!* That's not possibly –"

Paulo was at breaking point.

The magician looked at him firmly.

"That's totally impossible!" the boy insisted flatly.

"On the contrary; that would only be perfectly and absolutely normal, Paulo," Zeph replied calmly. "Everyone is exactly the same. *Everyone* here forges for himself a special identity based on some idea of a separate and unique life; a life balanced rather grossly, I must add, between soaring self-exaltation and glory on the one hand, and deep self-doubt and despair on the other. Nevertheless, try as you might, you *cannot* succeed in this effort: you cannot be different from others, not in any fundamental way."

There was a painful moment of silence during which the boy struggled with himself.

"Please don't misunderstand, Paulo: there is honestly nothing at all wrong with this; but it is much better to see this behavior for what it is, for your sake, simply because it is not a source of strength or happiness, but of pain. My boy, have you ever thought that perhaps the poor little wood seller is the identity you have carefully forged in order to separate yourself out from the One People, even though you claim to seek the wholeness of Love, and perhaps this is the reason it persists?"

The boy stared belligerently back at the wizard.

"Maybe you're stuck in your current imprisoning circumstance only because you have a secret, unseen investment in it; an unknown desire for it to remain. Who knows? The 'poor and unfortunate wood seller' is perhaps the way that you still unconsciously try to be someone unique, special and individual – in your own way, of course. The way you try to be *Paulo*. Yet all this serves only to describe the Maker-self you wish to make so important, real, and *separate*. And it has nothing to do with who and what you really are."

Paulo was thoroughly exasperated. He felt it was outrageously unfair he wasn't allowed to be special, to use his personality and the circumstances of his life in order to be different. *Why can't I?* he was thinking. What's so wrong with that? Why can't I be special and different when everyone else is making such an effort to show me how important and different and real *they* are? Why should they always be the ones who count and are noticed and respected?

He made his case to the wizard.

"But I can't just stop trying to be me. Even though I've been thinking about doing some other work, the wood seller is *who I am*. Everything you say about being special and counting is everything I think I am, and everything I do all the time. And everything everyone else does, too! I can't just stop all this. And all this can't be bad!"

The magician chuckled warm-heartedly. "Again, you must try to understand, my boy, there's absolutely nothing at all wrong with any of this as such. Pretending to be something you're not is just a game, that's all. It's not in any way a crime, but just a silly game, one of fantastic, heaven-shattering proportions perhaps, yet still just a simple diversion. But in our first conversation together in the market place some time ago now, you said that above all you wanted to learn to be happy. And I must tell you that you can't possibly learn to be happy and peaceful and strong while you still insist on remaining estranged from your own reality, and on ignoring that of your brothers.

"You do, indeed, try to be special, respected and recognized, Paulo. Just like the Mayor. Everyone does, even if that does mean suffering a great deal and being particularly unhappy and hostile. But that is precisely what causes the Love and Peace of the Kingdom to disappear from your awareness."

Paulo was utterly perplexed. "This just makes so little sense. All of it!"

"Just try to relax a little while I explain," the wizard continued. "It does makes good sense when you think about it: Desiring to be special and separate, to be known and appreciated as your small self, is simply the wish to be no longer at Home in the Kingdom, because in the Kingdom there is only One, not many. It's just a question of understanding that keeping separation in your heart is not a source of pleasure but of pain, despite what seem to be the rewards, because it hides the truth which is indeed something very beautiful."

Something glinted in Paulo's eye now like desperation, a fervent need to be told he would finally be happier when he was more successful, more respected, wealthier. But the magician couldn't agree with him…

"Being unique and specially known, or specially accomplished, is *not* the secret to happiness at all, despite appearances. On the contrary, it is a sure path to sadness, self-doubt and disillusionment. No doubt many villagers will, of course, spend their entire lives doing precisely this – developing their illusion of difference from others. And they do so believing this gives them some measure of satisfaction, security and substance. But, despite what the Maker convinces you are the gifts of specialness and individuality, you will never be truly peaceful or serenely happy, and you will never know who you really are if you follow this path."

"So what're we supposed to do?" Paulo asked plaintively. "Like always I'm supposed to change everything, right? To stop selling wood and become someone else?" He was thoroughly upset. In fact, he was far from convinced he really wanted to know the answer, or even to continue the conversation for that matter.

"*Looking* is what you do, Paulo. That's all."

The magician settled a wise, steady look on the boy.

"Until you are able to face your fierce determination to be someone special and separate, you will continue with the game of trying to be someone other than who you really are. So firstly you continue doing all the things you normally do every day and you begin to *look,* being exceptionally honest with respect to all the thoughts of difference and separateness you find within your heart.

"When you've found these thoughts, then you can become aware of the great cost of holding on to them. The cost, of course, is the glorious peace of your true Self that you're willing to barter for simple misery … the lifelong struggle to become the individual of your misguided imagination."

CHAPTER THIRTY-ONE

A Fine and Tangible Garment

"So!" Paulo huffed.

The wizard looked back at the boy and a playful grin spread across his face.

Frustrated with all these enigmatic responses, Paulo asked frankly, "So do I stay a wood seller or try to do something else. I've been thinking about this question for a long time – it's quite important to me. And please don't tell me it doesn't make a difference."

"Well, I guess you can stay a wood seller … or you can do something else, I imagine," the magician answered with equanimity.

The boy shook his head from side to side in disgust.

"In all honesty – I'm sorry I must disappoint you – it really *doesn't* matter at all what you choose to do. Because it's not what you do that can ever possibly change what you are, my young friend. You *will* find yourself, no matter the path you choose. What you seek to learn is always the same, no matter what you're doing, and no matter where you are. It's not, after all, your activities or movements we're trying to change, but the *purpose* and *reason* behind your choices."

The boy exclaimed loudly, "But how'm I supposed to succeed with advice like that? I just *have* to be able to make something more of my life. It's been a disaster till now!"

"My dear friend," the sage replied, "your life is not about making the best choices, or progressing along the richest path. Your life is about *learning.* You might of course become a great and successful merchant as part of your path, and there's certainly nothing wrong with that, but that isn't what your life is about. That's not why you came here, not this time."

"I didn't? That's not why I came? But I really want to do better and make something of myself!"

"Yes, I hear you. And the best way of doing that is by learning to *understand* yourself. You've got to learn to understand yourself first, in a different way, using the help of a powerful, gentle Presence in your mind to undo and replace that of the Maker. And for this any activity will do, whatever you feel attracted toward. You can learn to feel this wonderful Presence as a baker counting his loaves, if you so wish. Or as a farmer counting his chickens, or as a cobbler adding up his shoe sales. You will eventually learn to add correctly, to listen and to understand your world and reality properly, no matter the learning path you choose."

The boy was quieted by these words and sat there silently a while, contemplating.

"So then is the callous, arrogant Mayor any different from you, Paulo, or from the surly fish-man?" Zeph asked.

Paulo considered the question bitterly, and said nothing.

"Of course not. *Everyone* within his Maker-mind feels totally insubstantial, humiliated and worthless, and everyone tries to compensate for this in one way or another … *Everyone*. That's why everyone is always making such an effort to 'be someone', even when that means being hateful or judgmental, hurtful and inconsiderate. And even if that means suffering or falling ill.

"You see, there is not one person in the Domain who isn't constantly trying in some way or another to give himself and his life meaning and validity. That's because once a villager has lost sight of his own Reality, he'll feel a desperate fear in the deepest part of his mind that he's no one and nothing, and then he'll go to the greatest efforts to make his little self or his group as significant as possible. Nevertheless, as you can imagine, no possible circumstances or accomplishments could really keep such thoughts of self-doubt and insignificance away for long."

The boy interjected, "So there's no way the Mayor and I can be different? You're absolutely *sure*? We're really exactly the same? That seems just so extreme."

"The Mayor simply does exactly the same as you, Paulo," Zeph replied. "He wants to comfort himself in the same way you do with some feeling that he is, indeed, someone special, someone different, someone who counts. And above all, someone *real*.

"Everyone makes a separated Maker-identity for himself that is the focal point of his sense of reality. No one escapes this need, for that is why he originally leaves the Kingdom to go to the Domain. Upon settling there he immediately begins to fabricate this separated self, weaving it literally from thin air, plucking it from strands of mist and vapor and shadow. A mysterious and strange alchemical fabric begins to take shape before his eyes, starting from a base of carefully chosen looks and clothing and expressions. Into this cloth he then incorporates threads of well-considered thoughts and studied opinions. Finally he will work into it a pattern of vital life events, and a certain measure of unique knowledge and valuable experiences.

"All this is what he ultimately calls 'himself' which he slips on much as a suit, parading it quite proudly in public, quite sure he is wearing a fine and tangible garment. But he will discover the essential truth about himself only when all these tremendously important and most personal things are seen to be nothing at all. They are not good, and they are not bad. Just nothing and inconsequential, of no real meaning or importance."

The boy listened skeptically.

"Well, I'll do what I can," he pouted, "But I don't promise anything. Not for the moment at least. All that you spoke about still seems pretty important to me, although you obviously think it's quite stupid."

"Not in the least, Paulo. Once more, none of this is a sin or bad in any way whatsoever," the wizard reassured, "Nor worthy of criticism. But it is indeed a way of staying stuck in the exceedingly tiny home the Maker offers us instead of claiming the lovely, calm greatness of our Reality. In our real Home we don't need any exceptional accomplishments or qualities. How silly! We don't need any special knowledge, striking looks, notable achievements, or indeed anything unique to feel known and loved, to feel respected and worthwhile."

"How can you be so sure?" Paulo demanded. "I'm sure I'd be a better person if I was able to make more out of my life."

"When you go inside during a moment of quiet and remember your real Home, Paulo, you will *know* that you are perfectly loved and appreciated. You will understand that you are an innate part of the One Great People, deeply beloved of your King. And you will no longer need to see signs or proof of your worth or mask your feelings of insecurity. However in order to get there, it *is* necessary to look at all the ways in which you still attempt to make your tiny self-made home substantial, unique and significant."

Before Paulo was overcome with exasperation, Zeph added, "Until you get to this level of understanding, my dear and very capable student, you can stay with as many ideas of specialness and self-importance as you want."

Paulo looked at the magician almost suspiciously.

"When you finally decide that, above all other desires, you do indeed want to feel happy, content and safe," Zeph continued, "you'll need to begin by understanding the truth about yourself, as unpleasant as it might seem, instead of pretending to be something you're not. That's the sum of what I've been trying to say."

CHAPTER THIRTY-TWO

A Nice Face And Nausea

"Do you still want us to continue, Paulo?" the wizard proposed, offering the boy a moment of quiet. "Remember, I'm only trying to help. We can stop any time you want."

"Well, maybe I do want to be special, too," Paulo admitted grudgingly after a few minutes. He didn't like the fact that he was the same as the Mayor, but he could admit it. He had thought hard about the matter in the last few minutes and figured it didn't make sense denying what was so clearly true.

"But at least I don't get angry and spiteful at people like Mrs Belladonna. You can't change the fact that she can be really obnoxious to everyone. And *I'm* not like that – *that's for sure.*"

The wizard raised one eyebrow. "Are you really so sure, Paulo?"

Paulo didn't know what to say and certainly wasn't looking forward to the wizard's response. He stared back at the magician. "Do I really need to find out?" he asked plaintively.

"Maybe you don't get angry and critical quite like Mrs Belladonna," Zeph continued. "But perhaps you have a different way of expressing attack thoughts and violent feelings in your life." The magician looked at the boy kindly, still patient with Paulo's desire to prove there were indeed vital differences between himself and others. "Can you think of what that might be?"

"No! And frankly I don't care one bit either!"

Paulo was now utterly fed up and wanted to go absolutely no further with the conversation. He looked away and paid no more attention to the wise elder.

There's got to be another way of getting Home – without him!

He cast his eyes up into the branches of the tree and watched the breeze playing with the leaves for a while. But when his mind calmed down he found his thoughts insistently coming back to Zeph's question.

…In what ways might I also express violence and anger in my life?

Unfortunately it was only too easy for him to find some answers.

Zeph looked at the boy and waited patiently while he considered his response.

After a moment Paulo found the desire to continue. It seemed to him it wasn't really so terrible to speak the truth, not when he understood there was no real judgment waiting for him. Just Zeph's smile. After all, he figured, what could really happen to him if the truth were known? And in any case he was quite sure the magician already knew.

"I think spiteful things about people sometimes," he said. "I don't say them, but I certainly do think them. That's a type of violence, I guess. Sometimes I want what they have or I think they don't deserve what they've got. I think the world would be better off without some people, like some of my customers when they're being stupid, or when they're demanding and impatient. They should just disappear, or die or something, and then I wouldn't have to deal with them. But I put on a nice face instead and pretend everything's okay. Actually, that can make me feel pretty bad inside.

"It's clear I don't think they're like me, like we're one big family. They're just 'others', and have nothing to do with me. I even get sick in my stomach sometimes because of thinking thoughts like this, or it hurts in my head and throat. So I guess whenever I feel annoyed and upset like that, whatever the reason, that's a kind of violence. I don't show it or let it out but keep it inside."

He paused, thinking further.

"There's something else, too. There are times when I don't do what I know is best, even though it's good for everyone and even for myself. I pretend I didn't hear or didn't know, but inside I know I kind of did it on purpose and it makes a lot of trouble for everyone and even for myself sometimes. Or then I don't do things right and I do a bad job instead of a good one, saying I had to do it my way, even when *I'm* the only one that's hurt. It's like a part of me does it on purpose to hurt others and myself. Sometimes I feel I just can't stand to do what other people want or to do what's best or right. That's a kind of violence, I suppose."

Now that he had started being honest, he easily found other ways he expressed anger and hatred in his life.

"I think when I have an accident and hurt myself that this is maybe sometimes a way of being angry, especially when I know I could have done things differently and not get hurt. Mostly because I've insisted on doing something my way again, or haven't been thinking clearly. In any case I'm certainly not listening inside to any kind of quiet voice at these times. I'm just doing what I want and not listening at all inside for help or advice. I don't often think to ask what the gentle voice would want me to do and just do what I want instead. So I guess that's a form of hate, too, or at least it's certainly not love."

"That's very good, Paulo," the magician reassured. "Do you see these are your personal ways of expressing the exact same malicious feelings that you criticize so much in others? Everyone feels angry and upset at some deep, unseen level. And everyone chooses his or her own way of expressing this. A broken plough, a dispute with the baker, a sprained ankle, or the loss of a job or a friend: these events all derive from the same underlying miscomprehension of the nature of reality. Sometimes our inner, unspoken tension is projected outside and onto others, and sometimes it's harbored inside and is the cause of sickness and accidents. None of this is bad, of course, but it is certainly a source of distress."

Paulo was fighting hard with himself to agree with everything the magician was saying. Something stood in front of him like a wall, making it impossible to climb over and join his teacher. "Alright, so maybe I can also be a little angry and hateful, like Mrs Belladonna. But that still doesn't mean we're exactly the same." Paulo defended his point of view without too much elaboration. "We just *are* different!"

The wizard suppressed a chuckle and continued quite seriously, with just the faintest smile on his lips.

"Remember, my valiant young student, we *are* One. It is just *one* Spell … the Spell we all share, and no different from one person to another. One person cannot be better than another or fundamentally different, no matter how high, or how low, the social standing or achievement. As strange as it seems, this is just not possible. What you see around you is only different expressions of the same inherent condition within all of us. Each of us contains the same misbeliefs and illusions within the Spell; so we're each of us filled with the exact same intentions, motivations and feelings."

Zeph took in the boy's regard which was becoming more belligerent by the minute.

"We *are* identical, Paulo! That's why you'll eventually stop judging others: it becomes a most natural thing. If you're like everyone else and if everyone is exactly the same, then judgment has no real meaning. It makes no sense. It's just another game that you eventually cease playing, something you grow out of."

It's not fair! Paulo continued to sulk. *This has got to stop!*

CHAPTER THIRTY-THREE

Not On His Own

Zeph took in the deep frowns on the boy's face, and asked, a little amused, "You don't like to think that you're as nasty and hateful as Mrs Belladonna, do you?"

"No! It's not nice at all! I can't stand to think these things are within me," the boy replied vociferously. Then he added, woeful, "Zeph, are you really sure I need to look at all this just in order to get Home? Surely there must be an easier way!"

"Please do understand, Paulo," the magician smiled and replied, "it's really not a crime to contain such feelings of hatred, although it can certainly be very unpleasant. It's not a sin or a crime, and it's quite normal under the Spell. Despite the destructive tendencies you harbor, you're still one of your King's beloved People, and nothing you think or do can change this. It's just that perhaps now you'd like to discover what's really there within your mind, just so you can start to be happier. At first it feels quite uncomfortable finding out."

The boy didn't look particularly reassured.

"If it helps, think of it like this," Zeph continued, seeking another way to explain his thoughts. "It's normal that you should hate to think you're the same as the people you criticize – that's precisely *why* you judged them in the first place!"

Paulo's face puckered with confusion.

"Our habit is to judge others specifically for that which we don't accept about ourselves. This is the nature of *ridding*, the act of projection, which we discussed before: I feel there's an evil quality within myself and fervently do *not* want to see such horrors there, and so I pretend that it's not a problem with me, but with *you*. It's an automatic and unseen reaction within the false mind that whatever vicious or unpleasant tendencies you harbor within yourself and refuse to acknowledge and release, you will see in others. As if you can somehow become cleansed by expelling such qualities outside yourself and onto other people. This follows the law that *veiling* of what is within always leads to *ridding* without.

"In fact, Paulo, this might surprise you, but the way we learn the most about ourselves is by looking intentionally and purposively *at others*. We do this to determine exactly what it is that we most dislike and judge in them. This can be very important information for us, since whatever judgment we hold of another we can be sure is the perfect reflection of our *own* hidden nature."

The boy blinked – he had always thought he most condemned the people who were precisely *not* like him.

"Let me explain this idea," the wizard continued. "Most of us are usually quite ignorant of what we deeply believe about ourselves – this information is often very deeply hidden – and so it can be quite unproductive looking for our self-perceptions within ourselves. On the other hand, we usually have little difficulty recognizing our thoughts and feelings about other people. In fact in most cases these thoughts come quite unbidden to our minds, filling them easily with feelings of anger, frustration, scorn and the such."

Paulo smirked. He could in fact imagine the type of people Zeph was talking about quite easily, the type he had to face every day in the market place – and regretted.

"These people are very valuable to you, Paulo – yes!" Zeph emphasized the words to the boy who was now wearing a very sour grimace. "They are your *mirror* – and they will *set you free*."

This Paulo could hardly believe.

"In fact, the people who upset you the most are the most helpful to you of all!"

A look of utter stupefaction crossed the boy's face and he rolled his eyes skyward.

"...To them you look specifically to discover what you still believe about yourself, since this type of careful, analytical looking cuts neatly through all your attempts to avoid the truth. It's your hateful and judgmental thoughts about yourself that constitute the spell that confuses your senses. And so if you want to find the path Home, it will be absolutely vital to uncover these dark shadows. The only way to find them is to look for their somber reflection you have placed in others.

"Please try to understand, it is only when you can look openly and honestly at all the evil that is actually within *yourself*, at the things that make you most ill to your stomach, that you will make the darkness within you fade and disappear. Without completing this step fully, you will never be able to be wholly free of the darkness and pain in your life – *because you will still think they are real and powerful.* You will never be able to reveal the light that is already within you as one of the King's People, because you will have still kept a tight grip on shadows."

Paulo was listening very intently.

More than anything Paulo wanted one day to be able to feel again the warm light of holiness and be able to live in the resplendent sunshine of the Kingdom. And he knew he still had much work to do to get there. Perhaps this practice of looking at the thoughts he held about himself as reflected in others, as the magician suggested, might after all be the trick.

"True Forgiveness is only ever forgiveness of yourself," the wizard continued. "...a complete releasing of all notions and concepts of wrong with respect to *every* human being, a letting go of the darkness you harbor within yourself that has effaced the light. Begin now by seeing that it is not other people that carry the shadow of evil within them, but your own self-hateful thoughts you have cast upon them that imprison you. Then, remember ... you *do* have a choice, and no longer need to condemn and imprison yourself."

A look of despair now crossed the boy's face. "But this seems like an awfully difficult thing you want me to do, Zeph. I really, *really*, don't want to know about all these awful things inside me." He lowered his eyes downward. "I just don't think I'll be able to do it. How can I do this if I can't even stand to look?"

Zeph answered him gently. "You're right, Paulo, you can't do this, certainly not on your own. Trying to do things on our own is indeed how we made our first dreadful mistake, and now we must always learn to ask for help.

"There's only one way you'll be able to do this, Paulo, and that's together with my help, and with the help of the eternal kind Presence you carry within you. You can't do this alone because, as you say, you're far too scared; the evil seems altogether too great and frightening.

"But if I am next to you, as I am now, then you hold a bright light between your hands; and if you begin to look at your deepest thoughts of sin together with me, and if we take this brilliant light to that dark place, then I promise that you will feel safe and loved no matter how terrifying the visions there become. Then you can look at what seem the blackest nightmares and not be filled with your own terrible self-hate; because you will have my love and comfort next to you, and you will know that only Love for you is true…"

There was a moment of quiet. Paulo's thoughts stilled completely and just for an instant he held the idea of something most miraculous: the end of all hate and fear in his life, and somehow he knew that it was really possible.

He raised his head and looked solemnly into the wizard's eyes. The magician returned his gaze, a faint smile on his lips. After a moment, he spoke.

"Paulo, you should learn now that the problem you face is not the horror that you believe is there: that is not the actual problem, for there is no *real* darkness within you. You are only frightened now of what you *imagine* is there… Once, a long time ago, you had a frightening dream and imagined evil and hate within you which you immediately judged as terribly sinful. This act of judging made the hate appear as dreadfully real in your perception. Because of your fear of what you believed was a despicable *fact*, you ran away instead of staying to look. Today it is only your judgment of what you imagine is existent that makes it seem so true and terrifying."

The boy seemed to be following, and Zeph continued.

"By your judgment you rendered the Crime more real in your perception than it actually was. Your terrible condemnation of yourself caused you to *deny* its presence in your thoughts: it is only this resistance and denial that cause you pain now, not the actual object itself, since nothing is really there. There is no evil, there is no hate; there is no sin or crime. What you are scared of you will eventually discover is unreal … literally nothing at all … but you cannot do this until you take a step away from yourself and begin to look. And this you will be able to do only with our help."

Paulo became deeply thoughtful as the magician's words trailed off into a warm, comfortable silence.

Chapter Thirty-Four

The Paradox of Anger

Paulo thought seriously about the words his wise friend spoke, but then after some minutes seemed to find something that still disturbed him.

His face filled with concern and he turned toward the wizard. "Zeph, I feel badly for my brother, Fredo. Love's supposed to be there for us all, yet the blacksmith is a harsh master and often beats him for no reason. Why's it that horrible things sometimes happen to people like my brother, things we're not even responsible for? How's he to make his way on the path Home if he's always in such suffering?"

The magician took a moment to find his words, wondering seriously if he should reveal this important but very difficult piece of wisdom. "I'll tell you, Paulo," he said, "but I warn you it shall seem exceptionally strange since everything the Maker tells you in the Domain is so completely opposite to what I'm about to say.

"Listen now, open your mind, and try to understand… In the beginning when the King granted us the entire Kingdom as our own, he bestowed upon us a certain exceptional power. With this special ability we could receive everything we wanted simply by the power of our thinking about it. If you think about something, wanting it badly enough and accepting that it is normal that this should happen, then it shall happen as you have asked. That is the power we have in the Kingdom of Happiness: it is an extraordinary place and there we are an extraordinary people.

"Of course in the Golden City this power of ours functions very well. There our minds are clear and we only seek wondrous things for ourselves and for others. But in the Domain our hearts are secretly filled with evil and violence: that is the nature of the deep unconscious Spell within each of us. Influenced by this Spell, we unknowingly seek painful and even cruel, sometimes brutal situations for our Maker-selves, most often despite our best intentions and efforts.

"Each moment spent away from the Kingdom now is an instant of self-condemnation. This is quite normal: separating ourselves from our magnificent, natural state provokes in all of us a condition of terrible desperation, though it is of course quite hidden from nearly everyone. The result is that with this tremendous tension held unrecognized inside, we are secretly inviting punishment and constraint into our lives.

"Most people prefer to remain unaware of these self-destructive thoughts, and so unfortunate events and situations will appear to happen to them without any apparent reason. They seem to happen without any acceptance or responsibility on our part and take many different and disguised forms –"

Paulo started: "But…!" and Zeph answered the boy's question before it was even spoken:

"This is certainly not to deny that there are times when we are physically attacked by the actions of others; this is quite true. Perhaps by a situation, like your brother, or even by an illness," Zeph explained.

"– However, it is the *feeling* of being assaulted and victimized by a situation that is the clue we are fixed within the framework of separation and lovelessness. It is not the act, but our feelings about what is happening that we must pay attention to; the self-destructive thoughts we are looking for. All these thoughts permit suffering because they are inevitably self-condemning, starting as they do from the idea that our reality within gentle Oneness has been broken and destroyed."

Paulo was again plagued with frustration.

"I still don't see how it could be possible not to feel angry when someone attacks you," he exclaimed. "My hate of the Mayor and the local bullies is for a real reason, you know! And then you want me to believe that my anger will only turn against me and create havoc in my own life. It's so ridiculously unfair!"

The magician pursued his explanation. "Yes, it may seem like quite a paradox. Then let me try to make this idea a little clearer… Try to see, whenever we're feeling angry or hurt we're inevitably harboring some type of hidden attack against ourselves: such painful feelings could only come from having first accepted a self-inflicted, brutal separation from one's greater Self. Without the Exile in our minds, we can feel no sense of attack; there can only be a sense of strength … of peace and understanding, in which no actions of others can ever be perceived as truly harmful.

"But let me go one step further. There is only *One* People and *One* Life, Paulo, as I've said before, and so any anger toward any other person can only ever be an expression of anger toward *yourself*, and your own life. What you wish for another will always be your own wish for yourself, because there is no 'other'. In truth, *there is only You*."

Paulo was utterly confounded.

"Again, please understand, my boy, wanting to attack another is not a sin, and I make an effort to repeat this. There is nothing sinful in your anger, and your anger shall never remove your King's love and warm acceptance of you. Neither is the hate or destructive behavior of another a sin to be judged, nor could it remove him from his King's side."

So anger and hate are suddenly now okay, 'sthat it? the boy was thinking.

"Still," the wizard continued, "it is another principle of truth that anger and all expressions of hate can never be *justified*. Not yours, nor anyone else's. Anger is always purely a mistake – an error born of confusion and misunderstanding. This is so, as we have seen, because there is nothing outside of you that can cause you feelings of distress or injustice. Everything comes from within you."

Paulo now breathed a long heavy sigh of frustration, and he said: "Here we go again. 'What I feel is always my choice...' you're going to say, right?"

"Exactly... Your experience *is* always of your choice: either the peace and love that surpasses all things of this world, or your sensitivity to attack and victimization. If you remove Love from your mind and invite pain in its place, you may claim that the responsibility lies with another person; but by no means does this magically transform the other person into the actual agent of your pain. In no way *can* your brother do you wrong or harm – not to your Reality. If you persist with hurt and blame, it is an indication that you are simply frightened of Love, as we have said, and still need more time to approach this source of wonderful warmth and your unsuffering Self more slowly."

"I still think it's completely unfair," the boy cried. "And utterly crazy!"

"Perhaps it seems that way," the magician replied, still perfectly composed. "But think on this: it feels unfair to you, Paulo, for a reason, and a specific reason..."

The boy shot the magician a wary look.

"If this discussion makes you feel particularly uncomfortable, my dear student, if you feel it's unfair that you cannot *justifiably* hate a brother and suffer at his hands, it's because you don't want to give up the protection that you feel hate and victimization still offer you."

There was no way to impress the boy, and he wore a fiercely stubborn look. "I don't know what on earth you're talking about now – "

"Yes, hate and blame seem to offer you protection," the wizard persisted. "You believe there is a distance, a gap, between yourself and others, a gap which allows you to legitimately accuse and condemn other people, and you believe this space protects you from the truth. This gap is the illusion of separation. Without this so-called protection you are 'vulnerable' to the truth of Oneness and your inseparability from your brother.

"Protected by this space, this separation, you think you can condemn and attack with righteous impunity, and now you're seeing that perhaps this isn't possible. There are consequences to your deeply held beliefs in exclusion – all your personal feelings of fear, pain and isolation and the different forms in which they manifest.

"Yes, you can continue to believe that the Mayor and yourself are separate and do not share the same interests, the same path, and the same life; you can continue to believe that the blacksmith and your brother are unjoined and divisible, if you wish; you can continue to attack and judge the other boys in town: but you will never feel safe or peaceful, well or whole, as a result. And you will never know the truth and majesty of your true Self. To know yourself is to know your brother, and know that you are one and the same."

Zeph looked at Paulo, knowing well that he was unable to grasp the full meaning and importance of these many ideas. A look of patience crossed his face as he sought for a few more words that might make the challenging nature of the path clearer, and gentler.

After a moment he spoke.

CHAPTER THIRTY-FIVE

Remember Kindness

"Accept Love for yourself now, Paulo," Zeph said. "If it is indeed kindness for others you wish to feel in the place of your anger, then accept Kindness for yourself. It's that simple really… For then you'll naturally extend this Love, and in turn you'll feel the love you give.

"Look kindly now on him, your beloved brother, for in truth he is everything you wish to be. It is a law of the Kingdom that what you wish for another shall always be returned to you, because of the natural brotherhood you share. So if you wish to know peace and safety in your life, then ask for love for him, as well as for yourself. And don't forget to make a determined effort with those people who present you with the greatest challenge."

Paulo had grown quiet and said nothing.

"Despite your troubles and suffering, you have always been loved, my young friend, and this goes equally the same for everyone: Fredo, Mrs Belladonna, the Mayor, your mother, the other boys in town, the blacksmith… Everyone, yes, even your greatest enemies. Kindness *does* truly exist: an all-embracing, remarkable experience of peace and understanding. It is the original state of communication between all brothers and can still be your experience of life today, no matter what others seem to perpetrate upon you."

Still the boy sat on the ground in front of the magician, his sight turned inwards.

"It is simply your own hateful thoughts that now render you so vulnerable and sensitive, my young student. When you have made the deep conscious commitment to remember peace in the place of hate, you will no longer feel any fear because you will know all reality as unassailable. And you will then see attack as nowhere. In its place you will only hear the sincere calls for help and understanding that are really there."

The magician paused. The boy was deeply contemplative, making a sincere effort to let the wise man's words impress themselves upon his unwilling spirit.

"And thus to return to your brother and the blacksmith, Paulo, even though we're quite unaware, often we're wishing something harmful for ourselves simply because on a deeper, disguised level we're still holding on to a great deal of self-condemnation. Then perhaps something terrible might actually happen, and we wonder for goodness' sake why. So while Fredo finds himself in a challenging situation, you're not at all responsible for his suffering while concealed deep in his thoughts he continues to believe there is evil in him that needs to be punished. He'll unfortunately continue to see painful images before his eyes while his thoughts are still grounded in feelings of abandonment from Love."

Paulo felt despondent, still concerned for his brother for whom he should be able to do something useful, he thought. And yet there was not really much he could do.

"Please try to understand, Paulo, you are not responsible for the challenges other people face. You are not responsible for their choices and their experiences. You are only ever responsible for your own interpretations and choices and feelings; for the message you leave them in their hearts, for what you teach them through your actions and reactions.

"If there is nothing useful you can do for Fredo right now, then the best thing you can do is *remember for him*. Yes, that's already a great gift you can give. Remember that he has the power to change his mind about himself, about his work and his relationships. Remember also that he is accompanied at every moment by a wonderful, kind and comforting Presence. He, too, can learn to listen to the inner Voice of peace and this will certainly help him release his painful, self-imprisoning thoughts. Listening to the presence of Kindness will remind him that he has done nothing wrong, and that he is as innocent as the day he was created.

"The kind Voice will also tell him that, in his perfect innocence, he is strong and deserving of no punishment or imprisonment. It will say that if he desires, he may leave his current circumstance anytime he wishes. And he will hear that he is not bad or selfish, or worthy of judgment, if he does leave. But no matter what he decides, your role is to remind your brother of his essential strength and innocence, and this you can only do – how? – by *remembering yours*."

The sage examined the boy, questioning whether he had found the wisdom and comfort he was looking to communicate.

Paulo had indeed listened well, but now was gazing longingly along the stone-laid path that wound its way through the green-carpeted valleys, all the way up to the brilliant golden haze in the distance. His Home was still there, waiting.

One day, *one* day… he spoke to himself.

But in the meantime he could be patient while learning to be happy and less afraid, he determined firmly. Yes, he could certainly start by learning to be happier with himself, as happy as his King was with him. And certainly less afraid, too. That would also help his brother, Zeph had said.

Then he wondered: *afraid of what exactly*?

Zeph spoke, "Yes, it is a beautiful place, and it is *so silly* to be afraid, isn't it? But now it's high time you returned to the Domain. In fact I think you've had quite enough for one day."

That's for sure! Paulo responded inside, suddenly relieved.

"Certainly enough for the moment. Yes, we managed to cover a lot of ground this afternoon, much more than I thought you capable of – all to your credit, my young apprentice. I did say you would not be quite the same person as before our discussions, did I not?"

The boy now grinned a reply.

"Remember as many of these ideas as you can, my young friend. Remember above all that you can be just as happy in the Domain as here, as if you were sitting with me on the grassy, sunbathed hillside under this tree – no matter what might now happen to you back there in that dark place."

The magician winked at the boy, and put an arm around his shoulder. Together they walked back toward the giant wooden gates of the Door.

"Now you know that you can leave the Domain and come here to the Kingdom as easily as you wish, anytime you wish. You didn't have the slightest problem with the Guards this time, did you? You found that trick very nicely," Zeph said, proud of his young student.

"It wasn't so difficult to work out, really," said Paulo. "It's just *fear*. If you're not afraid, the Guards don't wake up, and you can walk right by them. It's everyone's fear that makes them come alive and look so dangerous. It's only fear that stops everyone from coming to this place. But the Guards can't hurt anybody, not really, can they?"

"Excellent, Paulo. Indeed, fear is the essential problem for everyone. And yet fear is nothing really at all; a pernicious, potent illusion. It's fear that provokes the things that terrify us, and not the other way around as most people think. Peculiar, isn't it? You've done well to discover this great illusion. Now, return home and, remember, *be kind to yourself!* Alright?"

Zeph patted Paulo on the shoulder and gave his hair a friendly tousle, then pushed him gently forward.

CHAPTER THIRTY-SIX

A Self-Fulfilling Prophecy

Slowly, hesitantly, Paulo made his way through the massive wooden gates and beneath the giant vaulted archway of the Door.

The sparkling sun-filled day gradually disappeared and gave place to the omnipresent misty-dimness of the Domain; the golden path shed its rich luster, becoming a slick cobbled street, damp from a recent rainfall; the broad fields of wild grass and flowers transformed themselves into the stony courtyard and mournful buildings of the derelict neighborhood behind the Town Hall. But Paulo didn't see any of these changes. He was still filled with the magic of Zeph's wonderful thoughts.

He spoke quietly to himself, "So, I just need to learn to be gentle and kind to myself. I haven't done anything wrong at all, and there's nothing wrong with me: that's just the presence of the Maker that thinks awful things. The truth is that my King still loves me."

He past unhurriedly amongst the sleeping guards, thinking, considering, and they didn't stir as much as a hair.

Now that he took a moment to look about him at the square, he noticed how thoroughly unlike it was to the place just the other side of the Great Door, so dark and dim and cold; and a disturbing thought occurred to him:

"But how can Zeph be sure there's really nothing wrong with me? How does he really know? It certainly *feels* like there is; it seems even *wrong* to tell myself that I'm okay and there's nothing wrong with me. No one else thinks that way – who else really thinks there's nothing at all wrong with me? *No one*, really; so how can that be right?"

A large fly landed noisily on the Chief Guard's cheek and he raised his lip in a scowl – still sleeping – to shake it loose.

As Paulo reflected further he felt like he was simply trying to convince himself he was good, but that the truth was actually something else, something quite unpleasant about him... "There must be some truth to this feeling if it's so strong. Perhaps Zeph doesn't really know me well enough yet. Maybe he's thinking of other people, but he doesn't really know what's in *me*. I'm *sure* I must be particularly bad – that's just the way I've always been."

The Guard snorted loudly in his sleep then scratched his nose with a fat, warty finger. Something was really bothering him now.

"Zeph doesn't know how I used to be such a bad boy, and mama would need to punish me often. He never asked me about the things that I used to get up to. I could be really disobedient. Even papa had to get angry to stop me from misbehaving."

As if waking from a dream, Paulo started and looked around him. The Door and guards were now some distance behind him, but he drew a breath, suddenly realizing he was at the place to which his mother *absolutely forbid* him to go.

"Mama *always* needs to be obeyed. If she *ever* finds out that I'm here, there'll be absolute hell to pay!" he realized with a shock. "I'd better get out of here – and *fast!*"

He took off and broke into a sprint, running as fast as his legs would carry him, holding tight to the oil-cloth roll still slung over his shoulder. But within no more than a heartbeat a great noise erupted behind him and a voice bellowed thunderously across the courtyard and resounded down the narrow alleyway:

"HALT! You there, HALT – *immediately!*"

Paulo spun his head around over his shoulder just as a terrifying sound reached his ears, that of grating and clanking metal on metal. And there he was, the enormous Chief Guard, hurtling toward him at frightening speed.

"Oh, *holy Maker* – now I've absolutely had it." Paulo thought of trying to outrun the guard, but knew it was hopeless.

The giant soldier came swiftly upon him and grabbed him tightly in his leather-clad fists. "Now, my friend," he sneered into Paulo's face, "you're in more trouble than you've ever been in your whole little life!" And he dragged him roughly down the street.

The Chief Guard hauled him by the arm all the way home, and Paulo thought that if his arm hurt, it was nothing compared to what his mother would do to him when she found out what he'd been up to. He thought about how stupid he'd been to have fallen for the Maker's ideas again, feeling rotten and guilty inside. And why? Just because that was the constant presence whispering in the back of his mind.

What had Zeph then told me? Something about making unfortunate things happen precisely *because* I think my evil should be punished. Well, I certainly did an *excellent* job this time! What will mother say? – she'll be so unbelievably angry!

Mama really doesn't like it when I do things she doesn't want; but why? Why's she so terribly upset if I'm near the Door? Maybe she's scared for me, she thinks I'll get hurt. Yeah, but that can't be all. Maybe she also thinks something can happen to *her* if she's near the Great Door to the Kingdom; maybe it makes her scared for *herself* when I go there. Yeah, that must be the real reason.

The guard continued to push and shove him down the path, giving Paulo the time he needed to think more about his current crisis.

But nothing can happen to her; not really, even though she doesn't know it.

Poor mama, she must be so afraid. She thinks she's never going to get it right, that there's always going to be something wrong with her and her life. She doesn't know, but she doesn't have to be worried about any of these things; not about any of the things she's so scared of and judges herself so harshly for. There's a remarkable Kingdom, and there's this lovely, amazing warm light of peacefulness shining on her all the time, just the other side of the Door. If only she could come there, she'd see. If only –

If only I could bring some to her…

CHAPTER THIRTY-SEVEN

Love and a Kitchen Spoon

The Guard pounded fiercely and impatiently on the simple wood door of the cottage; the old timber frames shuddered and began to splinter under the hammering.

Paulo's mother appeared in the doorway and Fredo peered out from the dim room within. The woman turned instantly chalk-white with fear when she saw the huge armored soldier with her boy.

"Mrs Vitali – just one more time!" the soldier yelled, piercing the hamlet's silence, and doors and windows flew instantly open on the neighboring houses.

"Just one more time – *do you understand?* – and your son shall be prohibited from ever coming into Towne again. I don't care if he never sells in the market again and you all starve. It's your job to control him. He is *your* responsibility."

"Uh, ah…" The poor woman wanted to respond but her tongue seized up, stiff and dry in her mouth.

The soldier loomed into the doorway and glared down at her from his giant height, his eyes bloodshot, his thick scars dark red and swollen.

"I don't think you understood, *Mrs Vitali,*" he bellowed. "This is absolutely *unacceptable!*" She winced in response. "Under no circumstances do we allow such behavior in the Domain. I shall now be writing a report to the Mayor… *Do you understand what this means?*"

There was an icy silence as their eyes met and the guard waited to see if she had registered his words. The terrified woman cringed lower.

"Yes, yes, of course," she finally managed to mumble.

The guard then dropped the boy and turned to leave. The peasant widow stood there, frozen and immobile in the doorway.

She closed the door in a daze and sat down slowly on the bench by the table. Paulo watched as her color slowly returned, then as her neck flushed scarlet and her face began to burn with a livid anger.

Without warning she turned on the boy and grabbed him tightly by the shoulders. She gripped him harder, sinking her fingers into his flesh, boring him with her eyes and rasped in a rough, dry voice –

"Don't think I'm ever, *ever*, going to let you forget this, my boy. Do you understand?"

Spittle dropped from her quivering mouth.

"*DO YOU UNDERSTAND*?"

Paulo winced at the screaming in his ear.

She didn't wait for a response but lunged over the table. A porcelain cup teetered on its edge then fell and smashed in pieces upon the floor. When she turned back to him she grasped in her hand a heavy wooden kitchen spoon. She grabbed his arm, spun him around until he was bent uncomfortably over her knee and then stretched her arm back over her shoulder. She took aim and brought the weapon down, hit him, then once more, harder, and then once more harder still.

Paulo held his breath while she whipped him and started whimpering, in fear as much as pain. He felt his emotions plunging, falling down a desperate spiral of hate and terror. Then descending further, plummeting rapidly toward crushing self-pity … and furious injustice.

WHY ME? WHAT DID I DO?

All was lost. All was becoming … hate.

I'M NOT TO BLAME.

Hate: there was nothing else; there was no hope; all was hatred.

I didn't do anything wrong.

Yet –

There was a moment of silence; a sudden, unexpected moment of peace amidst the chaos.

And yet –

There was a moment, the briefest instant of quiet, and the boy then felt something else, something that wasn't just hate. Something else was there, and Paulo stopped. He refused to continue.

This isn't right. This really isn't what I want.

Something suddenly, unexpectedly, stopped the tears from coming; something made him release his fierce grip on the way he saw the situation, made him let go; something in him didn't want to go on in this way, not down the same spiral of hate as always.

She hit him, and hit him again.

He remembered: there really was something else. The situation was not what it seemed to be. It wasn't really happening this way. It didn't mean what it appeared to mean.

She beat him more.

He remembered amongst her beatings. He remembered…

Another blow fell.

…there *was* no wrong, there was really nothing to fear, and nothing to protest. There was no real punishment.

– Nothing was really happening.

There was nothing to fear or to protest. Paulo felt, he *knew,* there was a place where none of this harshness was true or really happening. He knew that kindness was truth, and all this fear, this anger and injustice were just mistakes, misunderstandings. Not as serious or real as they seemed at all. He remembered all this, and then, for him, the fight simply stopped. It had no more meaning.

He lay there outstretched on her knee, sensing the fullness of his mother's fury. And he remembered more –

I'm not her enemy … I'm not her enemy, and she's not mine, either. I'm not the evil thing she thinks. And she's not the terrible creature she's convinced herself to be. No matter what we think about ourselves, there's something else here that's really kind and gentle. And yes, maybe we're not as perfect as we'd like to be. This is just a mistake, a misunderstanding, a silly misunderstanding, that's all.

This was all very strange for Paulo who was normally so furious with his mother when she beat him. Yet now there was no passionate and enraged sense of wrong, no feeling of helplessness. There was no hate and no enemy. No danger and no injustice.

'Mama's punishing me only because she thinks it's true what the big old guard told her, that she really is a hopeless failure. But she's not like the guard says. She's not what she believes about herself. And I'm not what she thinks about me. The guard is completely wrong, and mama doesn't need to believe in this anymore. I've seen the guard's nothing at all, as impressive as he looks. It's just our fear that makes him look so big and dangerous. But we don't have to believe in this evil anymore, not ever again.'

Meanwhile, Paulo's mother was also busy listening hard within herself, but to another, completely different voice –

And so it's true – I knew it all the time: I am truly, deeply evil. I've committed some terrible, terrible crime, the guard has made that clear. Everyone hates me, and for good reason.

First my husband hates me and dies and leaves me for good. Then the neighbors despise and judge me. Now my boy is getting me into more trouble than I can afford. Then they'll find out the truly hideous, murderous thing I've done, they'll find out that I… that I've killed the source of love. That's why I feel no love – I destroyed it though I don't even know when or how.

The King has gone and taken his Love away, long ago. He was there, and now he's gone. I killed my King, my father, love… and shattered heaven with my hate.

Paulo's mother was under a deep spell of powerful, intense self-condemnation, feeling the shame of some virulent but completely imaginary act of violence. She envisioned the enraged spite of some abstract, evil ruler returned from the ashes, come to condemn her for all eternity. A ruler, a king, who once had loved her, and yet whose love was now gone because of something atrocious and despicable she had done, she believed, and this was all too intensely, intolerably painful.

She was too scared now to permit her son to get her into any more trouble, to shame her further, to demonstrate her failings, and she needed at all costs to stop him. She tried so hard in every way to be good and perfect, to make things right, to redeem herself, make herself more worthy. And here was this tiny boy who managed so easily to demonstrate how stupid and incapable she really was. And how hideous.

'He *must* be stopped!'

Paulo started to cry again, but then it dried up. He held on tightly to his mother's leg but not in anger. Just to focus. It didn't feel so bad, like he had thought it would. He was somehow distant from the whole thing, like he wasn't really there, or was somewhere else at the same moment.

Mama just needs to see that it's alright. It's alright, it's not a sin, she's not bad. No one has done anything wrong. It's just silly, that's all. She doesn't have to think this way. No one does.

His mother turned him around to inspect the damage and scowled in surprise. She had expected to see him suffering terribly. She wanted – no, she *needed* him to suffer badly. His suffering was her only protection. She turned him and beat him again in desperation. '*I must correct him. This isn't right, this isn't good.*'

But the conclusion for her was only too clear.

She turned him again. Still she saw no pain in his face and was utterly confused because she saw only quietness there instead. She tried to hit him yet again, but only words of shame came forth within her –

This isn't good, this is no good at all. I can't win, not like this.

The hitting came more slowly.

It's hopeless. It's totally hopeless. I can't escape the truth. I'm a truly despicable person; a hideous, evil person. And everyone knows this is true.

Her strokes became weaker and more feeble until they finally stopped. Her arm hung limply by her side, then after a moment the kitchen spoon slipped from her fingers and clattered on the wooden floor.

Paulo lay there, listening. Then after some moments of silence he realized his mother was weeping.

She hung her head low, and spoke to herself in desperate resignation –

I can't change my loathsome reality, not by trying to be perfect in everything I do, not by defending myself constantly. And not by beating my boy. He's not really the problem. No. I – I'm the problem. It's too atrocious to bear. I can't win against my own evil.

Inside Paulo's mind, words of a different nature were being spoken.

'*It's all just a mistake, mama, that's all.* We didn't do anything wrong; you didn't do anything wrong, you were just afraid, that's all. And I didn't do anything wrong either. You were just mistaken about what you thought you were. You thought you were an evil person, but you're not. You're not even a person, not really. I've seen – you're one of the King's People. We've both been mistaken, but we're both really alright. You don't have to worry or be frightened now. There's nothing wrong with anything at all.'

His mother grabbed him and turned him around once more, her scarlet eyes full of a dry, aching chagrin.

Paulo looked back at her, and in his calm, still brown eyes there was no sign of hurt, of fear or reproach, anywhere.

She stared back at him in disbelief.

There was something there in him she couldn't quite fathom, and she gazed more deeply into his calm, quiet face. Something opened gently in front of her eyes, and slowly she felt herself being drawn away, feeling lighter and lighter, as if departing, leaving for another place, as her pain and confusion grew dimmer and dimmer

There was one intense moment of quiet, and suddenly she caught her breath.

In Paulo's eyes blazed something exceptionally different and otherworldly, and it made her own terrible pain and guilt subside to an unheard whisper. She looked again, carried away, far, far away... altogether elsewhere. A fragile remembrance was dawning softly upon her mind, something bright and warm, from a time ever so long ago...

And then she felt it – a magnificent Presence visited her. It came as a melody, a song, ever so slight but quite real, and strong; something at once kind and gentle. Warm, yes, a warm, comforting feeling that she had lost all possible hope of finding again. But it was *there*, it was with her in this moment. And it was *alive* ... not gone or destroyed at all as she had hopelessly believed.

Finally, after some moments, she saw him standing there before her, her boy, her beloved child, her son: blameless, whole, washed clean of all hate and crime. And in his kind, clear eyes she saw herself reflected for the first time, free of all blame and terror. She was just for this instant exactly like him, a calm presence of peace, and together they were exactly the same.

She lowered her head slowly. Tears welled in her eyes, quiet tears, soft tears of gratitude for the end of pain. Then moments later, deep and wholesome, shedding tears of release.

She brought her son to her chest, wrapped him tightly in her arms, weeping, as she let go of the hate and fear of unspoken, unremembered lifetimes. She had listened and she had heard: she was *not* what she had always thought, not at all. Love was really there for her, it had not left. She had not committed the most evil of crimes, love was truly there for her, buried and glowing deep within her own spirit. And there it would always live.

She held her son closely till eventually the crying abated.

"Paulo, I am so dreadfully sorry. So terribly sorry. But…" She placed her hands gently on his shoulders, stumbling to find the right words. "Please, Paulo, please try to understand. There are some things that are not good to do in the Domain. I am very afraid. I am very afraid… *for you*. Please, do not go back to the Door. Okay?"

He answered warmly, "Yes, mama. Please don't worry for me. I promise I'll never go back there again."

And she read in his face that he was sincere and meant her no harm.

CHAPTER THIRTY-EIGHT

Not Her Fault

That evening as they lay in their sleeping alcove and the warm glow from the fire-place surrounded them and cast flickering images upon the walls, Fredo asked, "How'd you do that?"

Paulo looked at his brother from his cot and propped himself on one elbow. "Do what?"

"It's a miracle, no?" said Fredo. "Normally you're so angry when she hits you. Then afterwards she's angry with me. Now she was so calm, almost peaceful. It was so different, strange; normally there's so much hate." He had been hiding but had seen everything, and couldn't understand what had changed.

Paulo answered, "I don't know, it just happened. It just didn't make sense to get angry, that's all."

Fredo waited for more, uncomprehending.

"It wasn't really her fault, was it?" Paulo tried to explain. "I mean, she was just listening to the same silly old hateful voice that we're all listening to all the time, that's all. That doesn't make her bad. People do wicked things all the time, but that's only because they're feeling evil and wicked toward themselves inside and don't even know why they really feel that way."

"I don't understand." Fredo couldn't make head or tail of Paulo's thoughts.

"Well, it doesn't really make sense to get angry at mama or be miserable, I figure. Otherwise it's like I'll be saying she really is a horrible person. Okay, she might hit me, but it doesn't really mean anything. Not really. I figure there's a choice, that's all. We don't have to blame if we don't want to: what good's that going to do?

That's the way I always used to feel, but it certainly never got me anywhere. We just have to remember there's something nice and kind around us all the time, if we want, that's all."

He stopped talking but Fredo still looked perplexed and intent on trying to understand what had happened. Paulo sought for the right words to help his brother.

"We're all the same, Fredo, don't you think? We all do horrible, stupid things sometimes, don't we? Me, too. We can't stop while we're still confused about what's going on, and when we don't feel good inside. That's why we should try to understand and why it makes no sense to hate. We're all the same; we're all listening to the same ridiculous, nasty old voice inside, and we're all trying to get rid of the wicked, evil creature we feel there. But underneath the hate we're all something else, too. All of us. Something nice in fact."

"Paulo, can I tell you something?" Fredo asked timidly, appearing on the verge of some great discovery.

"I think I understand a bit of what you're saying. Really, I do. You see, a similar thing happened to me today with the blacksmith. He was angry with me and this time for no reason at all. I think he must be a very unhappy person – he makes mistakes and then says it's my fault. He even hit me today because of something stupid *he* did, and then I ran and hid. But only for a minute. Then I came out and started to work again as if nothing had happened.

"I looked at him, he looked at me and I didn't blame him; he didn't hit me again and just left me alone. I think he was surprised, especially because he saw I wasn't afraid and didn't blame him. I couldn't see why I should be so upset, just because he feels so bad. He must be very confused if he thinks I'm the cause of his bad feelings. It's not really me that's the problem, is it?"

"No Fredo, it's not you that's the problem. And it's not *him* either. But he *thinks* it is. It's the Spell, like I was telling you. The Spell that tells us we're these disgusting people, that tells us to hate ourselves and makes us so confused as to what we really are. And it's in all of us just the same."

"But it's a pity he thinks this way, isn't it?" Fredo added. "I don't think his family must be very happy with someone like that. It must be very difficult for them sometimes."

Paulo said, "Yes, I think it's a pity we do such nasty things to ourselves. We really don't need to, don't you agree? I've decided that I'm going to stop. What about you?"

"Yeah! Me, too!"

As he lay there in bed, Paulo thought that life would probably be quite different now, if he could just continue to avoid punishing himself so much through the Spell. He didn't need to have any more thoughts of blame or injustice – that just wasn't really necessary any longer. In this way life would certainly be much more peaceful, he reflected, no matter what was happening.

"You can indeed be well all the time, Paulo," the magician's voice appeared quietly within his mind. "You can be very happy and well. In fact, it's quite important that you learn this, in order to understand the true nature of the King's Will for you and for all his people. His will for you is *happiness*, and not punishment or deprivation."

Paulo felt the warmth of these quiet words resound within him, and felt very tranquil.

The gentle voice continued in his thoughts, "There are still some situations where you are in pain, where you are not happy with your life, and the gift of these situations will be the learning they can still give you. Then there are perhaps other situations which you find difficult, situations that you must learn to walk away from, and you shall do so in gentleness, without regret, without condemnation and without anger. But remember, wherever you go, the King's Love goes with you no matter what decision you make.

Lastly he heard, just before falling into a deep slumber: "Don't be frightened now of being happy, Paulo, of being genuinely peaceful and well, even when others don't understand. Something inside them will understand even if it isn't obvious, because they will feel your respect and love for them. They will feel that you are not afraid of them, of their anger and judgment, because you will have seen that kindness walks with you, and with them, too. The air of the Kingdom of Happiness surrounds all your brothers, along with you. Knowing this, you will find yourself carrying the radiant light of your home with you wherever you go…"

And Paulo felt extremely peaceful, knowing he was breathing the remarkable, still air of the Kingdom even as he lay there on his bed of straw, and he eventually fell fast asleep.

Part 3

CHAPTER THIRTY-NINE

A Friend, and Brother

The weeks passed by, and a fresh new perception began to dawn, glowing and warm, on Paulo's mind. Though he hadn't understood all the wizard's many strange ideas, the essential message of Love and Kindness had come to take a place in his heart, and he was simply grateful. Over time he noticed the change in himself as he became calmer and distinctly happier; his days slipped by more easily, no longer filled with the same struggle and irritation, and his smile at the market place finally returned and came more easily, for everyone.

Nevertheless, he knew there was still a lot to learn. There were still a number of important obstacles that prevented him from seeing the Light the Domain contained, the wonderful Light from his Home the wizard promised him was always there. In fact, his new inner vision had helped him discover a constant sort of tension within his heart that prevented him from being fully peaceful with his world at every instant; and he was now sure there was something lurking there still in a hidden part of his spirit that didn't want to be found yet. Despite this, the darkness which he had been able to find and had so far managed to heal was already bringing him a great deal of joy and a particular kind of lightness to his days that hadn't ever been there before.

And strange, unexpected things were happening as a result. Filled with this new spirit, his customers now seemed to make a point of stopping by his stall on their daily rounds, quite often simply just to chat. Laden down with worries, their problems seemed to lighten immediately when Paulo smiled at them, and they laughed easily and joyfully at his playful, friendly way with them. Business was good, too, and there were other special compensations: Francesca now came over nearly every day from her stall to say hello. She also managed to find time in the hectic busyness of the market day to come and talk with him, which was certainly a good sign. And of course he especially liked being close to her.

Even Mr Bravuro now found more time for buying his wood, and that was certainly curious. He stopped by Paulo's stand more frequently to say hello and just talk a few minutes, though it was quite obvious he was still anxious about being efficient and punctual.

Mrs Belladonna, as an exception to the rule, did not stay especially longer than usual at the young wood seller's stall, but then that was partly Paulo's fault. In her daily rounds she still always managed to find something particularly problematic with the shopkeepers and stall holders, and so Paulo would then ask kindly but not without some provocation (and maybe just a little insolence):

"Madam, what would it be like to be happy with everyone – wouldn't that feel good to you?"

She would reply, "Well, Paulo, you know very well that you can't be happy with everyone. There are just some people who are absolutely impossible, you know."

"I think you might be quite right," he would answer. "There are indeed some people who are difficult, and sometimes impossibly so, as you say. But what do you think it would feel like *for you* to be happy, even if people weren't so nice? Would that be a good feeling?"

And then she would stare at him as if she hadn't understand at all what he was talking about, and quickly change the subject and move on to the next stall.

One day as he was closing his stall he noticed Francesca marching toward him across the market square, weaving a path amongst the last of the morning's shoppers. He watched her carefully as she approached. She held a resolute, determined manner about herself, and negotiated her way with a joyful confidence. Paulo liked that about her, and many other things besides. She stood there a moment before his stand, hesitating an instant, then she spoke.

"You're doing so well these days, Paulo. You must have more customers than ever." Her eyes flitted and danced amongst the strands of dark brown hair falling across her face which she smoothed behind an ear. Paulo noticed that she was wearing a red and white ribbon tied in a bow.

"Yes, I'm happy, I guess." Words didn't seem to come very easily at moments like these.

In fact, he wanted to say that it wasn't really the many customers that made him feel good, that it was something else. But after all he couldn't deny that the increase in business did make him feel rather fortunate. His mother had been pleased with him too, and had even suggested that he start looking for a feather mattress to replace the old straw one. That was certainly a nice change, as well as the rest.

Of course he still wanted to make more money and perhaps not stay a wood seller all his life, but there was still time for these things to fix themselves. In fact, he had begun to feel that life in the Domain maybe wasn't going to be quite so dreary after all. There was perhaps still some hope for finding happiness here, he figured. And maybe, just *maybe*, Francesca would be part of that dream. *Why not*, he told himself.

"How is it that you're always so smiling and happy now, Paulo?" she asked, curious. She lowered her voice, "Everyone is noticing."

"I don't know, it just comes more easily. But I know it helps a lot when I see you every day."

Francesca caught her breath and for just an instant tried to hide a smile. Then she grinned and turned quickly away.

If only I could spend more time with her, he thought.

The church bell struck midday and Paulo hoisted his empty oil-cloth under his arm and hurried down the lane that led toward the river. He jumped the steps two at a time and followed the dusty path along the riverbank. There, waiting patiently on an old wooden bench as had been his custom now for the past several weeks, was Mr Salvatori, or *Marco*.

"Well, my young magician friend, how are we today?" Marco called out the greeting. "And how's the weather, after all?"

Paulo raised his head skywards, laughed ringingly, and cried out Marco's favorite response:

"It's not too wet at all, dear sir, and I'm feeling *quite* well today, thank you."

The two of them had, in fact, bonded in a close friendship, ever since the older man had realized that there in the middle of the noisy, smelly market square, chatting merrily with the young wood seller, he had finally begun to find the answers to the most arduous, confounding questions of his soul. Now, he and Paulo met nearly every day after market to talk and pass the time. Paulo had learned quickly to appreciate the sincerity and courage of his older friend and was always glad to see him.

Marco had lived a good and long life and had done many important things, but still had not found the one quality in life he had been searching for: a sense of true happiness and simple peace had always somehow escaped him, and now at the end of his life he wanted more than ever to find it.

For years he had felt trapped in the prison of his same thoughts, feelings and reactions, and could find no relief. He had found it even amusing the extent to which he could be upset with the weather and preoccupied by the state of his health, but didn't know what to do. At least, not until he had looked into Paulo's face one day and had noticed something very different there. He had seen that the young wood seller was somehow not automatically bothered by things in the same way that everyone else was, and appeared to be quiet and content no matter what turmoil seemed to be brewing around them; as if the boy knew something else was true, something other than the mundane, depressing conditions of his life.

The old man thought Paulo was quite special and called him 'sagi', or *wise one*, and he had already found a great deal of comfort just talking with him, slowly learning to understand the obstacles he contained within himself to the peace he had so long sought. For Paulo had taken a risk, and one day had related to the old man the secret Tale of All Things, as Zeph had taught it to him, and had also explained about the accursed Spell of Guilt and Damnation.

The boy had then described in some detail the One People's separation from the Kingdom, and the origin of the Domain in their misguided decision for flight and escape. None of this had particularly surprised Marco as such: he had already begun to have many doubts and questions about the nature of the Domain; he had already become quite convinced that something else other than the fortress town he saw around him had to exist.

On the other hand, he had found it remarkable to learn about the reality of this other place, this *Home*, and was even more surprised to learn that an alternative existed to his daily experience of the Domain, a way of living in Towne without feeling like he was in a prison. He had avidly learned about the principles of *veiling* and *ridding*, and had tried his best to apply True Forgiveness to the relationships in his life, to use his relationships as a mirror and not as a battleground.

The idea that his personal sense of specialness and uniqueness was a gift to no one had been quite difficult for him to accept at first; but then he had come to feel deeply peaceful with the idea of a Love that was so vast and so complete that it ignored individual differences, actions and accomplishments, and excluded nothing. As he had said to Paulo one day, "I think I could eventually learn to give up wanting to be special if it has indeed been costing me an experience of true love and happiness!"

Paulo had been busy chatting with Marco as usual and then suddenly jumped to his feet. He stared closer at the old man's face, inspecting it, and Marco couldn't conceal a little smile; it looked like there was perhaps a small tear in the corner of his eye. Paulo was surprised by what he saw, then absolutely delighted.

"Oh, I'm so happy for you, Marco! You went, didn't you? *You really did it.* I knew you would! That's such great news."

Marco didn't need to respond, knowing that Paulo could well see the difference, the new peace that now filled his mind and had written itself into the features of his face.

The old man had listened carefully to Paulo the day when the boy had explained to him in detail about the Door and how to walk through it. And just that morning he had decided that it was worth risking everything in the world to try to visit, even for just a minute, the extraordinary fields of the Kingdom and breathe once more the fresh air of freedom from that golden realm. From *his Home.*

He had waited in the door recess before the forbidden square until he had felt completely peaceful and safe. Then, calmly and confidently, he had walked past the sleeping guards and straight onto the Golden Path. There was no describing the joy and serenity he had felt, and he had stayed there a long while relaxing on the grassy hillside, and then walking calmly through the quiet, sedate woods.

"I met a friend of yours there, Paulo," he said. "He is just like you said – exceptionally kind. He told me that I still had some things to learn here in the Domain because I was still too afraid to return all the way Home. He told me to find a certain Key, and some special 'Knowing'. He said that as soon as I saw the true reason to have no fear that I could follow with him to the Golden City."

The older man asked, "But, Paulo, did he tell you what it is precisely that we're afraid of? I don't quite understand that part. It doesn't seem there could be anything to be afraid of."

"I don't really understand either. Perhaps he thinks we'll be able to work it out together."

After their late-morning meeting, Paulo wandered back to the cottage, thinking all the while about the serious task they had set before themselves, and more generally about the many changes in his life since his first meeting with the magician. On the whole, things were going pretty well, he considered. Yes, there were certainly still many ups and downs; but there seemed nevertheless to be more happy moments than before, and it seemed easier to be patient with the difficult moments, too.

At home, things were still much the same. Paulo found his mother still made the same demands upon him and was just as anxious for him to sell well and bring good money home. She was still upset when things weren't done as she wished and wanted always to know that things were organized and where they should be. But there was nevertheless something slightly altered in the way she spoke; just a little less harshness maybe. She still demanded obedience, although she now seemed somewhat less convinced when she was angry that it was quite appropriate or the right reaction to the problem before her.

Paulo understood that it would take his mother perhaps a long, long time still to learn to trust what she had seen with him that special day. In one magical moment, she had felt a peace capable of erasing all her fear and pain, and had seen something new and fresh, something she could hope for beyond all the concerns and worries of her life. But it would take a long time still, and many similar brief instants of peace before she would make the final decision to become kinder to herself, and to stop blaming.

With his mother Paulo made a point of avoiding all subject of the Door. He had come to understand that it was important to respect people's fears, and now understood why Zeph didn't want him to take too many risks. That would only be unkind toward himself, and others. Besides, more and more he was understanding that the magician was as close as his own heart and not so far away at all. He didn't need to upset people in order to follow his path, to find a place to talk with the voice of wisdom and find the comfort he was looking for.

On the other hand, Paulo was still quite concerned for his brother. Fredo still found life hard since the blacksmith was a difficult, unforgiving master. He usually came home tired and very sore, sometimes because the master had beaten him, but mostly because the blacksmith insisted that they work very hard. The master himself was not happy – that was plainly obvious – because he too was tired and constantly worried about producing more. Fredo wanted to tell him that he would feel much better if he didn't demand so much of himself, but he didn't dare. He wanted to tell him that things would still be fine and he would be quite safe even if he managed to accomplish less than he sought in a day's work. But there was really very little he could do to try to change the unhappy man's disposition. He could only try to think things differently, within himself.

On occasion, when he was feeling brave, Fredo did think about leaving the blacksmith's workshop, but mostly he was too terrified of complaining about his work since his mother felt that any job the boy could get he should keep, even if that meant suffering a great deal. It seemed his mother believed that suffering was inevitable and had to be accepted; but Fredo just didn't understand why he had to remain in such a punishing situation. He had tried to see all this differently and had begun to realize that it wasn't his fault if the blacksmith was upset, or his mother, for that matter. He didn't have to feel affected when the giant man was angry, not afraid nor frustrated, and he didn't have to take his insults or his punishments personally.

Even when Fredo made a mistake, which of course did happen, the blacksmith didn't have to get angry. He could still be calm and help Fredo to do better. It was a choice the blacksmith was making to be upset because he was still listening to the Spell, believing himself to be damned and his life a hopeless effort to do more in order to feel better. But the blacksmith found it exceptionally difficult not to listen to the Spell, even though several times he had looked at Fredo and seen something kind and understanding there, something free of judgment, and patient.

Fredo just trusted at these times that the blacksmith might one day change, but it didn't look very hopeful.

CHAPTER FORTY

An Intimate Proposal

A week later at market Francesca raised her hand and waved to Paulo from her stall, motioning as if to say something. She crossed the length of the market square and came up to the wood stand. She stood before him, hands on her hips, cogitating.

"Paulo, what are you doing after market? I think we must talk." Her manner was efficient, her face wore a very serious, business-like expression. "It's quite important!"

Paulo couldn't imagine what the matter might conceivably be.

When market was over (Paulo could hardly wait) they took the lane that led down to the river and walked along its bank. Paulo was positively glowing inside just to think she should feel something was important to discuss with him.

"Paulo, you're a very good worker, I think, and people like you a lot." She looked him in the eye, and they both stopped walking. "And… and I think it would be very nice to work with you." She hesitated and it seemed she was thinking of how to say next what was on her mind.

Paulo raised his eyebrows, not quite understanding but delighted at these unexpected compliments. He didn't reply and simply bathed in the remarkable moment.

She turned and they began strolling again, slowly. "You see things are going very well for us on the farm," she continued after a minute, "and my brother must now stay and work more at home with father and the animals, so he can no longer come to market with me. But there is so much to do at the market and the crates are often too heavy for me to carry alone. Then there's the donkey which sometimes needs a strong boy to push when he's being stubborn…"

She paused, and Paulo was breathless.

"Paulo…" she said, looking at him expectantly.

He was unbelievably excited.

"…Paulo, would you like to come work at the farm with us and help me with the market?"

He couldn't say anything. It was simply the happiest day of his life. All he had ever wanted, valuable and rewarding work, and now the most wonderful, beautiful, and exceptional girl in the world was asking him to be close by her, side by side, every day. He knew in his heart that she chose him because she was very fond of him and not just because he was a good worker. And all because he had simply started to be happier and to consider that he was perhaps not the terrible, hopeless thing he had always believed!

He opened his mouth and was just about to answer when inside he felt Zeph's voice speak.

"Paulo, *wait!*"

Paulo frowned in frustration and began to get irritated. *What's he doing here?* he muttered to himself.

"Think carefully," the magician advised. "You need to take time to reflect. Be patient, take time."

What on earth could there be to reflect upon?

It was exceptionally irritating to hear a voice tell you to stop when more than anything you wanted to run ahead at full speed. After all, Paulo wondered, what could an old wizard possibly know of true love between a boy and a girl? Paulo, against his wishes, nevertheless paid attention.

"Just ask for a little time to reflect," he heard again.

He sighed silently, and replied, "Francesca, I think this is the most wonderful thing that anyone has ever offered me. I'm extremely happy that you chose me to work with you. But I'll have to ask my mother. Can you wait until I speak with her?"

Francesca agreed. "I do hope it will work out for us. I mean, for my family. It would so help my father to have a strong hand about."

Paulo lingered along the riverbank when Francesca had left, walking slowly toward the bridge and the path that would take him home.

He asked inside, frustrated, "Zeph, I don't understand what the problem could possibly be. This would be very good for me."

"Perhaps you're absolutely right, Paulo. I'm just suggesting that you take a moment to think about it. Try to find out why you think that this would be good for you, for example. Maybe this is the right thing to do now, and maybe not; just take time to think about it a little. Take advantage of the situation, to learn a little more about yourself.

"Ask yourself some questions: What am I looking for here, and where will I find it? What is my goal? And then try to let the answers come by themselves. I'm only here to help you find true happiness, Paulo; and it's only by asking some difficult questions and doing some searching that you'll learn to understand the true nature of happiness.

"If you feel that accepting this opportunity at this time will help take you toward what you seek," he continued, "then it is right and you must accept. If, having asked honestly, you don't have this feeling of 'rightness', then trust that all will be well and follow your path.

"I would just suggest that you try to become aware of all the many things that you still believe you need to be really happy, all the things you imagine this new situation might give you; things that might make it more complicated to see the right path. If you reflect a little, I believe you'll not find it quite so easy to make this decision as you think."

"But what you say can't be right. I *know* what's good for me – and this is certainly it!"

"I know it seems frustrating, Paulo, but try to understand that you don't yet really know where your path lies. I know you *think* you do; and over time you can learn to become aware of the best path for yourself. But just take a moment now and try to ask without insisting, to ask without *needing*; ask inside, and be willing to feel the right response. Try to leave your images to the side, to feel what is most *appropriate* in this particular situation, and be honest with yourself."

This was most exasperating advice for Paulo, and he brooded sourly as he walked along the road home. He sulked because he knew he had said that learning to be truly happy and present in the state of Love was his one and true goal, and he was wise enough already to know that this state didn't require any particular circumstance or change.

But now he had seen something special in the Domain, something extraordinary and truly exceptional: *The chance to work on a farm and be with the most beautiful girl in the world!* This was truly astonishing luck, it all seemed so very obvious and clear: he just knew the right response was to say yes. These were things a magician just couldn't know anything about.

He contemplated his bright new future as he walked.

Yes, working on the farm will be such a nice change. And what a change it shall be! It will certainly be different from the dead quiet of the Forest and being alone all the time. It'll be such a welcome relief to work with other people and have a change of activity.

Yes, working with animals will be quite a change; and quite nice, I suppose. I know I might miss the peacefulness of the Forest from time to time. But then I can always go back to visit … if I can find the time, of course, because I will certainly be very busy.

Raising animals. That's really quite different from collecting wood; I mean, they make a lot of noise, don't they? But I know it's better than collecting wood alone and in total silence all the time… Yet, what if it isn't really that much better? Well, in any case I couldn't possibly disappoint Francesca, that's for sure, and it's clear she'll be desperately unhappy if I don't accept. No, it wouldn't be possible to turn down such an excellent offer.

On the other hand – if I'm not happy there at the farm, then she'll feel it and maybe think it's her. She cares about me and wants me to be happy – at least, I think so. I know I don't really know her so well, but I'm sure she would be kind to me. Then again, what if she's not really as nice as I think? *But of course she is!* And *of course* I'll be happy there at the farm.

That's… obvious.

I think.

Oh, this is ridiculous – it's all so confusing! So many ideas of happiness, which could possibly be the right one? What's really best for me? What did Zeph say – trying to be happy in this way wouldn't be as easy as I thought? Well, it certainly looks like he might be right about that!

Paulo meandered further, lost in thought, failing to notice the light rain-shower starting to fall and even the swallows darting back and forth, feeding along his path home.

Yes, there's no question about it! Working on the farm would be an excellent change for me. I'll also make more money for the family. And Francesca! It's so obvious she's sincerely fond of me and thinks she'll be very happy with me. And she does need help, she told me so. That's important; it's important not to let people down, and to be kind to myself. And maybe they're counting on me at the farm. After all, it's not easy to find good workers these days, and that's why they thought of me. Good workers like me are hard to find. Yes, there are many very good reasons for accepting.

Paulo returned home to the cottage that day quite certain that accepting the offer was by far the best thing for everyone involved. Still he couldn't stop himself from wondering once more: *Why exactly was Zeph suggesting that I think it over so much? After all, it seems so obvious…*

He entered the cottage and closed the door, still with some confusion in his mind, and made his way slowly toward the bed alcove to put away his things.

And then he saw his brother.

Poor Fredo was sitting on the edge of his cot and it was clear he had been crying. He was hurt, desperately sore, and there were clear red weals on his face and body. Paulo came up to him and put his arm gently around his shoulder.

"Paulo, I don't think I should stay working for the blacksmith anymore," Fredo said, trying hard to console himself. "I must decide that it's not kind to myself to stay there. Even if mother gets very angry, I must find some other work." His thoughts turned inside a moment, and hesitated at the fear he found there. "I've decided… I've decided I shan't return to the blacksmith tomorrow, and I'll go instead to the market place to begin to look for other work. Please don't tell mother, or she'll be very upset."

Paulo just looked at him, and agreed to say nothing.

"Yes, it's a good thing to leave the blacksmith now," Paulo said. "Nothing will change the man right now, and it's really no longer good for you. You've done everything you can and you've learned everything that you can there. Yes, be kind to yourself my brother, that's what we're trying to learn."

Fredo looked up from the ground and his eyes met Paulo's.

"You must learn to face your fear now," Paulo continued, finding the encouragement he needed to get past his own fears for his brother, "and not let it stop you from doing what you know is right. There's no reason to feel guilty or bad because you couldn't make this situation work as you wanted. It doesn't matter. You've done the best you can; there's no doubt about this. You're a good person, no matter what anyone else might think or say."

"Do you really think so?" Fredo asked. And in Paulo's eyes he was gladdened to see that this was true.

CHAPTER FORTY-ONE

Impossible Dilemmas

All the next morning Paulo was disturbed by his thoughts. It was much more difficult than he thought giving up the work at the farm: he was already much more attached to the idea than he imagined. But now that his brother was desperate to find another job, it only felt normal to suggest that he take it in his place.

He reflected on what he had learned from the wizard about choices. Zeph had told him not to do what was *good*, but what was *appropriate* in this situation – *what felt right* – keeping in mind that the goal for himself and for everyone was to remember the all-encompassing nature of their King's Love; and thus it wasn't really a question of helping anyone as such, as the magician had said many times. "Help is available to everyone in equal measure, all the time," he had said. "Love and peace are available, and will remove all sense of pain and threat, no matter what is going on, for anyone who seeks to be helped and healed."

Paulo asked again inside to feel what was 'most appropriate' to do in this situation, since it was indeed clear to him now that he didn't really understand his own best interests on the journey Home. He started by trying to identify the things he was still hoping this new situation would give him, needs that now were obviously intruding on his clear, true-minded thinking:

"In what ways am I expecting this new development to give me happiness?"

He tried, as the magician wished, to understand that all his desires were perhaps still focused solely on images, on vague and varying concepts of joy and contentment, not on truth at all, and this was in fact the reason he couldn't see clearly.

He strolled further along the path thinking about Zeph's words, but peace just didn't come for all his trying. He swiped his boot at a stone and sent it skidding into the brush.

"This is hopeless!" he finally cried. "It just isn't so easy to forget the things I still really want."

He still felt a tug like a powerful force pulling him toward the things he needed – the work, the recognition, the money and the companionship he had always sought. The situation seemed more and more like a dilemma – a true disaster – that meant he would lose no matter what.

"Just try to relax a little, Paulo."

Zeph's voice was, as always, reassuring and made its way gently into his thoughts.

"Try to remember above all that your feeling of contentment doesn't depend on the outcome of this situation. Happiness is in you – because it is *part* of you. You can be happy no matter what happens, believe me. You must trust this above all. This is the only way you shall be able to find a peaceful answer – and return back to the path Home."

But Paulo's mind was now literally bursting with thoughts of sacrifice, deprivation and guilt.

I don't understand at all how to do this, he spoke to himself angrily. If I take on the work, then I feel it's not kind to Fredo and that I haven't been a good brother. But if I don't accept the job, I feel I'm denying myself something I've wanted for a long time, something that's especially meant for me. And I also feel that I'm letting down Francesca and her parents. Either way someone is going to be miserable, it's so obvious. *What an utter disaster!*

In addition, if I work at the farm I'll miss the quiet of the forest, but if I stay selling wood I'll be frustrated the rest of my life. It's completely unfair – *there's no possible hope of winning at all!*

He made his way to market slower than usual, taking the winding trail along the river-course toward the bridge instead of the direct high road, and made a more determined effort to reach the place of clarity and detached, uninvested observation – the True Mind – the magician had so often spoken about.

There must be another way to make this decision, he determined.

In fact there were two very different ways of looking at the situation, he saw. When he spoke to himself about the fabulous Happiness and Fullness of his Home waiting for him at every moment (though he might not see Them yet), he felt somehow stronger and more capable. When he remembered it was absolutely fine whichever way he chose – because the great experience he was looking for above everything else was always somehow present – he felt, and in some way *knew*, that things would just work out.

But when he thought that happiness, progress and personal value came from the situation around him, from the different people and activities, he felt weak, as if it was absolutely *critical* he made the right choice; as if his personal survival depended upon the matter.

He arrived at the massive curved stone arches of the bridge and crossed over to find a bench on the far side. He sat there quietly a moment before continuing on his way to the market square. His mind was gradually clearing, now that he had decided that remembering peacefulness was, after all, his ultimate goal.

"Now – what's going to work best for everyone in this situation," he spoke firmly to himself, "knowing that no one's happiness or safety is at stake – not mine, and not anyone else's?"

In the light of this new frame of mind, he saw that he could turn down the work, and that would be quite fine. It would be fine because either he would be able to achieve his true goals in his current position as wood seller, or in some other position that might come along later. Where he was and what he did was really not going to affect his path significantly. If his goal was to return back toward the Golden City, toward the reality of Love, then nothing – no earthly situation or condition – could possibly prevent him.

Perhaps the market square was after all the perfect place for finding what he still needed to learn. Perhaps he would be better able to learn how to be happier, freer, and how to undo the Spell if he remained as wood seller a while longer; and perhaps Francesca was not the only possible partner for him, if turning down the work meant that she no longer chose him. Riches and a partner could always yet follow: anything was still possible.

By the same token, this also meant that Paulo could accept the offer of farm work, and his brother would just have to seek another position: that would also be fine. Fredo's happiness, along with his own, didn't depend on the farm work. There would be other opportunities for Fredo if it was more appropriate at this time that Paulo accept the offer for himself. Fredo would then have to learn how to find a calm place within himself and manage his mother's fury at his loss of work.

"In light of my search for Love," Paulo spoke to himself, "what is now the appropriate thing to do?"

He thought lightly about the specific problem again, and tried to think of accepting the job for himself; but then something inside told him that this wasn't the right thing to do, not just now. He didn't know why, it just didn't seem like the thing to do. He contemplated more, and felt that it would be uncomfortable and rather silly to fight this feeling, even though he knew there was still a part of him that didn't fully like the outcome. In this way he became sure the right thing was to offer the farm work to Fredo.

Making the decision in this way Paulo felt strong. He no longer felt he was sacrificing his own happiness, he was no longer using the situation for his own personal purposes. He was not choosing based on his interests or needs, nor from a desire to make a sacrifice for his brother, or to please others. It was no longer a question based on anyone's happiness or well-being or personal value. The decision was made *for* him, he felt, as if he hadn't made it alone. The answer was there, as the obvious thing to do: it just clearly seemed that this was most appropriate. And he knew that only good would come from it, no matter what happened afterward.

Once the decision was made, Paulo felt very relieved. He strode down the path stronger, confident, and with peace in his heart.

Still, in the back of his mind he couldn't avoid reassuring himself: "This means I'll still be able to see Francesca because I'll obviously have to help them at the farm from time to time. She likes me – that's for sure – and that's why I always see her dancing blue eyes in my dreams. So it's obvious she'll still like me even if Fredo works with her. She'll understand. And besides, that's what good brothers do."

CHAPTER FORTY-TWO

Fredo's Relief

Fredo wandered past the church and hesitated a moment before the alley that would lead him into the middle of the noisy market place. He leaned a shoulder against the cold stone wall of a building. People poured into the narrow street from the busy square and he watched them enviously. His eyes moved quickly from one face to another. So many different lives, he thought. So many people who looked like they were happy. People who were obviously happy, he thought, because they had lives and work that were so well-ordered and predictable, and so respectable.

He took a deep breath and plunged into the crowd, struggling through the market square toward the wood stand at the far end. He waited till the last customer had made his purchase and left, then smiled meekly at his brother.

"Well, here I am. I suppose– "

"Your job hunt is over!" Paulo said, flourishing the words in the air before his brother. "I think I've found good work that'll be just right for you."

Fredo's eyes opened wide with astonishment. "What – *already?* But … how?" Delight and relief lit his face and gave Paulo the reassurance he needed to continue with his difficult decision.

"I'll explain everything later, but first let's see if my idea shall, in fact, work. I have to take you to see someone."

Paulo took his brother over to Francesca's stand and carefully explained the situation, asking if it would be possible for his brother to take the job at this time, who was also a very hard and competent worker.

Francesca's eyes narrowed in a dark frown of confusion.

"Does that mean you don't want to work with me?" she asked frankly, looking rather cross: this wasn't at all what she had had in mind when she had made the offer to Paulo.

"Oh, Francesca," Paulo felt a heavy weight begin to settle in his heart. "I'd like that more than you can imagine. It's just that I sincerely believe that Fredo would be the better person for the job right now, if you would find that acceptable, of course."

At these words the girl hesitated. She felt her face flushing with a hot irritation, but a feeling she didn't want. *This isn't right. This isn't the way I want to feel*, she spoke to herself. Still the young girl couldn't hide her look of disappointment and upset.

"It's rather difficult for me to explain right now," Paulo continued, reminding himself inside that all would be well. "I'd really like to work with you a lot, it's just that my brother is in greater need of work at this time, and he's also stronger than me, as you'll find out. But I promise that I'll come and help you as much as possible when I can – I do promise. Right now I just really think that Fredo is the best person for this job at this time and not me. *Please* try to understand, please try to trust me."

She looked from one boy to the other, and her thoughts flew suddenly inwards. "Please trust me..." she repeated Paulo's words to herself.

Her father's image came instantly to mind, the exact same words he had spoken to her on her very first day selling at market behind the stand. At the time she was very frightened, and distrustful... She would turn people away, he had warned her, if she didn't learn to manage her temper and quick impatience. "There's nothing to fear," he had said. "Please, just trust me, and all will be well."

She had then worked hard at the stand to please her father, growing in a steady, happy confidence which the customers appreciated; and he had discovered a real reason to be very proud of her. Now, faced with this unexpected turn of events, she wanted to understand and learn again, rather than judge as she might have done before. *I think I must still have something more to learn about patience*, she spoke softly to herself.

She realized as well that Paulo's thoughts were with his brother whose difficult situation was not unknown to her. Fredo's name as a disciplined and well-mannered worker would be familiar to her parents who would have to give their approval; they above all would want someone capable of fitting in immediately to the heavy work requirements of the position. Perhaps she had been thinking too much of herself, in fact, when she had suggested Paulo.

"This may work, Paulo, even though it's not what I had in mind. I will have to introduce your brother to my parents, though I think there should be no problem – if you still really believe this is right."

Paulo then reassured her that she wasn't making a mistake, and thanked her again. He and Fredo went back to the wood stall to handle the customers who had been waiting, and she stood there a moment silently wondering about what had happened.

She found it difficult to understand why Paulo wouldn't be able to join her since she knew that deep down he really wanted to. She admitted to herself she was upset, but not really because of him; it was just because she still found it hard to let life run its strange, erratic course. "*Stubbornness*, it's called, my princess..." her father had chided her playfully one day, "which you have clearly, though very unwisely, inherited from your beloved papa, I'm sure!"

But, as her father had also advised her kindheartedly, there was still time for faith and gentleness to come. And time as well perhaps, she reflected pensively, for the boy with the dark, soulful eyes to join her at her side. Yes, that would be nice.

Somewhere else, in another part of the market place, similar thoughts of frustration were crossing someone else's mind. Despite his brave performance, Paulo found it was also difficult for a part of him to understand what he had done. He had felt strong when he had pronounced his thoughts, yet still a part of his heart really didn't want to come to terms with it. *Just wait a bit… things may still work out*, he consoled himself.

That day, after helping at his brother's stall, Fredo went back to the chicken stand to begin learning about the livestock trade, and when all the shoppers were leaving the square at midday, Paulo came over to help them pack up the crates on the donkey cart. Paulo then went to meet Marco as usual for their late-morning discussions, and Fredo went to the farm to meet Francesca's parents.

Back at home Paulo's mother was delighted that Fredo had been able to replace his former job so easily, and with good, socially acceptable work as well. Fredo was overjoyed to leave the blacksmith's workshop and begin his study of farm animals. Paulo found it difficult to be completely content with the decision even though he still sensed it had been the right thing to do. He just didn't understand how it could be right if he still wanted so badly to be with Francesca and to change his work, the presence of eternal Love notwithstanding.

His brother now spent his working days at the farm and with Francesca at the market stand. Occasionally Paulo would help and in time he was able to meet Francesca's parents and came to like them very much; but he was busy every morning with his wood harvesting and the market, and there was a perpetually long list of chores to do at the house with his mother in the afternoon, so there was in fact little time to go to the farm after market to help out. Paulo also wanted to spend time with Marco studying their lessons and, unfortunately, it just wasn't possible to do everything he wanted.

Maybe things will still work out …

Chapter Forty-Three

Stinking Ducks

Several months passed by, and everyone was satisfied.

Everyone, that is, except for Paulo.

This wasn't the way it was supposed to be, he spat inside, giving his pile of wood a mighty kick as it refused to stay in place under its rain-cover. He lanced a spiteful look towards Benito and his 'putrid, reeking fish'. The fish-seller knew it was unwise to pay attention to the boy when he was in a mood, blew his nose loudly, and continued to ignore him.

– *I was supposed to be the one working on the farm and making extra money*, he fumed.

Then he looked over at Fredo and Francesca who were chatting merrily at their stand. Fredo laughed at something she whispered in his ear, and she placed her hand on his shoulder in a particularly friendly way. He stared at them disbelievingly.

– And *I* was the one that Francesca liked – not *Fredo!*

It's so incredibly unfair!

He knew it wasn't useful to be upset with his brother and didn't want to admit that his thoughts were black indeed because he didn't have what he wanted. But still it hurt to think that Fredo was the one that Francesca liked now and that she no longer came by to his stand so often to say hello.

– Why can't *I* have the girl with blue eyes? She liked *me* not him, and now I have no friend who cares about me. *I* was the special person in her life, not him. Am I no longer interesting anymore? Why do I punish myself this way? It's so completely unfair! Why am I always to be the nice brother – and *alone* and *poor*?

He stomped his feet on the ground, pretending to keep himself warm in the frosty morning air. It was difficult to remember the many extraordinary things he had learned since first visiting the Outside, when he felt that all he hoped for here in the Domain was being taken away.

What else is there to live for here now? he said silently. *Why on earth should I stay here any longer? What good is all this work if everything I want is being taken away from me, anyway?*

After market he walked along the river bank, whipping a switch of hazel wood back and forth, chasing stones and gravel from one side of the path to the other. He thought and contemplated, then thought some more … And then made up his mind.

He returned hurriedly to the empty market square and strode past the Town Hall into the dark, deserted neighborhood he now knew so well. He passed by the guards without so much as causing a whisper among them and marched through the Great Door, happy to have finally made up his mind about his one true goal.

– The Golden City, *yes!* That's all that counts.

The path descended quickly away from the Domain and the fortress wall, and passed over undulating fields towards a near range of higher ground. He felt the sparkling crisp air against his cheeks, and the fragrance of flowers and wild grasses filled his senses. The sun shone brightly and the Path glided by smoothly under his feet.

– Yes, the Golden City! How could I have ever wanted anything else?

He marched and marched and the time went by. The bright glow rested gently on the far-off mountain top and the path curved and wound through a series of low soft, green hills.

– *What could a girl and a job offer me that I won't be able to find in the Golden City?* How stupid I was for ever wanting such things.

There's only ever been one real happiness and I want it more than *anything* now. More even than, than … girls and stinking ducks! And that's that!

He strode further and the path curved, ran, dipped, and wound some more. The day was surprisingly hot and as he walked his feet began to chafe in his heavy work boots.

– *How could anyone not feel they haven't been cheated?* he thought to himself. I *have* been cheated, that's all there is to it! If only I'd been able to… to… I don't know what. Oh, there just *has* to be a way of finding happiness, this is so completely ridiculous!

The path rounded and mounted another hill and –

Paulo halted abruptly and stared hard before him, stunned. There in front of his astonished eyes appeared the giant Door of the Domain, set neatly and sedately into the cold stone of the Wall.

"No – It's not possible!"

His shoulders sank as low as they possibly could go, and he heaved a heavy sigh on the verge of tears. There was nothing to do, it was utterly hopeless, and he flopped down on the grassy bank on the side of the path.

He sat there for what seemed an eternity trying to understand what could have conceivably gone wrong, and not to feel desperately sorry for himself. There was no choice but to think that the Golden City was still extremely far away. And now so too was any type of happiness in the Domain.

"May I interrupt?" The magician's voice came from right next to Paulo, surprising him.

"Oh, hi, Zeph. This path of yours is really quite impossible," the boy said, trying hard to disguise his frustration – as well as his feelings of resentment toward his teacher. "I was sure that I'd made the right decision to leave the Domain. There's nothing there for me now, nothing at all."

The wizard looked at him kindly and waited for the boy to answer his own question. But Paulo was all out of ideas.

"What're you looking at?" he asked the magician irritably.

Eventually Zeph spoke. "You don't see the problem?" he asked.

Paulo's face was blank. *What's he talking about now?*

"Paulo, you were still under the Spell!"

The boy rolled his eyes. *No, surely not again!*

"You still think that you live separate from Love," the wizard explained, "and outside of the happiness you seek. That's all. You still think you have somewhere to go to find what you're looking for; but what you came here to find, what you're most looking for, is *still* right there in front of you. However, instead of seeking it, you must *remember it*. You just think that it has some form and place, when it doesn't. This happiness is simply part of what you are – once you manage to remember *what* you are."

Only more riddles – can't he do better than that?

Zeph smiled good-humouredly at Paulo's unspoken words.

"Let's get down to business now, shall we?" The wise man settled on the grassy bank next to the boy. "Tell me why, precisely, did you want to be with Francesca and to work on the farm?"

"Because I wanted to be happy, that's why," he replied gruffly, then added, "– of course!"

"But *where is Happiness*, Paulo?"

Paulo knew it was ridiculous to get frustrated with the wizard's impossible questions, and thought rather about what he seemed to be asking: *Where is happiness?*

Zeph spoke again, "What do you *really* think you want and need to be happy?"

Paulo tried to think some more, but was now looking at the ground and toying with a stalk of grass. He knew the basic answer to the magician's question – he just couldn't see how to make it work in his life. He felt his personal needs so badly, like a painful, yearning ache, and yet he knew he wouldn't be able to get Home until he dealt with that. For him the Golden City and all it symbolized was still too far away, and that was all that occupied his mind.

"Paulo, I promise: you *will* get to the Golden City. *Everyone* will eventually make it there. But how can you possibly leave the

Domain if you still believe you're giving up something important by leaving? Until you see there is nothing there – and I speak quite literally…" He wondered if the boy was still listening. "And until you see that returning Home is not just a wish of your soul, but *the* only possible wish of your heart?

"I know it is very difficult to understand at this point on your path, but just try to imagine that you give up nothing when you turn toward truth since, in essence, there *is* nothing there at all. Everything you like and want in the Domain is just as empty as a cold, bleak morning mist. All that you so ardently desire in that place of arid grayness is simply the qualities which the Maker has promised you these vague and shady pictures contain; but those promises are empty. This you will come to see and understand over time, if you are now willing to look clearly."

Paulo appeared not at all reassured by the wizard's words. Zeph looked at the downcast boy and reflected. His mind searched for another way to communicate with his young student and explain the true nature of his adopted, and very misunderstood, world.

"Here, let me tell you more of our story – remember? – the Tale of All Things."

The two of them settled themselves more comfortably upon the dewy grass amongst the fresh wild flowers, and the magician began to speak.

CHAPTER FORTY-FOUR

Siren's Song

"When the Maker made the world of the Domain," Zeph began, "he looked at his work and saw that it was not yet complete. He was desperate to ensure that the King's People remained in exile in his love-forsaken home, but knew there was still a danger they would wake from the Spell of exile and leave by the great Door that was eternally open.

"He had carved in everyone a deep, aching chasm: the emptiness made by the belief that Love had departed, the yawning hole that is the sentiment and conviction of evil, of something desperately wrong in the self. And he had hypnotized each person to believe that the only safe haven which now remained was his Prison Domain. He had filled our minds with a blinding terror, dominated by the belief that our 'sin' would be punished by a vengeful, violent – but, he failed to inform us, completely *imaginary* – Lord who dealt unforgivingly with his treacherous subjects. He had then ensured that we firmly believed the Door back to the Kingdom was barred and shut tight for our safety. Finally he had given us *veiling* and *ridding*, powerful mental weapons to defend these many myths and keep them from our conscious awareness.

"Yet the Maker understood he could *still* lose us. *But how?* Simply, he could not stop anyone from setting out for the Kingdom of Light whosoever deeply desired to do so, and believed it possible. He who felt the memory of the King within him and heard his Song, this person would find a way. Such a person would find a way past all the seemingly impossible obstacles the Maker had placed on his path, and eventually free himself from his belittled mind. Listening to the gentle Silver Voice in the place of the shrieking of the Maker would reduce the terror in his mind and the guilt imprisoning his spirit. Then, even if still afraid of the guards and haunted by the myth of the evil King, he would nevertheless be able to enter into the bright light of the Kingdom – as you have done – and would realize that the Domain was always, entirely a lie.

"And so to counter such a possibility, the Maker set about fabricating a special contrivance, an artifice, such that not one single soul would ever again seek to part with his cherished world of darkness He would fill his world with such sublime hope of happiness that never would it occur to a villager that another world might offer more.

"Now, what could the Maker have fabricated that would have such extraordinary power of entrapment over us?" The wizard looked at the boy, holding the question in his sparkling eyes.

Paulo was at a loss.

"It was a *diversion*, my boy," he whispered. "An exquisite distraction, a remarkable cover of smoke and mist. One that would so divert our attention away from our inner realms that we would never again become aware that such a magnificent Golden Kingdom might exist outside of his world.

"And of what, then, was this diversion composed? Of what remarkable substance and fabric was it woven such that it contained the power to render us unconscious, even to the point of mindlessness?

Paulo breathed shallowly, hanging on to each of the wizard's words.

"*Objects*, Paulo. And *situations*." The wizard pronounced the words slowly and carefully. "An entire universe of such exceedingly special objects and situations as would confuse and bewilder us, enchant us and astonish us. He spoke to us of such things that would have extraordinary – no! – *phenomenal* power to make us happy; things to make us content and satisfied beyond even our wildest dreams – and eventually beyond our own hardened guilt and misery. Such was his promise.

"And so the Maker set about weaving a powerful binding spell, and the words he spoke reached our ears, tempting us, calling us to delve deeper and deeper into his kingdom of illusion. He whispered deep into our inner minds and his promises began to glow and shine, and stood out like golden beacons luring us toward magical circumstances brimming with attraction and potency. Toward brilliant, gleaming objects, astounding situations of recognition, comfort and influence, and positions of overwhelming reward and freedom."

Paulo felt an ache grow within him, a desire to reach out and touch these remarkable imaginary things.

"Have you not ever thought of such things for yourself, Paulo?" the wizard asked temptingly. "What would they be for you, I do wonder…?

"Let us think a moment. We'll begin with something simple, I think, like shiny new boots – yes! with leather thongs as laces, not nasty string that breaks and cuts your hands; and burnished, sturdy brass buckles, that would start us off nicely. What do you think?" Before waiting for an answer, Zeph rolled on. "And how about an embroidered waistcoat, of the finest lambs-wool lined with red and silver trim, fastened with buttons of gleaming black ram's horn? Not bad at all, if I do say so myself. Something, my boy, you can be truly proud to wear and to be seen in, not like these old and worn things you're wearing now."

Paulo looked down at his patched trousers and faded shirt; and suddenly he felt embarrassed, which he never had before.

"I'm not finished!" The wizard commanded, pulling Paulo's attention back to him. "Your stomach! Yes, to fill an empty stomach, we would need something truly delicious to eat, no? We should set before you a steaming, heaping platter of savory and tender meats, all simmering in a sea of turnips, potatoes and gravy. And to finish off, something marvelously sweet – like, like, a basket of honey-coated pastries sprinkled with sesame and hazelnuts – there we are! – and a crusty baked pie of apple and peach and strawberry."

Zeph surveyed the boy whose eyes had started to glaze, and continued. "But then let's move on to something else. There is still so much more – *so* much more! Company, friends, yes! You will then obviously need good company, I should say; but charming, sympathetic and generous friends – only that kind will do, I believe, of socially important status, nothing less. And trustworthy, ever trusting and trustworthy; never let you down, these friends, no!

"But of course, we should not forget a special companion for you: one special, magnificent person. Let us imagine romance then, tenderness, sweetness, and loveliness; love to fulfill your heart's most burning wish to be known and cared for. A soft hand to wipe your brow at work, a warm smile to light your cold nights. *Why not?*"

A haze had instilled itself in Paulo's mind, a swimming feeling like desire and mystery and excitement all mixed up, and floating in the middle of it all were Francesca's lovely blue eyes and strands of dark brown hair and soft olive skin.

"And then you should not go unnoticed within your community – that would not do! Yes, we would need you to hold a place of high public standing. A special new post in Towne – *chief of market activities*, there it is! And a rewarding position it is too; never shall you want for a silver crown or two to bestow upon those less fortunate than yourself. You shall rule the market with justice and benevolence. People will love you. And the Mayor himself shall come to fear the sway you hold on people's hearts..."

Paulo's mouth hung wide and his eyes gleamed brightly back at the magician at the mention of all these unbelievable things.

"...Yes, my young friend," Zeph's tone changed, becoming softer, slightly sad, "an infinite variety of spectacular and important things such as these, the Maker promised us; things that would satisfy our insatiable need for feeling good about ourselves – safe and content within the insecure, impoverished little lives that he himself had bestowed upon us. Our secret hunger would impel us to strive for the myriad glittering things presented to our blinded eyes, with one pure intention: that we should think of naught else but this frantic search. A search that would begin ... but never end." He drew a breath, then repeated, in a whisper, "Never – *ever* end."

Paulo continued to listen, rapt.

"Indeed, there seemed a means now, one last remaining way to find happiness once more in the midst of our desperate, wretched lives. But it would require our constant effort, our eternal striving to satisfy this aching need within us. And we strove, we strove...

"Suddenly, magically, despite our constant pain, no place could compare to the loveliness and beauty we found within the Maker's prison of destitution. Useless it would be to look elsewhere for satisfaction or peace of mind, we concluded – only too hastily. 'Why search elsewhere?' we asked. 'There is no other place: the Golden City is destroyed, the evil Lord has exiled us. All we want can surely be found right here!'

"Only one solution existed: the perpetual search for these objects that glimmered in the obscurity of our cold new home. And whenever the appeal of some beloved situation or cherished object diminished, there was ever yet another flashing toy, another fascinating place, the guarantee of an even more exceptional person or circumstance to take its place. There would be no end to the things the Maker promised us would satisfy the pain and hunger that constantly gnawed and chewed at our entrails. There was relief, but only in his world: such was the Maker's promise ... and this promise we profoundly believed, and even worshiped."

Paulo suddenly removed his eyes from the magician and cast a searching gaze around the far countryside. He stared vaguely, abstractly, into the distance as his mind turned over the wizard's words.

He was contemplating his recent dilemma, his failed plans and longings, his needs for change, comfort and recognition. He drew a deep breath and the air passed heavily between his teeth.

He murmured quietly, half to himself, "It's all wrong, isn't it? All these promises and pictures of happiness, they're all false, aren't they?"

He looked straight at Zeph, disappointment etched deeply into his face.

"It's all rubbish and lies, isn't it? It's all based on nothing. There's nothing there at all, in fact. Everything I think is so wonderful and magical, well, it's not really that way at all. It's just what it is, but not really everything that I make it out to be. I just want it to be that way."

Zeph smiled warmly, and looked kindly at Paulo. He understood only too well what the boy was going through, the wrenching away of so many beloved images and long-held hopes. He had been there, too.

"I'm glad you can start to see this, Paulo. I know it's hard, very hard, but it's really the only way. How else could you learn to see properly?"

Paulo sighed again, faced with a truth he had absolutely no desire to acknowledge. The images he had so long cherished could not possibly contain the extraordinary power over unhappiness he claimed. Yet there seemed to be nothing to replace them.

"But how… How is it that I'm so unable to see clearly, to see things as they really are? Why wasn't this clearer from the beginning?"

The wizard prepared a response to the boy's question.

"The Maker's plan is thoroughly diabolical, Paulo, but it is not without a measure of logic. His bewitchment of our senses remains *unseen*, and this is its reason for surviving in the mind.

"Yes, the Maker would have us first imagine an irremediable banishment from our Home, an unhappiness and lack too great to describe; and, yes, he would present us with contrived images of magical pleasures in an attempt to ease the pain and keep us focused outside the Mind; but then he would have us *entirely forget* the path we followed to this point. All traces of our journey have been erased from our memory: nothing remains. It requires now a tremendous effort of will to uncover the hidden steps we have taken away from our original state of wholeness and plenitude. It is possible, but at the cost of the pictures in which we have so invested."

Paulo asked solemnly, "I cannot have my pictures?"

"Of course you may!" the wizard answered brightly now. "But real happiness can never *come* from these images. It is just impossible. The two are not joined in any way, since they operate in completely different realms. But we don't see this, and that's why it remains.

"So it's not a mystery you didn't find the problem, Paulo. Most people never do. It's extremely well disguised, and it takes someone with the greatest sense of self-honesty and courage to be willing to face the problem as it is. After all, it is a truly terrifying prospect: the end of any dream of happiness in the world."

Feeling suddenly very weary, the boy said, "But there's something in me that really doesn't want to know all this. My will isn't that strong. I still want so much to believe in my dreams. Why?"

"Let me explain: this is really quite important. There is, of course, a perfectly satisfying alternative to the empty and disappointing dreams of the Domain, but our Maker-self now has no interest in letting us find this. That specific part of us which is now accustomed to independence and separation in essence obstinately refuses to acknowledge any power other than the material world. Yes, we continue to want happiness, but not as It really is, and we insist on believing in an impossible dream despite all our experience that would teach us that our path has failed.

"Again we have to ask, *why?* Why should the choice between Truth and illusion, Happiness and disappointment be so terribly difficult? Simply because this cherished independence and separation would uphold that our tiny individual self is real and true and the foundation of our reality. We are all faced with a choice we *desperately* do not wish to make: between original and real Happiness on one hand, and our miniscule, empty lives on the other. Instead of reasoning the problem through, we simply occult the dilemma altogether from our view. *That* is the cause of the despair each of us feels when he deeply questions the value of his beloved objects. His very existence seems to be endangered by these questions."

"Yes!" Paulo exclaimed. "It feels like there's something dangerous there. And I hold on tighter to my dreams and then look for others."

"Quite right, my boy. When the memory of Love encroaches upon our minds, we brandish our cherished objects and situations as we would a protective talisman. The assault of tenderness and kindness slows and ceases, and we return to the familiarity of our dreams, empty though they be. It is likewise with all experience within the Domain. We will seek powerful sensations and emotions, whether exalting or depressing, in order to return our minds more firmly to the Maker realm; and the door that Love offers us back to the Kingdom closes and finally disappears from view.

"Thus, far easier than confounding and terrifying ourselves with these questions, we continue to claim there is no alternative to the promises of the Domain. Yet, beneath every hope of earthly achievement, lofty and glorious as it may be, lies deep the thought of futility, and the empty, eternal charade of life within the Domain."

Paulo flopped suddenly back on the grass and closed his eyes.

How did I get myself into this mess? he spoke to himself and shook his head. *I just wanted to feel happy and well again – that's all! That's not too much to ask, is it?*

He crossed his hands behind his head and opened his eyes, staring upward into a deep azure-blue sky, perfectly cloudless from horizon to horizon.

CHAPTER FORTY-FIVE

Shadows of a Dim Lantern

Zeph paused to scrutinize the boy.

Indeed, laid flat on the grass and staring into space, Paulo was busy wondering at that moment if he had made the right choice to follow this path.

"Are you okay, my boy? Do you wish to return to the time before you had met me, is that it? The time before all of this strangeness?"

The wood seller closed his eyes a moment. He lay there and allowed a memory to return, his first unexpected meeting with the infinitely kind, wise man when he ran terrified through the streets of Towne escaping what he thought was a sure thrashing. He opened his eyes and stared solemnly back at Zeph.

"No, I wouldn't go back. Not for anything would I return to my life before, despite the shadows I see everywhere at times."

The sage waited a moment. "Then I should continue?"

The boy nodded.

The magician desired indeed with all his heart to help the boy move past this confusion and sorrow, but only if he still wished to do so. He was quite sure that Paulo had already gone past the point of returning, and only needed a little more help to find the traces of real hope along his way; but he would still always give him the choice to go back if he wished.

"Questioning your dreams will indeed lead you into this despair, Paulo," he offered in a soft voice after some moments. "But then it will kindly lead you on further, toward happiness, toward freedom… and back into the soft embrace of Love. Not before great darkness, this is true, and this is perhaps where you are today, the dark and terrifying night the soul faces on finding itself caught between two worlds: the seductive material existence of the illusory Domain; and the purely joyous but supremely abstract reality of the Kingdom."

Paulo raised himself on one elbow and stared at the ground, contemplative, still deeply unsure.

"You have only one real need, Paulo, not the many needs of your life as you now see it," Zeph continued, seeking to reach through to his young apprentice. "And this need is already wonderfully, beautifully satisfied within your heart, within the quiet place of your own mind. There you will find all that you seek. The Love and Joy you have sought *are* there, but they are densely covered by this Spell of false wants – this illusion of lack.

"Let me explain further perhaps. This Spell of lack is no more really than an idea, a conviction, just an unquestioned conviction of need and emptiness. It has also been called the *Principle of Scarcity*, which is a law that has come now to dominate the Domain and every aspect of its culture. This personal feeling of insufficiency arose instantly at the moment we left the state of Fullness. Though self-inflicted and completely unnecessary, it is nevertheless a most powerful, devastating feeling, capable of driving people to ruin and to satisfy their every need despite the consequences. So powerful, it might one day lead to the destruction of their beloved world. And so there would indeed be no hope at all for the Domain … except that this scarcity and disorder are ultimately still only images in the One Mind, and can always be changed there.

"Just look at your own life, Paulo. This aching need you have for special situations to make you feel better is just another expression, an *experience*, of this scarcity aspect of the Separation. You needn't feel so bad, my boy. This isn't really a serious problem, as you think, though it *has* been the cause of a lot of unhappiness for you.

"Imagine: without this sense of rupture from Home in your heart, there would be no more experience of personal want or lack. In the place of that ache and frenetic need, there would now be just a simple sense of fullness and peace. If you felt only the true wholeness of Love in your heart and mind and understood the loveliness of your reality, you would in fact feel no more needs at all. Then when you made choices they would no longer be based on a desire to get anything, but simply on the movement of your life at that time."

Paulo continued staring at the ground for some time, then broke the silence. "Do you really believe I can do this, I mean really, Zeph? Do you think I'll be able to do what you say and finally get to this place of fullness you speak about? I don't feel very full on the whole."

"Paulo, my friend, I have the deepest faith in you," reassured the sage. "You are very capable of walking this path and making it through this dark phase – please try to believe me. Every time you make even a small effort, you make a correction in your mind. Every time you suggest to yourself that there might indeed be another way of looking at your life experiences, you are making progress and changing your thought patterns; you shine away a little more of the shadow there. This prepares your mind for understanding and feeling things it is not currently able to. Every moment of effort brings you closer to Home because it makes real and lasting changes within you –"

Paulo blew out a long, whistling breath in the middle of Zeph's speech.

Frustration edged his voice, "But how can I really be happy without the things I want in the Domain?" he said. "Frankly, it just doesn't make sense to me – my needs and desires are just there. I don't have the things I want, and that's why I'm not happy! It seems that simple to me. It sounds quite bizarre, this idea that I can just feel that I'm somehow complete. The person I am doesn't feel very complete at all!"

Zeph had expected this reaction at some stage from Paulo, and was quite pleased to receive it openly. However, there was only one wise way to respond…

"Perhaps the person you think you are is not the end of the story, Paulo, and that is maybe where you need to begin to look. Maybe, in fact, you are not at all the person you think yourself to be…"

Paulo flashed his eyes to the wizard in surprise.

"Okay," the boy said, "I don't know what I am; but whatever it is, it's complete, right?"

"Let me explain further," Zeph said. "It isn't a question of just feeling complete, or *pretending* to be happy and satisfied. It isn't a question of convincing yourself now of something you don't really feel. You see, the feeling of sufficiency and plenitude is more than just a state of mind – it comes from a natural and implicit understanding of the true nature of reality. Of *your reality*. That is why I say perhaps the problem begins not with your circumstances but with your self-conceptions. Remember, as we have said once before, what you think you are is the starting point for all your experiences and perceptions."

Paulo struggled to express his feelings, embarrassed. "Zeph… I really don't understand how to make these ideas work. They just don't seem to agree with the world I see at all! The 'me' I think I am seems very much to be in this world where there are real things I need and want, and I don't feel much like something else."

A pleading note entered his voice. "I know you believe in me and that you really want me to make it back Home and all. And it's not that I think you're wrong, but…"

"Look at it this way," the magician broke in, having found what he thought might be the problem. "Let us try to imagine for a moment that the real you is not what you have always thought; is not, in fact, a body at all. Let's imagine you are not this little creature of bone and flesh so familiar to you: yes, let us imagine that. Let's say in reality you're actually a great and extraordinary Light, a brilliant and magnificent force of luminosity, why not?

"But now this great, wonderful Light has undergone some mysterious change and has somehow welcomed into itself a sense of limitation and constraint, and has become very unhappy. It is now more like a tin lantern or a cheap oil lamp and shines weakly and sadly. Not more than a fraction of its real light escapes and glows depressingly in the dark. It wants to be happier, so in order to cheer itself, this lamp has discovered a particularly curious form of entertainment: it fabricates strange, beguiling images and shapes, attractive to its eyes, it devises these shapes and then casts them onto a tall wall surrounding its home, making them move and dance and jerk, and giving them in all ways a complete semblance of life and independence. Do you have that now?"

The boy seemed able to grasp that. It reminded him of the shadow games he played with Fredo in the bed alcove at night with the firelight on the walls of the cottage.

Zeph continued, "The lamp is enthralled by all these fantastic shapes and pictures that now dance and flicker all around on the walls of its home, images that somehow appear outside of the light, and quite separate from the lantern itself. Nevertheless, you understand, the images have no real existence outside the light itself. They still remain shadows and pure fabrications of the light. This, Paulo, is in actual fact the nature of the world you perceive around you every day in the Domain.

"Every day you look at these vague images on the walls of your home and you give them a value, a power to keep you happy and joyful, or else an ability to make you miserable and sad. It doesn't really make sense, but it is a game we have agreed to play. How logical is it, after all, to feel a desire for a shadow-picture, or to be sad because it is not there? What could achieving a certain pattern of images accomplish for the lantern? What does it serve to acquire a certain shadow above another?"

The boy shook his head; the magician continued:

"Nothing, really. The aching feeling that troubles you is because of a problem maintained within the light, not because of anything unpleasant seen before the eyes. The only real need we now have is to see through the game itself, to undo the confusion, and remember that we are the great and perfect Light itself. Yes, the only happiness we can find is to undo the spot of darkness that has so strangely entered the lantern and marred the Light's brilliance. That's obvious."

This seemed relatively clear to Paulo, thinking of uncovering his hands from in front of a candle flame.

"But let's now say that we wish to change the moving shadow-shapes we see upon the walls of our home. For whatever reason, we think it's time for the pictures to change. What should we do? Should we run up to the wall and place our hands on the shapes there, pushing and pulling their outlines into other figures? No, that would be quite silly really. Under normal circumstances, we wouldn't go up to the wall to work on the shadows there, would we? Rather we would go to the source of the moving pictures: we would go to the lantern itself and work on the light there that was making the shapes and images, don't you think?"

Paulo seemed still to be following. It all seemed quite logical up till there. But now their was a wariness in his spirit, as if some danger or disappointment lurked within the magician's words.

"So it is in the Domain as well," Zeph continued to explain. "Whenever there is an experience or condition there you wish to change, for whatever reason, it is an indication of something that must be done within the lantern, within the *light in your mind* – not with the reflected images and shapes themselves.

"And so on the path Home we are guided to work first on the thoughts held within the mind that are affecting the light coming from that magical place. Remove the shadows there, and then our experience of our world will change. When the shadow is lessened, the experience changes, and the outside condition can shift and become something else in turn.

"So before seeking to change an outside condition, first seek to shift your experience rather than move and alter images and conditions before your eyes. When you perceive unhappiness, look closer and try to uncover the darkness that is hiding the light rather than fight and blame. The condition and its reflected images may not change immediately, but your experience will certainly become one of much greater peace and enjoyment."

Paulo stared silently back at the wizard, his lips held tight.

"This may be all quite bewildering, Paulo, but try to keep certain things straight in your spirit. You may still feel that you are not the source of the images in your world, that they come unbidden with a life of their own. You may yet be convinced your interest is with the shapes and circumstances of your life, not with the lantern itself. You may even confuse yourself with an image on the wall, believing that *you* are one of the shadows there…

"But yet your reality, your Mind, like the lantern, always remains outside the reflected images and above the moving pictures on the screen. You remain your *Self*, the great Light, despite any perceptions and experiences you might have to the contrary."

But still Paulo said nothing.

Zeph tried to find a few more words to encourage the boy.

"Here, I shall give you some good news, Paulo. The good news is that the images in the Domain need never affect you if you wish, because your Mind is always the origin of your experience and the home of the happiness you seek. There, what do you think?" he asked gaily.

Paulo's mood didn't visibly brighten in the least – this wasn't at all the type of good news he'd been hoping for. His gaze turned vacantly back toward the horizon.

"And that also means," Zeph continued cheerfully, "that you can change all the pictures and situations in the Domain and have precisely *all* that you want…"

Paulo looked up swiftly now, his eyes keen and bright with hungry expectation.

Then Zeph finished his thought, "…anytime you're willing to undo the obstacles within you."

Despite this last piece of annoying information, Paulo nevertheless found a glint of light, a spark of hope of finding happiness and satisfaction as he still saw them in the Domain.

"The circumstances of your life are nothing more than images that follow from the thoughts held deep within your mind, my boy," the magician explained further, "and that's why they can always evolve. As I mentioned before, your experiences will always flow like a stream from your deepest thoughts; and your thoughts will continue to issue like a fountain from your founding beliefs about yourself. If the fountain holds thoughts of suffering, then the waters will be darkened and bring suffering. Or poverty. Or a failing body. Similarly, if in the deepest part of the spring there is the clear and pristine thought that happiness, sufficiency and wellness are normal and appropriate for you, then these qualities will gently flow into your daily experience of life.

"There is no evil and uncaring god that destines you for misery, my friend. When you understand this, you may begin to release your own secret insistence on pain and lack. At that time, the images you see before you can begin to reflect this change of mind.

"But while you still unconsciously believe suffering and limitation are appropriate, even *justified*, you will certainly prevent yourself from finding true happiness and its symbols in the Domain."

Paulo took in all these wise words as best he could. But still a question framed itself in his mind, a doubt for which he still had no really satisfying answer.

Chapter Forty-Six

Where Happiness Was Entrusted

"If my needs are still there inside me," the boy asked, "you say I can really get what I want, and that's not so bad?" Paulo came back to the essential sticking point, as he saw it.

"But of course you can!" the magician reassured loudly. "However, there is a paradox here. For this to happen, you must teach yourself one simple rule: You must learn to understand that it is not the worldly circumstances themselves which contain some magical power of happiness or contentment.

"There, I've said it all. Does this now sound a little familiar? You could say, my friend, that the first step in finding what you want is to take your burning desires and wants – a *little less seriously*. And the only way you can do this is by learning patience, complete trust and –"

"But I *do* take my wants seriously," Paulo interjected furiously now. "They *are* important – to me."

"I imagine so! Everyone's wants are important to them. And they always seem to be especially, particularly justified. And they shall certainly remain a long while yet in our lives while we are still so frightened of Love – as a protection, as a shield. But perhaps we can *learn* to take our desires a little less seriously. Just try, Paulo."

The boy showed not the slightest sign of wanting to do so, not even for an instant.

"Just try to take a step back and look at yourself desperately wanting all sorts of things to happen, *as if* there were a real solution there. Try to see the pain and frustration that you think will disappear with the objects you might gain, or the joy and relief you believe will come with a new situation. Then try to remember that the only solution that can bring real relief to your aching heart is the love and comfort that you have banished. Not the comfort of another person, or of a special situation or position, but that remarkable presence which you have refused to let enter your mind. *Love* – love that is not of this world, but that you can welcome again.

"Then sit down and make your plans, and work hard to achieve them. It's that simple really. Don't give up your wants and goals and images now. Just remember that while you work toward your long-held dreams, your happiness is in every moment, and not when you finally arrive. In this way you turn your goals into a powerful means to happiness, instead of a path to some futile, empty end."

"But I feel bad when it looks like I'm not getting anywhere."

"When you start to feel unhappy because your plans aren't working out, just remember that the disappointment is because you've slipped again into thinking that achieving your goals would change your experience of life. It won't, not really. That's just a mistake, but a mistake we will all make time and time again and that will guide us back to the truth: that the real Happiness we seek is here and now already within us, and not in some far off picture."

Paulo ran his fingers through his hair and gripped his head hard in his hands. He let a sharp breath of frustration escape between his teeth.

"But…" he began, then hesitated. "But if everything is really all absolutely the same," he asked, exasperated, "how on earth am I supposed to decide on what I want, and which direction to go in? There are some directions that look better than others, but if they're really all the same, what am I supposed to do about making my choices? And in any case, things are really not the same for me – not at all! I'm not trying to be difficult. That's just the truth."

Zeph smiled affectionately; he was really quite delighted with Paulo's progress, though it was clear the boy himself felt he was going nowhere.

"How do we make our decisions, you ask, is that it?" the sage repeated. "Yes, in the Domain we will always be called upon to make choices, and to desire one thing or situation over another. That strange world brims with images we must decide between every day. While this certainly demands careful consideration on our part, we can perhaps begin to turn these desires into *preferences* – and to make our decisions based on what we would *prefer*, rather than on what we feel we *need*.

"That's not really answering my question," the boy pouted.

"Think of it this way – selling wood, raising chickens or baking bread, being with one person or with another – it's all your choice. But these decisions of yours don't have to be based anymore on *need*… Not as if another activity or person or another place or situation would improve your sense of peace, well-being or fulfillment. Your decision can just become a preference for something else.

"You see, your choices no longer have to be urgent and critical, to be a series of needs, to escape some desperate situation, for example, or a person you don't care for, or a job that drives you crazy. In plain words, your decisions don't have to be driven by anger or frustration or fear. They can simply come from the awareness of a time for change, based on respect, appreciation and a desire to continue your lessons somewhere else – don't you think?"

Paulo was struggling to understand. He was maddened by what he felt was a vicious circle: the impossibility of being happy with the situations he needed in the Domain; and the difficulty of seeking some pure, abstract form of happiness and being content with what he considered 'nothingness'; but realizing that that was perhaps the only way he was ever going to experience true peace.

He cried, beyond distraught, "But I can't simply give up wanting the things I want. It's just not possible! There are some things I still really need and you're saying I'll never be peaceful that way. I mean… there are some things, some situations which are still really important to me!"

He was still thinking about Francesca (he had no intention of letting the magician know that) and deeply felt that living without the promise of her company would make life seem utterly hopeless.

"– That's just the way I am, and the way my world is!"

The magician's eyes opened wide and his mouth twitched into a smile. "But I don't believe I heard anyone say you had to learn to do without the things you want – did anyone here?" Zeph looked around as if searching for someone hiding behind a tree. "Is there anyone there I failed to see?"

Paulo looked sheepish. He understood that in fact the magician had never reproached him for his desires and wants, nor had he even implied there was anything wrong with them at all.

"No one is saying, Paulo," the wizard continued valiantly, "that you must do without the things you believe you need. We're just trying to understand where *unhappiness* comes from, so we can eventually understand where happiness *is*. Remember, I'm only here in your life while you wish to continue learning. It's simply honest and sincere happiness we're still trying to achieve for you. But you're free to do as you wish, as long as you wish, and there shall never be any judgment of your path."

He interrogated the boy with a kind regard. "Do you want to go on?"

"Okay," Paulo mumbled begrudgingly, "– I'll listen."

A warm smile of understanding lit Zeph's face a moment; he knew only too well the boy's frustration and inner conflict.

"Let's continue then a while longer, okay? There are perhaps indeed some 'situations' as you call it" – he winked cheekily at Paulo – "which you must still explore and discover for yourself. This is only right and good. After all, how else would you be able to learn if there were no longer any movement in your life?

"Let's take an example. For instance, in the Domain there seems to be nothing greater, nothing more wonderful and exceptional, than the finding of a special partner who seems to make your life complete and utterly joyful."

Paulo didn't react and stared all the more sullenly into the wizard's face. He was committed to ignoring his teacher's provocations.

"Nothing makes us feel so whole, so fulfilled and worthy as the attention and devotion of an exceptional person in one's life. These special relationships are the best way, perhaps the only way, to learn about the true nature of love. Your feelings of need for another person come from deep, unspoken places within you; and it is only by exploring these depths that you will uncover the real source of your needs.

"The desire to join with another is the profound call we all feel for becoming whole. Ultimately not joining with another person – but returning into the embrace of that wonderful wholeness we all have left. All relationships can remind us of the possibility of becoming whole again, and of the family we all come from. So you see, there is really nothing wrong with seeking out your special partner."

Paulo was not sure if he should feel reassured; he was suspicious the magician was in fact trying to trick him, and that there was still something wrong with his needs and wants. He couldn't believe that the wizard would really agree that wanting a *girlfriend* could be a good and spiritual thing.

Zeph tried to respond to his unmentioned concern. "Believe me, Paulo, I'm quite serious. There is really nothing at all wrong with your wants and needs, even if that does mean desiring a wonderful companion with all your heart and soul, or desperately seeking another work situation.

"Still, as on the day we first met," the magician added, "when you ultimately decide you wish more than anything to feel profoundly safe, happy and peaceful, you must learn that it is not in such situations that you will find what you are looking for. It's not *in* these things, but *through* these circumstances, that you will find what you are looking for."

Paulo rolled his eyes. "Here we go again," he said. "I can't have what I want and be happy, is that it?"

"It would be better stated otherwise, I think," replied the sage. "Let's say that it's an irrevocable principle of Truth that you cannot have the things of the Domain *and* be happy – not if your *reason* for having such things or circumstances is to attain happiness. You may certainly find what you are looking for, as many people do; but if you want them purely for satisfaction and fulfillment, you will find the end result ultimately quite disappointing or short-lived. In some cases you might even find the effect tragically disturbing."

"But why?" the boy demanded.

"*Why?* Simply because needing any circumstance in the Domain for the sake of happiness contradicts your reality, your true existence. That is why. Maintaining such an inner contradiction in your life cannot *conceivably* leave you peaceful or satisfied.

"As you are, you are already complete; and your original state of completion *is* your happiness, as obscure as this might seem to you right now. What you are *is* happiness itself – it is your natural state of being. So needing special things outside yourself is simply an act of self-denial, a way of refusing to accept and understand your true nature."

After a moment, Paulo let out a long, heaving breath. "So there's really nothing to be done. I suppose I should just stop wanting things altogether and learn to live with nothing, like a some type of hermit. You want me to go into the Forest, build a hut of twigs and branches for myself, and stay there, waiting to understand my 'true self', is that it?" He folded his arms and stared crossly at the magician.

At this point the magician had to chuckle. He was quite aware of Paulo's inability to understand his true meaning: this would only come with much time and patience. Paulo still conceived of reality in terms of 'either-or': either happiness as he understood it, or else unhappiness; and could not yet grasp the sense of a constant happiness that already filled the world of his Mind in all his many activities and pursuits.

"I'm very glad to announce, my young friend, that you can still have whatever you wish in the Domain. Living in the Domain is not a question of doing without things – no, not at all. It is normal to have things in the Domain, since it was conceived of as a place of objects and situations.

"So, please, make the fortune you seek, and share your wealth freely. Find the love you are burning for, and then help others understand the nature of the love you have found. *Nothing is bad in the Domain*. There are no unjustifiable possessions or inappropriate situations, and you can have whatever your heart desires. Everything is perfectly neutral. It is simply that nothing there has the special powers you believe – that is all. Neither to make you feel pleasure, nor to make you feel pain."

There was a moment of silence. Only the whispering sound of a warm breeze in the tall grasses could be heard.

"Right. So, I'll try harder … *Again*." Paulo spoke determinedly, with just an edge of annoyance in his voice.

"Just remember when you do," the wizard advised, "that the Maker has no interest whatsoever in you finding your real Self, and this is the reason he will insist time and time again on your many needs. 'Don't seek there where you would find a useful answer to your needs', he will warn you, *'but do seek here where you will never find one'*. That is the sum of his message – to confound us and totally preoccupy our hearts with endless, useless searching.

"This strange creature, Master of your thoughts, Ruler of your emotions, will tell you that the goal of your many life choices is to make your individual self feel better and more comfortable. But how totally absurd! Your *Mind* – far above your individual self – is where happiness can be found and the only place where you can possibly claim it, because that is where it was entrusted.

"You see, the good King is most kind. He wished you never to be without happiness, and put it in a very special place where it could never, ever be taken away from you, no matter what transpired, no matter whether you lived or died. And where is that? He placed it right there within you – within the holiness of your very own Mind."

CHAPTER FORTY-SEVEN

The Battle for Peace

Paulo dug his fingers into the soft grass and took a moment to ponder the magician's outlandish ideas.

He tossed and turned the thoughts relentlessly in his mind but it was impossibly difficult to make them stick. It really felt like he would be better if he were there right now, holding hands with Francesca, and working on the farm with her parents in his brother's place.

"Paulo, please try to find just a little acceptance within yourself," Zeph replied to the boy's acute dilemma. "There's really nothing wrong with these wants of yours. For a long time still you'll seek things in the Domain to feel better. It's inevitable: your wants *constitute* your classroom, and it's only by pursuing them that you'll come to learn your lessons.

"I might suggest, though, that, as you busy yourself with your goals that you begin to look at how you earnestly wish for certain things to have, indeed, special powers to satisfy you."

Paulo tilted his head to the side, listening intently.

"Try, for example, to observe how you sincerely want friends to be a certain way, to have certain special qualities in order to please you. Look a little at how much you depend upon jobs and money to fulfill you, excite you, satisfy you. Discover the vital importance you give to certain happenings in the world, or to specific bodies of knowledge. All of this simply represents your intention to anchor yourself in the world, a way of making the world and your self always more real and important in your senses."

The wood seller asked, "All I need do is just look at that, you say?"

"That is indeed the first part. The second part is this: when your expectations are no longer fulfilled, notice then the pang of disappointment that invades your heart. Notice how rapidly you become disenchanted if friends change or fail you. Or notice how you become mystified at the loss of excitement of a familiar activity, or perhaps at the disproving of an important idea."

Paulo looked dubious. "And this will help me see how things don't really have the power I want them to have, is that it?"

"Yes. That's all you need do for the moment," Zeph answered. "I promise that one day you'll understand all this much better… one day, in the not too distant future. In the meantime, however, it may also help if you tried this: if you started to consider that all the things you want in the Domain, all your cherished objects and situations, are sort of like the things in a sleeping dream at night."

What … ? Paulo frowned heavily.

"Do you see what I mean? All events and objects in a dream at night are perfectly the same, right? That's because all dream things are simply in your imagination and not real at all. That's quite simple, no?"

What's this craziness? No, it's not simple at all! he spoke to himself.

"Once awake, you know that one dream-event or dream-object was no more real than another because it was *all* make-believe. No matter how real the dream appeared, no matter how thoroughly convinced you were while you are dreaming of the importance of an object or event, you know upon waking that nothing there was real. It was all just images. Even the things of the most fascinating beauty, the most startling horror, were all just images."

A wave of indignation swept across Paulo's face. "But the *Mayor!*" he cried, returning to an old and favorite battle-ground.

"But I still think the Mayor is terribly unfair with the stall-people. What he does is *very* wrong, and *very* unjust. That's just the way it is! I can't just go around telling the other market people 'it's not important because it's all just a silly dream', and that I don't really care what he does. I do really care – *and so do they!*"

Zeph replied calmly, "You are absolutely right – and that would indeed be quite unwise, and unkind, too. In the Domain we will always be taking positions to respond to the many complex situations the Maker has imagined and fabricated for us. The Ruler of that world provokes us to take all this as very important, and as very distressing. But perhaps we can start to learn that the issues and challenges that arise before us every day are not important in quite the same way as we always imagined; perhaps because they are literally in *every way* all just situations in a–"

The magician stopped in mid-sentence, turned to reflect on some place within him, then continued more slowly.

"Paulo… things can be different now, if you want. Easier. We can make all the declarations we want in the village and state our well-thought opinions – but we can begin to express ourselves *differently*. With less judgment perhaps, and certainly with less tension and frustration. And we can take our positions with just the faintest, tranquil smile on our lips. Why? Perhaps because we remember: the world's condition is simply not the whole story.

"We will make our important declarations and remind ourselves of the truth at the same time: that we are all indeed quite safe and whole, despite the many dramatic and often tragic happenings around us. We do not see the Kingdom nor understand its perfect nature, we cannot yet comprehend its unassailable integrity and our place within it; nevertheless this does not mean it is not there or non-existent – no! *The Kingdom is safe*, regardless of what seems to be happening here within the chaotic world of shadows. And our inner reality is firmly located still within that calm, magnificent place."

"But the Mayor…" the young boy insisted stubbornly, an unmistakable glowering look flickering across his face. "The market people just don't have any power to make things right. And he only looks out for himself and his own special friends…"

"Do not judge some people as sillier than others," Zeph managed to suggest in between Paulo's protestations, "simply because of what they are seeking and the way they seek it. You do not approve of what the Mayor is seeking – the recognition, influence and power so dear to him – and how he seeks to fulfill his needs. But, dear friend, are your personal goals really any wiser, any saner, than his? When you consider that anyone who pursues his dreams in the Domain in the hope of satisfaction or safety is mistaken, then are you not all the same? Do you not still have many of your own goals that resemble the Mayor's?"

He glanced at Paulo and his eyes only met his student's barely veiled sullenness.

"*All* the villagers are mistaken, Paulo. And equally so," Zeph concluded.

"Let me repeat," the wizard tugged Paulo's elbow, pulling his unwilling attention back to the conversation: "*none are better or worse for what they seek*. This is a very easy point to miss, because it will still seem for a long time to come that some goals and behaviors are more acceptable than others, and some decidedly inferior! But none are better or worse for what they seek in the Domain. Any path there can lead toward truth, even the most earthly or the most bellicose. And other paths of seeming holiness and benevolence may lead precisely away from understanding and compassion."

The wizard looked down at the boy, a smile warmed his face and he spoke encouragingly, as he said:

"You, my fine apprentice, will still be tempted to fight many battles in your world, that's clear. Perhaps it's in this special way that you'll finally learn the nature of true happiness and peace. Perhaps in this way you will eventually come to understand an important but obscure lesson: that there are no critical situations in your suffering world that you have to right; that there are no battles there essential to win. There is in that dark world only a vital *understanding* to seek and to find. There is in essence nothing outside of yourself that you need to accomplish in order to fulfill the meaning of your life, this being all that truly matters."

"Are you sure?" questioned Paulo. "But I just know there are some situations that have to be corrected. That's just normal!"

"There are certainly situations that are more *preferable* than others, this is sure," the magician responded quickly, "and we should unquestionably work toward these over time, on the level of your own life, and the township as a whole.

"But the accomplishment of your inner well-being and purpose, or of that of any other person, does not depend on any outside situation being righted – can you understand that? This stands to reason, for the King would never deny even one of his children the possibility of perfect fulfillment within Himself. It is the great temptation of the Domain to believe that peace shall not come before certain worldly or personal conditions are corrected. But this is yet another way of staying focused in the wrong direction, and on the wrong relationship to true peace."

"It seems very strange," the boy said slowly, shaking his head slightly. "It just seems there's still so much to do, to fix."

"There are still many things to do in the Domain, Paulo," the magician suggested somewhat solemnly, "but nothing more to do for the reasons you always sought and believed in. You shall still act and speak on the same matters, with all your courage and determination, but your actions and words shall now carry a different message. When you manage to disengage even just a little from the significance of your goals, then your language and acts will automatically carry with them a power, but a power that will not be of yourself alone.

"So please do keep on pursuing your goals and strivings, Paulo. But understand as you do that no earthly peace or justice that you might manage to establish in time by your efforts can ever resolve the basic problem on which the Domain has been founded. It takes great reflection to understand how the Domain was purpose-built from its inception to be a place of lack and conflict. And so to put the world in proper perspective, it is essential to know that if understanding and wisdom are lacking, then conflict and deprivation will inevitably return in one form or another."

Paulo stared directly at the wizard, but his sight was inward. For an instant a remarkable new world seemed to appear in his thoughts: All people were looking within themselves to understand the nature of the hate and conflict and the Love that were there. Only then did they bring themselves to act; and their actions and words were filled with wisdom and grace and understanding.

"Until there is a greater understanding of the origin of conflict and the real cause of peace," the magician expanded, "we can only be patient and compassionate with our brothers as they pursue their ill-founded solutions. We can only smile quietly to ourselves at their forceful insistence to secure something that is quite illusory, and then continue on our path – reminding ourselves constantly of the work that awaits *us*."

So I'm first supposed to work on me, I guess, Paulo thought.

"That's right," Zeph responded to his unspoken words. For each of us, our work is first and foremost within *ourselves*. We can only ever help others by our example, by our unemotional attachment to the results or changes we seek in the world. In that way we leave a place for the peace and acceptance in us to speak in the place of our passion and judgment. And we learn to understand that no brother deserves condemnation simply because he doesn't agree with us, and needs for the while to continue following his goals. Nothing is ever truly at risk: he can do no real harm." The wizard glanced at the boy. "This does seem strange, no?"

Indeed Paulo was feeling this was not only strange, but truly impossible to comprehend. *So the Mayor doesn't deserve condemnation – that's new!*

The magician explained his thoughts.

"Your brother, the Mayor, is frightened, Paulo; that's all. But then who among our brothers isn't? He is scared, as are all the villagers, of his real Identity which is not the identity he is most familiar with and has so long invested in. And it's this acute fear of not being the self he has so long imagined which causes him to react without consideration and reflection. It's the same fear we all contain in coming to the Domain, and so in being patient with *his* fear, we learn to accept our own. This is the secret to understanding."

Zeph paused, seeming to prepare for his next thoughts. He filled his lungs deeply a few times, and when he finally spoke, he expressed a calmness and poise that came from some other, peace-filled place.

"The villagers are in pain, my boy," he spoke slowly, "but can sense no true relief in their lives. They seek, but do not find; they have felt a need but cannot understand the problem. Vainly and despondently they seek where there is no solution, and fight battles with no reward. What the townspeople search for endlessly is not in their world at all, but in their confusion they will fight for many randomly chosen solutions, firmly convinced that these will supply them with the safety and justice they crave.

"Paulo, in this ill-founded search we are *each of us* identical: all of us have failed to understand the problem, and have failed to identify the solution. But you, Paulo, do not need to do so any longer, to live this life of sad desperation any further... You can change all this now."

The sage's words filtered through Paulo's thoughts like a healing rain. He so desperately wished to believe in this new vision of life, a life free of weakness and hate.

"And so I no longer need to fight, s'that right?" he asked.

CHAPTER FORTY-EIGHT

No Dream of Malice

"I can give up fighting and just see what happens, is that what you're saying?" Paulo couldn't quite believe this is what the wizard was saying, but it seemed a little like it.

"Please, my young friend, don't misunderstand: you won't suddenly stop taking positions or opposing now. But you'll no longer do so by fighting and struggling in the same way, believing that you're removing evil and injustice from the world and bringing happiness and freedom in their place.

"You can't possibly shed light through angry opposition or resentful resistance, you know this; but you *can* bring light to the world by your understanding and patience, even if you do feel the need for determined, forceful action. You've learned by now that evil is in the *mind* – but in the mind of *everyone*. So too is Love, and that's where they must both be seen, and selected from. The world will then come naturally to reflect what has first been chosen in the mind as one, and *that* is the secret to peace in the world."

Desperation and incomprehension edged the boy's voice now, and he declared, "But the town is a terrible place filled with angry, violent people who don't understand *any* of what you're talking about." He took quite seriously the magician's words, yet found tremendous difficulty managing to believe such ideas could possibly work in practice. "It's true, what I'm saying."

"You're quite correct, Paulo," Zeph responded patiently; "and I know that your experience of the Domain has been one of great disappointment; and perhaps you still believe you're all alone in your efforts to work things out there.

"But let me tell you this, Paulo, and do please try to understand, *you are not alone*. And you *can* leave the violence of the township whenever you wish, whenever you come here to meet with us."

Paulo was listening carefully now.

"You can find remarkable peace and comfort in your life, even within the violence of the Domain. But you will not be able to find this comfort until you accept one imperative point: there is nothing *powerful* within the hate and cruelty of the Townspeople. Nor within the devastatingly inconsiderate and short-sighted things that appear to happen in that world."

He spoke calmly but his words had a great effect on Paulo. The young boy struggled to understand their full meaning, realizing there was some essential truth hidden there within these perplexing thoughts that still escaped him.

"There is nothing powerful about hate, anger and selfishness, and their effects," the wizard continued, responding to Paulo's confused look. "This baffles you, I see. To understand how this might be so, my young student, you will have to learn to think quite differently about your world, and yourself."

Paulo found inadequate words to respond. "How could this be true? How … all the violence and selfishness?"

"My dear friend," the wizard said quietly, "simply because no dream of malice and insanity could ever alter in any true way the quiet and gentle reality of the King's People and their true Home… All is well, and it will forever be."

Paulo was left with the strange feeling of not being able to truly comprehend something he knew was a great gift, a gift of exceptional hope and beauty.

"Despite the many scenes of violence there in the world of darkness, you can find the peace and happiness you seek," Zeph went on. "Whenever you find again the deep Peace that is there present within you, you will remember it is the truth of all things. It will transform your vision. Nothing you see thereafter will seem quite the same, quite so convincing. No expression of hate or chaos will be able to alter the firm impression of what you have seen within that serene, holy space."

The boy was lost in thought, deeply touched by these words of his teacher. Yet still more was to come from the sage…

"Paulo, you have everything you seek as of this moment, because the good King has already *given* you everything, and it is all there within you even while you reside within the Domain. The peace you seek *is* there. The Maker's darkness cannot remove it from your mind, just as it could not close the access to the Kingdom or render you truly sinful; and that is why this insane Ruler so desperately tries to keep your attention on the world's problems, precisely so you will never look inside yourself.

"If ever you looked within your heart for just a moment, with openness and a sincere desire to know, you would find something far more worthy of yourself than all the shimmering gifts of the Domain. You would find within your heart the song of ancient Harmony that still sings of your beloved Home … and *that* is indeed worth finding.

"Listen to me now, my boy, and pay close attention–"

Paulo looked far into the magician's eyes, which seemed at this moment to reach deep into another world.

"Try to understand: you have everything you could ever want and seek because you *are* everything the good King has given. You *are* everything the good King created, and what he created is supremely good. There is nothing else to seek and find. It is all there lying in wait within you … within your holy Mind."

There was a silence as the boy listened intently, listening inside to another perfectly still place. For a time the entire world was utterly quiet.

The wizard paused to see if Paulo had returned. He then said matter-of-factly:

"When you asked what was the right thing to do with the farm work and Francesca, *you knew*. You didn't make the decision alone, you were quite sure. Now you must learn to trust. You don't yet know what surprises the path of learning might hold for you, so you must learn to wait and be patient.

"When you saw that perhaps your brother was getting the special situation and attention you hoped for, you became upset. A part of you still hoped you could push and command your destiny and get the particular things you thought you needed to be happy. You listened once again to your Maker-self, and you believed that these things were truly enchanted and would deliver all the happiness you missed in your life.

"But if you did feel it was right to give the work to Fredo, then you must learn to trust that your true happiness does surely come from within you, and another appropriate situation will present itself at the right time. Releasing your fear and tight hold on situations is the way to allow other things to happen in your life. We do not *need* something else special to happen: we release the situation from the importance we gave it so that it may be replaced by something else, even if that process takes time."

He smiled kindly at Paulo, slightly amused.

"You'll get everything you want, Paulo, I promise," the magician reassured. "– Even a special girlfriend and new leather boots, if that's what you really want. There is no sacrifice on the path Home. Just trust."

Paulo thought the wizard might be making fun of him and he just stared into space, looking pensive and pretending to concentrate. He was still very tempted to think that another person had got what he really wanted, what was his *due*, he felt. And had got it *now* rather than later as the wizard promised *might* be his eventual reward. But he was also upset with himself because he had felt unkindly toward his brother whom he loved.

The magician picked up on this concern of his. "Paulo, do you really think that you can love your brother while you still feel so incomplete within yourself?"

The boy turned to look back at the sage with eyebrows raised.

"What do you mean?"

Zeph paused an instant before finishing his thought, his hands resting placidly on his knees, his gaze placed lightly on the boy in front of him.

"While you still feel so unfulfilled within yourself, you'll be liable to imagine that your brother can take or withhold something you need, or something that you can lose. You will, in effect, remain continually suspicious of him. But this isn't love."

The wizard paused once more as his eyes searched for a response in the boy.

"Remember, no one can take away anything you really need... No one can take anything you cannot afford to part with, because you can lose nothing of value. This is ultimately why you will learn to love your brother, and love all your brothers together. You need no longer feel defensive or protective because you can truly be deprived of nothing. You cannot be stolen from, and you cannot be hurt. So you can begin to relax and to forgive all those you once believed could steal from you, who are many in your thoughts.

"Look over there now, Paulo," the sage said commandingly.

The boy looked quickly in the direction of the wizard's pointing finger, toward the gentle brightness of the Golden City glimmering tranquilly in the warm afternoon haze.

"The Spell tells you that you lost everything that is beautiful at the moment you left the Golden City. It whispers that you shall be without beauty and love forevermore, and that you must now substitute for this loss however you can. But this is not true; you can see that now. The City is not gone or destroyed – it is right there, and it is waiting ... *for you*. And nothing else can ever provide for the absence of the Kingdom in your life, no matter how alluring its promises.

"You learn about love and comfort by remembering what is contained within you, and not by insisting on outside conditions to sustain you. *The path Home lies inside.* And you will find it again by learning to listen to that special gentle Voice whenever you are still tempted to follow the counsel that would keep you plunged in darkness. When you feel the great Silver Presence within you, you will *know* that you lost nothing at the moment of departure from the Kingdom … You will know it is all here, right now."

The boy seemed to understand better, and nodded.

"You're not staying in the Domain just to satisfy your desires and appetites and ambitions there. This is what you believed, as do all the Townspeople. Do you remember why you're there now? You're staying for another reason – do you remember what it is?"

Paulo remembered it well. He thought about it all the time – when he wasn't thinking about Francesca.

"Yes," he answered confidently. "You say the Key to the Golden City is in the Domain, and some kind of special Knowledge, too. You say that it's only my fear that stops me from finding them. And now you're saying that I don't need to look anymore for my happiness there in the Domain, if I don't want to. Is that right?"

"Correct. Very good. Not in the *things* or *situations* of the Domain. Happiness is there in the Domain, because Happiness is in *you*. It cannot be separated from your Identity which you take with you wherever you go. But I see you were coming to understand this all by yourself, don't you think? I believe you were starting to see that it's just not possible to make decisions contrary to your deepest feelings, and still feel happy. Happiness is found by following the wisdom of your heart when your heart is clear and detached, and not by insisting on the simplistic solutions the Domain seems to offer."

Zeph rose to his feet and placed a kind hand on the boy's shoulder. "Trust me, Paulo. It is true what I say."

Paulo didn't understand all the magician's many thoughts, but he knew they were very important. He knew it would still take many months of practice in the market place, maybe even longer, to learn all their hidden meanings.

Zeph then said it was time to return to the Domain and walked him slowly back to the Door. This time Paulo crossed back through without a problem, the guards remained peacefully asleep, and he wandered calmly back to his cottage on the edge of the forest.

CHAPTER FORTY-NINE

Gentle Classroom

"Is everything really alright, Paulo?" Francesca's voice rose sharply.

The market place bustled around them, clients were lining up behind each other at the stall, and Fredo hectically prepared eggs and chickens for sale.

"Great!" Paulo paused. "*Why?*" His delivery to a customer on the far side of the square had passed close to their stall and he had stopped by to exchange a brief hello. But now he wondered what Francesca could be seeing in him that worried her.

"Nothing. Just … Fredo and I just wanted to make sure everything was really okay. That's all." She stumbled to find the right words.

"Honestly, I'm feeling fine," he said. "Sincerely fine. Please don't be concerned for me."

But what's changed so much in him? She had asked herself the question several times over the past month, and had found no really satisfying answer. Even Fredo, when she had asked him, didn't seem to quite understand the difference in his brother. But he certainly wasn't the same.

There was about him a calmness, a joy and happy playfulness that clearly hadn't been there before. *No,* she reflected, *he wasn't like that before.* It wasn't so long ago, she had remarked to Fredo, that he had become taciturn, even sullen. He had stopped coming to the chicken stand to say hello and had even turned down offers for tea with the two of them. That *was* definitely strange.

But now all seemed surprisingly well with him.

Yes, really well, altogether.

Paulo was happy. Far happier, in fact, than he had ever been before in his life. He had noticed himself how much more relaxed he had become since his last secret visit to the Beyonde and his lessons with the sage.

"You and Fredo should come by my stand," he offered to Francesca now. "Things are going well and I can buy you both tea. Will you come sometime?"

"Of course. We ... I ... would be delighted to come," she replied a little nervously.

After the last intense round of discussions with Zeph, Paulo had returned to his daily life and had decided to redouble his efforts to apply the ideas that formed the magician's obscure and demanding – not to mention highly *bizarre* – curriculum. He collected his wood, went to market, dealt with his customers – and the Mayor; and in all his many activities he tried to see in what way the wizard's teachings might be able to help him.

He found that he called more often on Zeph now for advice, and always when he had to deal with his customers did he make sure that the magician was somewhere there in the back of his mind. It astonished him how much lighter, in fact, he found his work when he felt that his wise teacher was with him as a sort of constant companion.

Though his customers were still often quite irksome (sometimes downright obnoxious), and Benito's fish still smelled horribly (especially on warmer days), Paulo began to focus on the special Presence he had been told was also there, despite the fact he couldn't yet see it or feel it clearly. The soldiers would still harass and bully the market people and the Mayor would serve himself a basketful of apples from someone's stand and grin obscenely without paying; the braziers wouldn't burn properly because of the drizzling rain and the smoke would drift in Paulo's direction and burn his eyes; a customer would complain and short change

him because he thought his bundles of kindlin' weren't big enough
to start his fire.

And Paulo would look out at the many scenes before him,
shaking his head slowly in bewilderment, and tell himself – "*All
this is somehow just a show*. Underneath there is something else
here: nothing terrible is really happening, not personally to me,
and not to anyone really. We're all making this up together, these
pictures. And there is something else, something … *hidden* under
all I see."

Somehow, somewhere, he now mused back at his stand, even
here in the market place with these harried people rushing and
pushing at the stalls is an extraordinary Knowledge, and *that* is
real.

He looked again, staring.

It had to be there, somewhere out there.

…Where?

At the same time as these questions were going through the
wood seller's mind, a solitary old man was slowly winding his
way into the market square from one of the many side alleyways.
Entering the bustling place, he picked his way carefully among the
market stalls but he didn't appear to be shopping or looking for
anything special, rather to be just looking around. He said a quiet
hello to some of the people he crossed, but on the whole he simply
smiled at the many passers-by.

In time he came within sight of the kindlin' stand and made his
way toward the busy young wood merchant. Paulo finished with a
customer and caught the approaching figure out of the corner of
his eye, and a grin broke out on his face.

"Greetings, young man!" the figure called out from underneath
a wide-brimmed felt hat, and came forward.

"Hi, Marco. What brings you to the market place this
morning?" Paulo asked.

"I've lost something important and now I'm looking for it," he
whispered. Then he stepped back a pace, took off his hat and

exclaimed laughingly, "It's such a dreadful bother! Be a good friend now and help me find it, would you?"

The wood seller grinned. "Now what could you have gone and lost, I wonder?" Paulo asked, though it seemed he already knew very well. His eyes sparkled as he said: "A smelly old fish, that's it! You've lost a fish you bought from Benito a week ago. No, I've got it – it's a bundle of sodden kindlin' that won't start your fire you bought from me. No, that's not right either..." His eyes narrowed in concentration. "Let's see, just maybe it's something that I'm also having a hard time finding, 'sthat it?"

Marco's face lit with a wide smile. "Don't give me that, you rascal!" he replied, chuckling, and put his hat back on, drawing the brim down low again. "You know only too well, my boy, this blessed thing that's still so elusive to me. No need to tell you, of all people!"

He lowered his voice as if to tell a secret. "But now we're just going to have to get much more serious about this search. Time's just not going to last forever." He tapped the center of his chest. "I feel it here in these old bones of mine. So, I'm setting us a challenge, the two of us. Today and for several weeks to come we'll both try to work more thoroughly with our perceptions and self-concepts. I've been thinking that they're perhaps the secret Key our strange magician-friend has been speaking about. What do you think?"

Paulo nodded vigorously. "Sure, let's try that. I give you my word I'll do my best." He threw his arms wide, "And look! If I'm not already here in the best of all places in the whole world to put it into practice! Hundreds of opportunities every day, right here! So, let's look all around us really carefully, then dive down deep into our thoughts just like real explorers do and find the path there back Home. So, till the next time we discuss our adventures: good luck, Marco!"

"Have faith, my friend!" Marco called to Paulo as he turned to go. "We'll yet find the secret passage Home – soon, *I feel it*. Till our next meeting at our sacred riverside sanctuary – the old bench!"

With that the old man left the market place, and Paulo turned to face the next customer hastening toward his stall.

Waiting patiently behind his wood pile, Paulo did over time manage to discover his buried opinions, to draw his mind away from his automatic behaviors, and back to the stories Zeph had taught him – the *other* explanation for the world he perceived around him.

"While you're in the market place, Paulo," the wizard had counseled him, "look specifically at your *inner reactions* to the events around you. This will already give you a very clear indication of your perceptions and interpretations – the unseen contents of your mind. Doing so will help you discover what is all the same and one."

And ever so gradually things did actually begin to evolve in his sight. The individual interests that had so divided the merchants and town officials – pitting one against the other in constant battle – now more often appeared to resemble each other in his observant eyes. The upsets and dramas around him inevitably contained precisely the same motivations and purposes, he saw: the desire to feel safer, more respected, comforted, and justified. Behind their needs and irritations, their dreams and crises, Paulo found the same background thoughts and beliefs in all the Townspeople. And in a curious, mysterious way, this seemed already to bring him a lot more peace than he had ever previously known in the market square.

Somehow just knowing it was all a great mistake, just a mistaken understanding of their common dilemma, seemed to help him find more ease of mind. The peacefulness was all the greater when he remembered the reason why the drama and pain were of no great substance or consequence: because Love would never have allowed this chaos to become truth in the place of peace. Nothing had ever happened to that Love; it was still there … whole, perfect, waiting and expectant.

Even now.

CHAPTER FIFTY

Waves of Fury

One morning, some days after Marco's passing by, Paulo was kept busy by a constant stream of customers. There seemed to be no end! He wondered even if something wasn't occurring within him that was now becoming visible on the outside: the number of customers coming to his stand to buy wood seemed to be growing week by week. He was a lot busier than before.

Fortunately, he was now able to collect wood more easily since he was no longer afraid of harvesting right alongside the Domain's Fortress Wall where kindlin' was always more abundant. He would stack the piles of wood on a small two-wheel cart he had built, and trundle the entire load to market to satisfy the unexpectedly large number of customers now appearing at his stall every day.

"Here you go, ma'am," he addressed the busy baker's wife, and handed her two piles of kindlin' tied with string. "If you care to pay when you come tomorrow that would be quite alright."

"No, dear boy. I have a minute now." She fished in her purse for a coin, handing it to him.

He glanced at the money then prepared her change.

"That's quite fine, Paulo," she said. "Please keep any extra for yourself."

He thanked her kindly and placed the coin in his pocket. When she had left, he pulled the coin back out again and looked at it. He held the tarnished copper piece in his palm. 'It's so bizarre,' he mused to himself. 'I was sure that money was such a problem. It seemed so hard to fight for all the time. Why do people now insist on leaving me more money than necessary?'

He quickly stowed the coin back in his pocket to serve a grim and somber customer now arriving at his stall.

Moving with surprising speed, the man suddenly stretched out his hand and grabbed a bundle of wood which he stuck under his nose. He sniffed loudly and scowled, then bent his eyes down to the young wood seller.

"Boy, you'd better change jobs. This wood's damp! Here, take this, and consider yourself lucky!" He flicked a couple of pennies on the ground and turned around to go.

Every muscle in Paulo's body went instantly taut. He tried to breathe calmly, but felt a sort of explosion erupt in the pit of his stomach. The sensation rose rapidly through his chest, coursed through his throat and tightly clenched jaw, and within a heartbeat fiery waves of scorching hate broke like a geyser upon his mind.

"There's absolutely no question about it - Life would be finally so much better if I didn't have to work here and face so many stupid, inconsiderate, not to mention thoroughly rude, people."

The hateful thought forked through Paulo's mind like lightening. But he noticed its devastating passage, and closely followed its course.

After a minute he unclenched his fists.

"I'm not feeling good – not at all."

He waited another moment, then the conclusion rang out softly: *"I do have a choice."*

He listened once more to the gentle silence that he knew now filled the empty spaces of the noisy market place, and found the counsel he needed. "My true goal isn't this hate. I don't have to feel hurt. There's always something else…"

And suddenly the magician's voice came through to him, clear and convincing:

"Paulo, would you really be feeling so upset if you felt a warm and tender Presence here with you in the market place? After all,

what you're looking at in this man isn't the truth, but simply more
hateful and confused images cast by darkness. There's no need
anymore for hate or hurt; you can ask for something else in the
place of those tired old feelings."

Paulo's heavy, angry breathing slowed further and his irritation
began to pass. He couldn't deny that he would feel much better if
kindness and calmness now filled his mind instead of this burning
injustice.

"Is it really satisfied, respectful customers you need to feel
well? *Is that all?*" Zeph probed. "Or perhaps it's something even
more important than that now? How about the remembrance of
that special quality that links yourself with this man?"

Paulo reflected hard. All these thoughts and questions passed
through his mind within a flicker of time. He understood by now
that they were the key to finding peace amidst the countless upsets
that assailed him every day.

"Paulo, try to understand," the wizard counseled, "you don't
need to suffer any more – being a victim belongs to the past now.
You don't need to be bothered any longer by what you think are
the faults, sins and injustices of others. What you're really looking
for beyond your daily upsets is present. *Something else is there …
even now.*"

Paulo looked towards the customer as he hoisted the wood
under his arm, and summoned within himself the willingness to
find something else within the situation.

"*Something else is here,*" he declared firmly to himself. "This
anger is definitely *not* what I want right now. Despite what I think
and feel about this person, above and beyond all the noise and
hate – *something else is also present.*"

He stared fixedly at the man's back and found another thought
appear within his mind, an idea that was less familiar, but not
unpleasant.

He saw that what his customer had really wanted from him
was something other than what he had actually come looking for.
The customer came to the wood stand seeking good, dry kindlin';

and he himself was looking for money and respect, things that a client should give him. But that wasn't the end of the story. They seemed to have different goals in the matter, but in actual fact they shared precisely the same deeper interest…

Paulo began to smile quietly to himself. *Something much bigger, greater, and far more wonderful than any dry wood or silly copper coins,* he reflected.

Paulo turned to the man who was stomping away in a cloud of righteousness.

"Yes, sir, perhaps you're right. My wood might be slightly damp today," he said calmly and naturally, and turned to greet the next customer, thinking nothing more of the matter. The man shot a confused look at Paulo, then left.

And inside Paulo felt deeply satisfied.

Free.

Later that morning the customer returned to the stand and held out in his hand the coins in full payment for his bundle of wood. He didn't say a word but just extended the money towards Paulo.

Paulo's face lit with a slight, knowing smile.

He was happy – but not because he had been paid. He was freed from his own hate and judgment and was happy even without the payment. 'That's the freedom,' he said to himself. There had been no real injustice; no harm was done. The irascible customer could not ever have removed that which Paulo so sorely needed.

'I was upset, yes – but not because of what the dour-faced man did to me. There's no reason I can justify to be angry with him.'

His brother, the customer, was distressed about his personal sense of being – as was everyone in the market place. That morning it so happened he thought he would feel better if he took something from someone else without paying. 'That's certainly common enough.' Paulo could understand this desire all the more because he had done the same with Zeph in the market place. And it was just another silly error, that's all. 'Everybody does that', he said to himself, 'try to take things they haven't been offered.

They're so eaten up by feelings of deprivation and lack and injustice, and think they need to take something without asking in order to feel better.'

Of course that's not how you feel better, he said to himself.

"You can feel better only by remembering the presence of Love within your true Self," he remembered the sage telling him once. Yes, everyone was just looking for something else ... They were all simply looking for that forgotten mystical feeling of Love, that exceptional feeling of being whole and complete again, and unmarred. The extraordinary sense they had all lost and that left them adrift, lacking, constantly searching, and constantly irritated. And yet the very same feeling that could be found anywhere.

Even here.

Paulo returned to serving the following customer but was still preoccupied by the morning's event. There was something else there, some other niggling issue he was missing understanding; and then it came to him.

For a fleeting instant he had been furious with the customer, yes, but even more so with another person. With *himself.*

'That seems odd. Why would that be?'

In fact he had been particularly upset with the man's actions, he saw, because it had had thrown him back into the whirlpool of his own self-doubt and spite. It had reminded him that he still felt his life was impossibly miserable because he thought he should be doing something more worthwhile and better paying than selling wood. He had thought the man was somehow right: "You'd better change jobs..."

The buyer's attitude had brought out in Paulo his own belief that life was unjust and cruel. Unfortunate situations constantly seemed to appear in his life for no seeming reason, as if some evil Lord still sought to punish him and keep him imprisoned.

Yet none of this was true.

None of this was accurate but purely the mischievous activity of the Maker in his mind. It was the depressing identity he still contained which was tied to the world and its situations of chaos.

When his mind was lost in thoughts of separation from his Home, he felt that life would never change or improve, and there was nothing he could do but learn to suffer with more patience and swallow his pain and resentment. He felt locked in an interminable prison, trapped by the unkind will of some harsh and thoughtless Ruler.

But it wasn't true, just an unhappy game, since freedom, love and strength were available to him at all times. When this awareness returned back to his mind, Paulo knew he was never far from the happiness and peace he sought. He knew also that he was always capable of making changes in his life if he wished to improve his situation.

He drew in a long, peaceful breath, and now sent his inquisitive eye back out into the market place, wondering what further havoc the Maker could possibly be preparing for him there.

CHAPTER FIFTY-ONE

Real Help

Images of shoppers and soldiers, travelers and tradesmen of all sorts jostled and bumped before his eyes.

'It's just here somewhere, in this crazy busy square,' Paulo spoke to himself. "Yeah – that Presence of light the magician constantly speaks about, some understanding of the perfect nature of all things.'

No absence or error in life, nothing missing or scarred in all the universe – that is what the sage had taught him was real. Everything he was looking for was right there. And so he began to listen even more carefully inside in order to detect the unseen presence of this pure, remarkable vision.

He surveyed the next customer: her head high, her chin pronounced and her eye's flitting nervously in all directions; a small kerchief held daintily to her nose to ward off the foul odors, the young and impatient doctor's daughter arrived at his stall.

She rarely came to the market place; only, in fact, when her mother was otherwise occupied. Paulo avoided meeting her eyes as she cast a brief, chill gaze upon him. Were it not for the daily need for the wood, she wouldn't come by his stall at all, he was quite sure.

"Yes, she too contains what you seek, Paulo," the magician whispered. "There's no reason to think there is something wrong with you because she might judge you, my boy. Tell me, why do you think she might disapprove of you?"

Quite obviously because he was only a poor wood seller, came his immediate response; that he was nothing in comparison to the respectable daughter of a doctor. This thought upset him a lot. He was still tempted to believe it was true – that he would never amount to much in terms of the village and its people.

He hesitated, and noticed the error.

He asked to understand and then a light came into his mind. 'Why, the doctor's daughter only judges me because she judges herself! Of course! She's also lost in dreams of darkness, and she's listening to a terrifying voice telling her she's worthless.'

"Quite correct, Paulo," Zeph spoke. "Yes – she can't bear to face the judgment she's laid upon herself. It's excruciatingly painful for her to face these evil thoughts. So it feels altogether normal and certainly more comfortable to see these thoughts portrayed outside of herself, onto other people such as yourself. She feels in this way reassured that although she might contain some faults, at least she's less severely marred than others."

Paulo relaxed. The way she looked down upon him in fact had absolutely nothing to do with him at all. Surprisingly, he found himself suddenly feeling a warm compassion for the doctor's daughter in place of his habitual judgment.

'This is no true solution for her, he concluded. She needs to know she's already perfect and exceptional, a wonderful and holy part of the One Great People – like us all. Just the *same* as everyone, not better than us because of her special status in Towne.'

The young woman huffed and fidgeted as Paulo prepared the package of wood. He confidently placed the bundle in her basket, and his eyes gleamed with a kindness and gentle laughter. There was really nothing wrong with her after all, he thought. Nor with him.

She stretched out her smooth-gloved hand with a coin and placed it gingerly in his palm. He gave her the change for her wood with ease. *Something bright flashed in his mind.* He let his eyes now rest upon her, and suddenly the image of a perfect equal came to mind, strong and lovely … infinitely acceptable.

The doctor's daughter glanced at him a faint instant, and hesitated. Just for a second, the briefest moment, Paulo saw a question in her eyes, a confused, relieved surprise. And behind the question was a spark of remembrance in her mind, of Love, of Kindness and Beauty, of *her* beauty, of worthiness, and homecoming.

On the other hand, the young woman's mother, the doctor's wife, when she came to fetch the family's kindlin' which was most days, would carry a look of great pity and sympathy in her big dark eyes for the poor wood merchant, and would always give him a little extra money.

Paulo didn't mind the money but felt strangely uncomfortable with the way she was charitable with him. *How would Zeph explain this?*

"She, like her daughter, also senses there is something acutely wrong with her and feels trapped, invalidated, even desecrated," the wizard explained. "But her way of finding comfort is different. She would find people less fortunate than herself and demonstrate great pity with the suffering she finds in the world. Though she appears quite loving and generous, she is secretly reassured to find other people who are weak and needing her help. This is the way she reinforces her feeling of personal strength.

"Within her darkened imagination she is remade whole again, because she sees others who are a little more condemned than she is, people she can help. And in helping others, her attention is diverted away from her own abject condition and onto yours. Within her cheerless world she is a little safer, a little more blessed and comforted because it is obvious the Lord has looked more kindly upon her than upon others. Somehow, she reasons, he must have judged her more favorably. This is the reason for her helping others.

"This behavior can be a rather unpleasant, even devious, strategy for staying locked within the confines of the Maker-personality. It is a way of wrapping oneself in special favor, a way of keeping valuable differences between people to avoid recognizing the strength and hope in all members of the One Great People."

"Okay – but I can't honestly say that I mind the gift of the money," replied Paulo. "Could that be wrong?"

"Not in the least," Zeph replied. "We can help others materially as much as we want, and we should. Learning to be helpful in terms of this world is important. All those stuck in the Domain need assistance at some level, and everyone there is in some way sick and needy of healing.

"But anytime we focus on the problems or weakness in another person as an indirect way of supporting our own imperfect self-image, we are keeping him imprisoned. If we manage to offer others the assistance they need materially, all the while remembering the inherent Strength in the spirit of each villager, then we give them the *real help* they need, and not just a few simple coins."

The boy frowned. "But what about people who really *are* in desperate situations?" he asked, somewhat perplexed. "How can they possibly feel everything's okay?"

The magician answered thoughtfully, "It's certainly very challenging, trying to look at situations that seem disastrous in order to perceive them differently. And we should above all *never* presume to tell someone they're incorrect for feeling suffering – that would be very unjust and unkind. A brother who is faced with a desperate situation must first be understood in terms of *his* perceptions, which are undoubtedly very real for him. He is afraid, and in his fearful state he sees frightening images coming to hurt him and maybe even those he loves. That's why before trying to help others, we must first learn to put ourselves in their shoes and remember that, if we were them, filled with their same thoughts of vulnerability, we too might find it difficult to find the comfort that's there.

"Still, this doesn't mean of course that relief and help aren't there with us. Despite everything that might be going on, Love and Strength are *always* available. When a brother feels pain, he is in reality afraid of the peace that is already present there for him. The pain is a screen, a protection against the Love he believes will enter his mind and erase the images he has made, as we have discussed before. And so to protect himself it is certain that he is still condemning himself, and perhaps others, for the vicious, unresolved crime he keeps within his mind."

Paulo then asked, a little incredulous, "And then they're just supposed to find peace with the difficult conditions in their lives? And that's *all*?"

"Well, no. That's not all," replied Zeph calmly within Paulo's thoughts. "Over time as we're able to release more fear and guilt, to remember the peace waiting for us beneath the frightening circumstances, then changes can begin to happen in our lives. When self-judgment begins to loosen its fierce grip on our minds, our personal experience of the situation evolves and becomes lighter, freer. Then the outside conditions can begin to reflect this fresh new experience."

The boy replied, "So then the outside will get better."

"That is not necessarily so. While a person still tries to block out Love, his mind will remain tightly netted within the identity of guilt and specialness. In that case, sadness and suffering will be inevitable, even if the outside physical conditions do appear momentarily to improve. But when we do manage to free ourselves even just a little from our self-condemnation, then we free ourselves to real peace of mind. Simultaneously we free the outside to become something new that reflects the Beauty we've found inside."

"So then what do we give others if it's not really money, for instance, that helps?" the boy wondered.

"But do indeed give money! Paulo," the wizard advised, "and any other material assistance, if that's how you feel moved to act. It's not after all what you give, but *how* you give, that will make the real difference to someone. Once you begin to release yourself from your own personal need to help, then everything you do for another will be filled with real healing.

"When you sense Love within yourself, when you feel the Peace that is there for you in all your own difficult situations, then your gifts to others will always be maximal. The person whom you help will *feel* the choice for peace and self-forgiveness you have made, and will be encouraged to do the same. That is how you can be helpful. At the same time, if offering money or any other material help is the way you enter into a healing relationship with another person, then all the better.

"Paulo, look now around you right here," the sage requested of the boy. Paulo cast his gaze in a wide arc around the square, at the multitudes of Townspeople filling his range of vision.

"There is no one here in this market place – *not one person* – who does not feel in some way that there is something deeply, horribly wrong with him. But this is only his current unconscious choice. It is because of this choice that he is present here in the Domain at this time – because he has made the decision to separate his mind from his original abstract condition of holiness, and has become lost in dreams of form and individuality.

"In every instant of his life he carries Light and Strength within him, although he is completely unaware of them. In every instant, all those you see as suffering and unfortunate remain the beautiful and powerful People of the King, far more important than any role or condition they might have adopted for themselves in village life. In every instant, you are capable of seeing the astonishing illusion of weakness and pain around you, and simultaneously the powerful Light everyone carries within him that comes directly from the Kingdom.

"Not for the last time shall I say, and you must perhaps forgive me for repeating myself: the world is made of many different *chaotic appearances,* but of only one same *magnificent Life.* So, now bring the multitudinous appearances and problems you see around you every day, bring them all to the same understanding, Paulo. *That* is how you will resolve the enigma of the Domain.

That is how you will find the Knowing and release your mind from its prison.

"Try now to let nothing be an exception to this rule, something that would stand outside the truth, to be the one thing that would confirm separation, sin and suffering. Your King is kind, and would never bless some with more and others with less. And he would never divide his People into these many separate and warring parts. This chaos is not his work.

"There is only *one* People of which you are all part. All conflict and chaos you see are part of the same collective desire to manifest suffering in order to keep Love at bay. A question of form certainly, but not of truth or reality. Don't be fooled any longer..."

And so it must be possible, Paulo whispered to himself, surveying some fancily dressed councilmen now disputing with a group of ragged peasant farmers – *No differences and only one peaceful Life we all share.*

So it's not really the rich town administrators and elected officials who are the nasty, evil presence in our lives... Look at them, after all, those despicable, selfish, arrogant, thieving... no, wait! That can't be right.

"Zeph, what do I do when I find all these ugly thoughts in me, judgments like this?" he asked.

The magician responded with a simple answer: "Just don't take them too seriously, that's all.

"But what does that mean, more precisely?" Paulo demanded curtly.

"It means don't attack yourself for the condemning thoughts you'll still find within your mind. And don't believe in these judgments and criticisms either. Just notice them, and allow them to be corrected. These thoughts are simply incorrect, based on false assumptions, and a mistaken attempt to try to find peace through attack and difference. You're well aware now that peace can't ever come from attacking or condemning someone. That's just silly. And your confusion, as hateful as it may be, isn't bad or sinful –

it's simply a mistake, as is everything, and again just requires correction."

"Please, Paulo, while you're in the market place, use your time here for a special purpose: use this as your own special classroom to uncover the contents of your mind, and learn to bring all your dark thoughts – without exception now – to the light of understanding. You won't be able to come with me along the Path and enter the Golden City while these shadows still cloud your mind: because while you condemn you'll still think that your condemnations have power and purpose, and you'll want to remain here in the Domain to pursue this purpose, and the sense of power and reality this gives you.

"Just relax and let the importance of your judgments be gently corrected for you. Let their meaninglessness be shown to you. Now let that become your mission in the market place…"

CHAPTER FIFTY-TWO

The Best He Could Do

Over time Paulo did finally become more aware of the real purpose for his being there at the stall in the market place, of selling his kindlin' and dealing with all the different people that came into his life. More people came now every day, giving him plenty of reasons and opportunities to release his misconceptions – to practice the special art of *True Forgiveness*. In this way the fatigue and ennui of his work that had always weighed so heavily on him every day started to disappear altogether. He knew *why* he was there: the same old activity, but seen in a completely different way.

Paulo found himself one morning at the market looking around the square as he had done so often in the past, a break in the flow of customers allowed him a few minutes of quiet to be with himself.

'Many different people, *just one Life,*' he spoke to himself gazing at the scenes before him, 'as Zeph has said so many times.'

The lives of the many Townspeople that crossed his path every day were really *exactly* the same as his, he was coming to see. The same confusion and fears were in everyone, he saw, not just in him alone, and this understanding always lightened his mood.

Even when his customers came to him upset or were difficult and complaining, Paulo could now laugh and smile with them. That was a pleasant change! Their problems were really nothing more than the mistaken thought that there was something deeply wrong with them and their existence. And under that dark thought was the even more terrifying vision of some violent, wrathful King.

'Just mistakes, that's all,' he would tell himself.

Yet all these frightening ideas occupied the villagers' minds, he now understood, purely in order to avoid confronting something they feared even more. What they were all really scared of was the plain truth: the magnificent truth of their Reality. How bizarre, he thought, yet it was true. They feared the wonderful reality of their One undivided Being even more than the image of some terrifying, vengeful God they imagined rampaging within their minds.

But despite their most fearful convictions about the nature of Heaven, there was really nothing to be frightened of. Okay, so Love was great, and Oneness and Wholeness certainly appeared intimidating, but it was only another mistake to believe that any harm could come from such gentleness. No, within the joyful experience of Acceptance, they would remember happiness and Home. They would remember *Themselves*.

These thoughts and other observations turned over in Paulo's mind now as he stared at the busy comings and goings in the town square. He prepared himself for a customer coming in his direction, smiling at the harried buyer as she approached his stall…

How can I help?

The best he could do, Paulo had come to understand, was to help his customers see that their upsets and problems were perhaps not as terribly serious as they believed; that they did not necessarily have the meaning they were giving them. Something else was still present, something their anxious minds were still covering with countless layers of difficulties. And this *something else* was not dangerous, but extraordinary.

His customers, in turn, seemed to understand that something had changed in the young wood seller. They returned more frequently to his stand, often just to say hello, and sometimes they came bearing gifts of fruit and handcrafts. More and more frequently they refused to accept the change for their purchases, and Paulo thanked them sincerely.

With the cheerfulness and joy that he now shared with everyone, indeed, Paulo found that over time more and more customers came and left increasingly large sums of money at his stand. Shoppers would come with cups of hot tea delighted to be able to share a few minutes of their day relaxing and chatting with the happy, calm wood seller, and this pleased the boy greatly.

In this way Paulo found that he had more money at the end of each week than he could ever have dreamed of, though now he was no longer surprised. In fact, it felt quite normal. His mother was delighted, of course, and let him finally buy the feather mattress he had always dreamed of, and a nice woolen coat and new leather boots, too. But these things were really quite unimportant to him. More than his fine clothes and comfortable bed, he felt blessed because the sadness, the anxiety and resentment that had permanently haunted his life were finally disappearing.

All these material changes helped Paulo understand the important lesson behind it all: that he was now *free*. He was free to be healthy and well; he was free to have friends; he was free to be sufficiently provided for. But most importantly he was free to feel the warmth, the deep love and the great appreciation of his elder brother, Zeph, and of His King. He was quietly happy with what he had come to feel within. Inside was now at last a far calmer, more restful place.

In turn, as a result, the outside was becoming a place of far less restriction and aggression. Gone were the harsh feelings of frustration and resentment as he made his way to market; not a glimmer remained of their past intensity. Gone too was the constant irritation and complaining, the victim-hood he had worn for years like protective clothing. When he woke in the morning, his heart no longer weighed with leaden feelings of regret and anxiety. Somehow the Domain no longer held such powers to assail and unbalance him. His existence felt lighter and less vulnerable, no longer defensive, as if his foundation were less rooted in the happenings and circumstances of the world around him.

He perceived what happened in the dramatic events around him, but they no longer seemed the anchoring point for his feelings, as if there was a slight distance between him and the world about him. Another realm was being born within his calmer mind, a place that held far greater promise for happiness and satisfaction than he could ever have imagined.

The Domain, it was clear, was not in fact as he had always insisted – the heavy sadness in his heart had only ever come from his way of perceiving his life. Another way of seeing and knowing his universe existed, and from that angle the world had in fact very little affect on him. Almost as if it were not even there…

Little by little, the market place did indeed become for Paulo a place of wonderful freedom (who would ever have imagined that!). While he was still tempted at times to re-live the old familiar feelings of irritation and imprisonment, he had now come to see the cost of doing so to his happiness, and the ludicrous beliefs on which these feelings were based.

Everyone he found in town was, in fact, looking for the very same remarkable happiness he was – despite what they *thought* they were looking for. Yet Paulo nevertheless still had to remind himself nearly every day what this quality really was: it was only *Love*, the Love that was the very Life itself they all sought… The Love that would replace all the false imaginings from which was born every day in their minds the hostile, unforgiving world of the Domain. The Love that embraced them all completely, magnificently; silently, and just out of sight.

Somewhere, indeed, very close by now…

CHAPTER FIFTY-THREE

A Splendid Marriage

As Paulo came to better understand his customers, he noticed just how many of them – like him – appeared under some tremendous, unseen pressure to perform better in life in order to feel happier about themselves. Though he often enjoyed talking with them now (a very pleasant change!), some of them, he saw, appeared disturbed by terrifying thoughts of incapacity.

Mr Bravuro for instance still needed to return home promptly after market, believing he was otherwise being exceptionally inconsiderate to his wife. He would hurry through the market place buying things as quickly – and cheaply, of course – as possible, and then would arrive home precisely at 12 o'clock in order to begin preparations for the midday meal.

How unfortunate, Paulo thought. *And how unnecessary.* But for Mr Bravuro it was really quite serious.

Mr Bravuro apparently believed there was something seriously wrong with him if his wife ever became upset, no matter what the problem was, and so he tried to avoid this as much as possible. The great strain and fatigue of this effort were obvious to Paulo but he felt there was little he could say.

Paulo wanted to talk to the gentleman about gracious self-acceptance and self-forgiveness, but it didn't seem appropriate – Mr Bravuro could easily misunderstand him, and become upset or frightened. The young wood seller didn't know how to begin to be useful to him, so he tried to let the magician speak for him in these conversations instead…

"Sir, if I might ask, why do you think there might be something wrong if you didn't manage to return home on time?" Paulo asked one day when Mr Bravuro appeared particularly stressed.

The gentleman eyed Paulo anxiously from over his spectacles. "Of course there's something wrong if I'm not at home on time, my boy."

"I'm sure you're right, sir, that it's not good to be late. But, sir, is there something wrong *with you* if you're not home on time?"

Mr Bravuro didn't know quite what to say but regarded the boy with curiosity, and became thoughtful.

In this way, Paulo tried to help Mr Bravuro see that he could certainly make the effort to do things well for his wife – indeed, try to do all things in life as correctly as possible – but didn't need to think there was anything wrong with *him* if he failed to. The gentleman showed sincere interest at this idea and smiled, and just for an instant his eyes lit with joy.

From that moment on, the gentleman's visits to the market place became surprisingly more frequent, and Paulo noticed that he no longer seemed in quite the same hurry to return home at midday. Apparently he had informed his wife that he now had some 'important business' to attend to in the market place; business, he insisted, that just couldn't be hurried. He would stay and chat with the wood seller who had now taken to presenting the gentleman with more challenging thoughts, asking him startling, bewildering questions on the subject of being happy, matters that the older man had never thought about before.

One day Mr Bravuro surprised Paulo, declaring that he finally wanted to find out why his wife was so perpetually unsatisfied, something he had never questioned till that time. Why exactly was she unhappy – for example – if things weren't done precisely as she wished, he wondered.

Paulo was impressed. It seemed Mr Bravuro was coming to see that his own sense of peace didn't necessarily depend on his wife's happiness, though he might nevertheless try in every way to fulfill her requests.

"Couldn't she also learn to be happy with me, regardless of my actions and decisions, as I'm learning to be with her?" he asked Paulo. "What do you think she would say?"

That very same morning the gentleman came hurrying back to the wood stand looking particularly flustered. "Young man, I think I might need some more of your assistance!" It seemed the conversation with his wife hadn't gone so very well.

In this way Paulo and Mr Bravuro began to spend many mornings together, drinking tea and discussing all manner of subjects. Mr Bravuro was delighted to be able to join in such wise conversation with the astute young wood seller. He would stroll up to Paulo's stand with two steaming cups of sweet tea, and, standing and sipping in the market place, they would work through the different questions that occurred to him.

The older man wondered, for example, what made people want and need things, and what made them get so upset when they didn't get them. He said the answer could help him a lot.

Standing there amidst the bustle of the town square, Mr Bravuro would then listen transfixed as the wood merchant related to him the story about the Separation and the coming of the Maker, events which had instilled them all with a powerful feeling of lack. As a result, Paulo explained, everyone constantly sought to do certain things in order to make them feel better – as if there was *something important missing* in their lives.

Obviously nothing other than the experience of the exceptional Love from their Home could ever satisfy the People's true need, Paulo explained. As he said, nothing outside their *True Mind* contained any real miraculous power to create pleasure or happiness. Belief – even conviction – could never render any objects or situations or people capable of answering a person's deep need for inner well-being and happiness.

One day, during their usual conversations, Paulo shared with Mr Bravuro the idea that this painful inner lack and sense of evil was also what motivated people to hurt each other and fight.

A look of profound upset swept across the gentleman's face. "I… I don't know quite how to say. I also fight sometimes, and, well, can get quite angry really." In fact, he felt deeply ashamed about his behavior.

Paulo laughed gaily. "But that's just the Spell, sir! Nothing more than that!"

Mr Bravuro stood dumbfounded.

To the older man, fighting with his spouse was proof of his wickedness. He was capable of screaming and even of wishing his wife's death, and this was entirely unacceptable to him.

"But that's just more of the belief that Love's disappeared," Paulo would cry, "which is the cause of the whole problem in the first place!"

Mr Bravuro frowned heavily, totally confused.

"Dear sir, *please* try to understand … you're *free*!" Paulo exclaimed loudly in response to what he felt was the gentleman's ongoing self-condemnation.

And the older man looked into the boy's gleaming eyes and felt touched by his wide, carefree smile; and somehow in that moment he knew that freedom and release from all his sad, desperate thoughts about himself and his life had to exist.

Paulo tried hard to find the right words. "You don't have to feel bad about yourself just because you've been thinking you're in a prison. It's normal to make mistakes when you're not thinking clearly, when you're feeling such terribly unkind things about yourself. If you can forgive yourself and understand why you do such silly things, you can forgive your wife and then won't be so upset when she makes mistakes and is harsh with you.

"If she's confused because of the Maker, then she'll naturally be very unpredictable and likely to say and do some very hurtful things. She might even hate you and wish you harm, but that's okay. That's quite normal and you can expect that. She's just feeling pain and fear, that's all. It's not sinful, of course; it's just a mistake."

Mr Bravuro responded, "Just a mistake? Quite normal, you say? Why, that's quite amazing, I think. And there I was filled with such bitter feelings for her."

Paulo continued, "She tries hard to throw this terrible feeling away from herself, and then it falls upon you. Or it could fall on someone else, or even on herself as an accident or sickness. It doesn't matter, it's all the same mistake. Just try to watch your reactions to it, and try not to judge it all. Remember that everything you're feeling for the moment is just a mistake, because you don't really see anything clearly yet. You can even watch yourself trying to explain and justify your criticisms and feelings, but it won't be right."

"So I must observe my reactions – is that all?" the gentleman asked.

"The best thing we can do when people around us are upset," Paulo answered, "is to try to remember the *real* problem, sir, and not just see what's going on in front of us. When you remember that you're both upset just because you're both still secretly afraid of Love, and *not* because of what the other person said or did, then you'll feel calmer and will think of something better to say. You won't need to attack the other person or justify yourself because you know that's not any kind of a solution.

"You just want to remind everyone that you can all feel a kind of *gentle peace* no matter what's going on, no matter what's happened – and *that's* the answer. Maybe you can't say it directly, because sometimes it makes people feel even more scared and angry than they already are. But *you* can feel it inside your heart. Then you can relax and try to think of something better and more useful to say."

Mr Bravuro seriously considered these thoughts.

"You mean, she's not really angry at *me*?" he asked hesitantly, and pondered some more. "What you mean is that she's upset with me only because inside herself she feels this pain, this rift and hole you speak about, and then she claims the pain is because of *me*, is that right?" He considered further. "That's really quite… *strange*, isn't it?"

He smiled behind his spectacles and his eyes gleamed brightly with delight at his discovery.

"Yes, right!" Paulo answered. "*All* pain starts with this going away from Love. The hate and anger are only because of this scary story which keeps going on deep within our soul, none of which is true. There's no battle against some mighty King who's set out to punish us for our sins. There is no hateful crime. And there is no Love gone."

The gentleman regarded the boy with awe.

Then Paulo heard himself say, "It's all a myth, sir – an *illusion*."

Mr Bravuro sought for the right words. "So … you're saying that it's all present, right here. Right now. The magical thing we have always believed we have lost. That special feeling of warmth and kindness."

"Exactly," Paulo replied.

The next moment the boy was lost deep in thought himself. He paused and let his eyes search outwards. *Yes, it's all here… somewhere. That's what Zeph says. But where?*

Mr Bravuro then told the boy that, in his thoughts, his wife had always been the cause of all his misery. But in actual fact, he now felt, he had only ever been *using* her to this end. He said he suddenly felt freer, because he could begin to see that she really had nothing at all to do with his unhappiness. *Or* with his happiness.

"What a strange thing relationships are," he said to the boy. "My wife still thinks that I'm the cause of all *her* problems." He laughed heartily. "We certainly seem to have been well made for each other. Thank goodness I've been able to find some peace in the matter."

He had in actual fact been wondering recently if his wife wouldn't be able to follow these same lessons of peacefulness. "Wouldn't she be so much happier?

"Paulo, just think! Both people in a relationship learning how to be happy – but *not* because of the other person! Both people learning finally how to be kind toward themselves, and to free themselves from pain. What a splendid goal for a marriage!

"Wouldn't it be marvelous if we could actually look together at how silly we are, being upset with our partners and blaming the other person for our problems and feelings? That could even be fun, don't you think?"

Paulo reiterated an essential principle the sage had taught him. "Certainly that'd be wonderful, sir. But I think your only real goal for the moment should be trying to understand your own confused thoughts. Once you do this, then everything you say will be kind and a good example to everyone else. We don't ever need another person to change in the way we think they should, or to believe like us to make our way Home."

At this information Mr Bravuro looked thoughtful.

Paulo continued, "And, yes, it's certainly important to remember that we can all have wonderful, great happy lives – if we wish. We can all have lives that're completely free of upsets and full of Kindness. That's really normal."

Then when Mr Bravuro had left his stand, Paulo would spend a moment repeating these ideas to himself: "Yes, we can all remember true Love if we just wanted to, and it's possible and quite normal... It's normal because ... because –"

And this is where he would get stuck.

CHAPTER FIFTY-FOUR

An Amazing Thought

There was still some block within Paulo.

He wanted so desperately to accept that he deserved the magical blessings about which Zeph spoke constantly; but it was really difficult. It seemed maybe possible, but Paulo sensed there was still some engrained doubt within him. A block.

A certain key was still missing.

He knew he would need to find the proper willingness, since the magician had said he would have to learn to live perfectly happily there in Towne in order to grow accustomed to the brilliant light of his Home. How else could he be comfortable at Home, if he couldn't first accept its golden reflection in the world of shadows?

It's just really not so easy to do in practice, he puzzled. *How could I never again know a moment of fear or lack of peace – ever! – as Zeph says?*

This was the question that Paulo found so difficult to answer, and when he stood alone waiting for customers he would think about it over and over.

Looking around him in the town square, it was only too easy for him to hear the dreary refrain still chanting away in the hidden corners of his Maker-mind: "Really, Paulo, things could be much better, you know: it's really not adequate that you're still selling wood, and that you have no special friend to take care of you."

Yes, over and over it could still say the same old stupid things.

In spite of everything, despite all the amazing things he had seen and learned, it still seemed quite easy to find the reasons why his life could be miserable, sad, and totally insufficient. Though he focused on these feelings far less, and had come to much greater peace with the limitations of his life, the possibility of being upset was always there. It was difficult, even strange, to think that all experience could finally become one of an absolute happiness, without so much as the slightest shadow of fear or sadness.

And this begged further questions he now grappled with.

Was there really no possible way the world could affect him, not through sadness and suffering, and not with any pleasure or happiness either? Did the actual place of his experience really stand somewhere else outside the world around him?

He was coming to see that this was maybe exactly what the sage had been trying to say to him all along, at least when his thoughts and experience returned back into the clear-seeing True Mind. It seemed like the True Mind was maybe not really in the Domain at all.

But is there actually no real link at all between me and the outside world?

Though the idea seemed quite incredible, even impossible, it still needed to be considered. And it begged a further, disturbing question…

'If all the magician says is true,' he wondered, 'if one day I'm no longer bothered by anything in the world, if there's no real link like that between the world and me, and if my feelings come only from some other inside place – then who on earth is this person, *Paulo*?'

Other thoughts came to mind now, and he reflected once more on the questions of the farm work and Francesca. It had indeed been some time since they had caused him any concern.

Paulo had received a great deal from the market place conversations with Mr Bravuro because he saw that his own life still reflected similar difficulties. The nervous gentleman was thoroughly preoccupied by the questions with his wife, and he,

Paulo, had been similarly engulfed by his problems with work and companionship.

The older man and the younger boy had both made progress, but the class wasn't yet over. Yes, Paulo was now making good money selling more wood than ever. But that didn't seem to have fixed anything, not really. The money wasn't making such a big difference.

There was, he had to admit, still that tension, that deep seeking after something, perhaps the company of Francesca, that would help him feel better, more complete. Mr Bravuro tried to fix the missing part of himself by pleasing his wife; Paulo thought he would still very much like someone else to please and to care for.

So the real problem remained. He, too, still felt an absence within him. He could still be tempted to listen to the noisy discord and insatiable needs of his Maker-self. And that was why his feelings for Francesca were still tender. Though he was much closer, he hadn't yet really seen, not yet *known* the loveliness and fullness of that great Presence of Love of which the sage spoke. He had learned and seen so much, and yet there still seemed to be a gap – much smaller, but still there – between what he was looking for, and what he saw and felt. A gap that seemed occupied by a lot of boisterous wants, needs and questions.

And he wondered, 'What could help me stop paying attention to the Maker's crazy ideas and now come to some real peace? What kind of strength do I still need to get Home? And what can I do to finally remove this stupid Spell from my life? There *must* be a solution here somewhere…'

CHAPTER FIFTY-FIVE

Of the Bridge and the Purse

Paulo left the town square at market end and strolled down the path to the river. He walked slowly along its bank, then wandered up to the bridge. Over the balustrade wall he looked down at the enormous stone footings of the bridge's massive arches and the water that rushed and curled around them. The water swirled into whirlpools, washing and splashing into powerful currents that eddied down the river and all the way to the distant bend.

Intrigued, he dug his fingers into his satchel and took out the little black Spell Purse, placing it on the stone wall that overlooked the rushing waters. He took a step back, placing his feet squarely on the rough cobbled surface of the bridge, and sank his hands deep into his pockets, ruminating.

"The herbs inside this Purse must be very potent indeed."

The Spell, he noticed, seemed to have an effect on absolutely everything he thought and felt. It made him think exclusively in terms of himself, his life, his body, how it was feeling, where it went and what it did: its dramas, its aches, its conflicts and conditions, and generally exclude totally the Light from his awareness.

But there *was* Light, there *was* Life – he knew. *Somewhere.*

One exceptional, extraordinary Life, where none of these special, personal concerns were important anymore, he felt. And now he was learning that he didn't have to think or feel this preoccupying way about his own particular life any longer. He didn't have to think he wasn't worthy of kindness, or of knowing the truth. There was indeed a type of Love that didn't need him to prove he was worthy or special. There was no real lack within him. An *ocean* of Kindness was available somewhere without any constraints. He knew this…

But how do I get there?

He approached the wall, studying the Spell Purse more closely, placing his hands on the cool stone on either side of it.

Just one little movement of my hand, one little flick, he spoke to himself, and this little bag and all its silly magic would go over the side, gone forever, washed away. And then I'll never have to worry ever again about the evil Spell and the preoccupations with my life. Just one little…

He thought deeply.

– *No, that can't be the right answer.*

"Excellent, Paulo!" came Zeph's voice suddenly and clearly. "The answer is in learning that *the Spell is nothing*. The black pouch and its magical beliefs, the body and all your concerns, *are nothing* and have no power if you choose not to make them overly important.

"There is indeed Life, my friend, an existence *much* bigger than your personal life, your body and its concerns. Much bigger than *anyone's* life and concerns. To understand this you don't need to throw the Spell Purse away, or condemn or destroy it. The Spell Purse and the body are not the problem, neither is the Spell itself the problem.

"The problem is still simply within your continuing fear of That which is there on the other side of your illusions. Don't condemn the body now, or seek to reject it; that would be most unworthy. Just keep practicing smiling and laughing, and learn to be patient when you find yourself still getting caught up in the concerns of your life, that's all."

Paulo put the herb pouch back in his satchel and looked toward the distant horizon which was now cloudy with a late morning haze. He sighed, tired from all this thinking and reflecting.

Zeph's voice returned. "Paulo, my fine young apprentice in whom I have so much faith, just try now looking past the mist."

Paulo stared again toward the murky cloudiness in the distance.

"Pay no more attention to the Spell," the wizard continued. "That is no longer your path. You are nearly Home. Soon now you will be there, *I feel it*. There is an opportunity before you. You've done very well and now may start to feel the warmth of your Home already here. Just look through the mist."

Look through the mist…?

Paulo stared out at the grayish daylight covering the river and countryside. He turned around now and surveyed from afar the town center where the Townspeople were hurrying on their way home for the midday meal.

…What mist?

Part 4

– CHAPTER FIFTY-SIX –

Marco and the Old Bench

Marco Salvatori wandered slowly and quietly through the village streets, quite at home in the crowded alleys, twisting passage ways and dim cobbled squares of the ancient medieval town. 'This strange and hostile world…,' he whispered to himself as he went. '*And this, the loveliest place on earth, I do believe.* Here live my friends. No! – not just my friends, but *my brothers.*'

Presently a shutter creaked open.

"Ah, there, Master!"

A woman's face popped out of a narrow window followed by an arm waving a white kitchen towel. "Over here!"

Marco stopped and turned his face upward to the open window, and a broad smile lit his face. "What is it, my dear lady? What can an old man like myself do for you?"

"Do wait! I have some freshly baked bread here. I seem to have a loaf or two too many, and I would be grateful if you would take one off my hands."

The face disappeared from view and a minute later the front door of the building, an ancient slab of worn and carved oak, creaked open.

A round and pleasant, ruddy face greeted Marco on the doorstep and placed a warm loaf wrapped in the white dish towel in his hands.

"There you go! It would have been such a waste, and my husband would have only given me grief. Do us both a favor and take this home with you, please."

"I shall be only too happy to render you this small service," he said, and his eyes gleamed with warmth and good humor. "But I do not really doubt for a minute your ability to count your bread making, and so I thank you from the bottom of my heart for your generosity. Accept my blessings, dear lady, for both yourself and your husband." He tipped his hat and turned to go. "Good day to you, and thank you again," he said quietly, and left.

Marco had become happy – genuinely happy.

For the first time in his life, he was simply and undeniably peaceful. In his many daily meetings with the villagers he had finally discovered the particular quality of spirit that had escaped him these many years past; and in this search he was surprised to find, *delighted* to find, they were all perfectly equal. No matter what harmful and vindictive things they managed to get up to, he understood that the villagers and he were only motivated by the exact same desire: the deep wish to find release from the Spell, and further peace and comfort in their lives.

The Townspeople had unknowingly helped Marco, and he was sincerely grateful.

A hidden sense of superiority had come to his awareness during the course of his inward journey, and had felt insurmountable, a bane, a dark spot lying deeply rooted in his character. But countless moments of finding himself faced with the perfect likeness he shared with the Townspeople had allowed a real shift toward humility, toward self-forgiveness. And this in turn had permitted an opening, a passage away from his solitude, relief from the isolation that had become his routine experience of life.

A real and genuine kindness did in fact exist, Marco had found, something above the sense of condemnation he had constantly harbored for himself which had pushed him to seek comfort in seclusion. And he had decided that helping others to find this remarkable presence in their lives was really the only role that made any sense for him now.

It was clear to the villagers as well that something important had altered in the solitary old man. Their regard no longer turned away from the stranger as he passed by, wrapped in his cloak of indifference. They approached him, greeted him; and he in turn accepted them, welcomed them, and warmed them in his company in a way that managed to calm even the most suspicious, agitated mind.

As only a true brother could possibly do – *he loved them*. For Marco had finally managed to see past their fears and spite, past their squabbles and gossip, only to discover the quiet inner spirit they secretly all shared. He had found the Kindness that loved each of them as one, despite the foolishness each and everyone got up to. The Townspeople had felt this remarkable transformation in the once friendless old man, and for this blessed reminder of their true state, as subtle as it might have been, they were very grateful indeed.

It sometimes happened that Marco would speak to the Townspeople about the gentle truth he had learned. But for the most part he just let it filter through his eyes and the happiness he felt in their presence. They were, indeed, his true friends – all of them, good and bad.

Yet of all his friends, Paulo had perhaps become his favorite.

Together on their beloved old bench by the river, discussing the profound questions of their souls and their most cherished dreams, Marco and Paulo had shared many remarkable moments. Trying, always trying, patiently and diligently, to see their brothers differently and better understand the truth about themselves. Sometimes they just chatted, simply spending time together, and at other times they spoke earnestly about their path so that they could learn to understand and remember. To understand and remember true happiness ... and to make the journey Home together to the Golden City.

But now they sensed that time was getting shorter; they both knew that their work was not yet done. Their one remaining task was still to find the Key and gain the understanding, the special Knowing, that the magician constantly reminded them of. Only in this way could they possibly hope to undo the Spell, and finally release their imprisoned vision of the Domain, once and for all.

Their sight was not yet completely clear; yet together they could work through the remaining obstacles, and finally return Home. More than anything, a desire now filled Marco's heart to enter within the Golden City and live once more in the full presence of his King, his beloved celestial Father.

One day (a day that really should have been like all the rest, but was not to be), the old man and the boy sat on their worn wooden bench by the river, watching the barges and boats go by as was their custom, and they spoke of their last lingering resistance to True Knowing.

"Marco, I'm sure the time is coming now," said Paulo pensively. "You know, we've got to think about taking the final steps. We've a lot to do, our friends need us, and we still need to discover the complete meaning of the magician's words. It's a responsibility we took on our shoulders. We still don't have the understanding or true vision he's told us about so often. Our eyes aren't fully open yet. So let's work it out now; help me to start to see it all more clearly."

The old man listened attentively to the boy as he continued.

"Okay, so we've learned that the magical thing we're looking for is somewhere here right in front of us, before our very noses. We've learned how to know our brothers and sisters much better here in Towne. And we know that our goal is Happiness, some kind of joy that's beyond any words we could find here in the world to describe."

He turned his head upwards in thought, then brought his regard back to Marco.

"So here's my question – if this incredible joy is really inside us and always there, then why don't I see it properly? From time to time I can see that a special kind of happiness is right there in front of me – sometimes I get just a glimpse, a second or a minute, but then it can be gone again just as quickly.

"For instance, why does it still sometimes seem to me like a different situation might make me feel better? And why am I still concerned that something here in the Domain will make me upset and angry again? I mean, *why isn't Love fully here in my mind all the time now?* It's so frustrating! It just doesn't make sense – not after all we've seen and discussed already. I know it's silly, but I still think sometimes that I'd be happier if I were somewhere else doing something else. It's like a feeling that *life should still somehow be better.*"

Marco suggested, "Maybe because you still believe you're not loved, so you look in these other things for the gentleness you think you're missing."

This was precisely the perception that Paulo had gained in the market square with his customers.

"Yes, I see that now. But how could I *really* be missing this wonderful Kindness if I've felt it inside before? I mean, if Love is really there, then it must be there *all the time.* And if I'm not seeing it, then it's not because it's not there or somehow gone. I'm still really confused about all these things, but now at least I think I've an idea why…"

Marco looked back at Paulo with interest.

"This is what I've been thinking," the boy continued seriously, and put forward his suggestion. "Maybe the Spell actually makes a solid cover like a kind of dense smoke before Love, and I can't see anything at all clearly then. I can catch glimpses through the fog, but don't really get the whole picture. Maybe all the problems and questions I've had, like about the farm and Francesca, like my customers, the Mayor and the town officials and all the other problems that have been so important to me, maybe they're all just smoke from the Spell that actually makes me totally blind." He looked back at Marco. "What do you think?"

Marco's eyes widened in delight. "This is *very* interesting, my boy! Yes, yes, I think you might just be on the right track. Perhaps as you say, it's all nothing more than a dense smoke before our eyes."

Marco then went on excitedly, and suggested, "Maybe in fact *all* the many questions about trying to find happiness that have filled our mind have together been part of the Spell itself. What if – what if the Spell is so intensely strong that it confuses us with an infinite number of questions and problems in our lives that seem undeniably important, but really aren't so at all!"

Marco paused and his sight drifted for a moment out to the river and then further toward the distant line of hills.

"Maybe, just maybe…" he drew himself inside, "Maybe in fact it's all much – *much* – simpler than we both have thought."

Something suddenly burgeoned in his mind, a fresh awareness, something remarkable and completely new…

"Paulo!" he cried unexpectedly, startling the boy. "Just look at us here, sitting like two old roosters on our bench. Why, I do believe that there is indeed a wonderful warmth and kindness – but it's *right here, now*. Look there, *look* – out there!"

Paulo stared into the distance, wondering what Marco could be talking about. The older man stretched his arm and waved an open hand before him, a grand motion that seemed to embrace the entire countryside: river, houses, fields, forest, lakes and villages. It was a gesture that encompassed everything, everywhere. And it was clear Marco meant *anywhere*.

"Maybe everything we've ever sought is indeed before our eyes and has been sitting there all along. It's actually quite simple!"

Marco now clapped his open palms together noisily, then cupped them before him and continued his explanation.

"Listen – maybe the destination we've always sought is precisely here within our own hands, Paulo. The beauty we've struggled to find for so long, all the knowledge and freedom – we just don't feel it. But it is true, *it is there!* It is smoke, Paulo, but *just* smoke, and not reality that stops us, nothing more than that. There really is no solid barrier or obstacle."

Paulo considered these ideas seriously. He thought about how his life had been busy lately with so many things as usual: tasks, jobs, questions, goals, concerns and obligations – *only just smoke?*

He reflected more intently – his thoughts, his ideas, all his problems, his opinions, good and bad, all his many preoccupations with the things of his world, his trying to work things out, to find his path and make a place for himself. His daily struggle, his terrific, heroic, desperate struggle to work out his life, all perhaps … just *mist*? In the clarity of that precise moment, it certainly seemed plausible.

"Perhaps you're right. It might really be like you say," Paulo said, thoughtful. "All of it – just smoke."

"The answer, the Love, must be here," Marco insisted excitedly, "but rather *in spite of* our lives. Maybe our entire lives – and all life everywhere, for that matter – are part of the smoke-screen that preoccupy our minds so intensely, so completely, that we don't see the truth. An immense diversion! These lifetimes of ours are perhaps thoroughly *insignificant*: all our goals, our efforts and interests, even our greatest intentions and strivings. Even our individual being itself…" Marco pronounced the words with great intensity.

Paulo, his head bowed in solemn concentration, fought to find the sense behind Marco's thoughts. "So you're saying that perhaps we have to put away all our questions and preoccupations now, is that it? It seems they were maybe stopping us all this time from uncovering our treasure. Somewhere right here," he said, looking down at the ground in front of him.

"Maybe…"

A strange thought occurred to him.

"Maybe in fact we first have to learn to welcome, like you say, the *unimportance* of our lives … in order to gain the first step."

Paulo paused and then repeated to himself under his breath, "Somewhere right here … beyond any thoughts of self."

The young wood seller knit his brows and turned to his older friend. "But, Marco, why on earth don't I *see* it?" he asked, somewhat exasperated. "If the King, our Father, wants nothing for us but this remarkable great Life and if he really did place it within us, then it must be present here *now*, as obvious as…" He looked out at the river, "…as these boats and fields right in front of our noses.

"The wizard constantly tells us that what we're looking for is always right here in the Domain, that it's *everywhere*. He said that if we don't see it, it's certainly not because the Gifts aren't there, but because something inside us still really *doesn't want* to find them."

Marco replied, "Perhaps just so. Perhaps it's the entire belief we've placed within our self and its life in Towne that is our refusal of Love, Paulo.

"But now, my young friend, how are we going to take these last few steps, and finally end this fruitless searching?"

Paulo went silent for a moment. He then suggested firmly, "We'll have to ask within our hearts, Marco. That's how we'll find the answer."

CHAPTER FIFTY-SEVEN

The Blessing in a Smile

The two friends sat there on the bench, Paulo closing his eyes and Marco gazing far over the river, and both asked the same question inside.

"Where is the presence of warmth and love I seek?" They whispered the words into their hearts, and in that same breath each tried to reach past the wall of his personal preoccupations, past his own sense of being.

"This is now my deepest desire," they each spoke. "I understand all that I wished my life to be and to signify, and I let that go. Above all things now, more than everything I have believed important and real, I wish to feel the peace of my beloved King, and to know what I truly am."

Paulo focused intently, and quieted his breathing further, but after a few minutes he found it difficult to concentrate. Something quickly rose up to disturb him. He tried again, and asked yet more sincerely. He then felt something, but it was not a comfortable sensation, a feeling that before long made him shift and fidget in his seat. The something he was feeling was not at all kind or loving, like he had thought. Rather it was unpleasant, cold like stone, and harsh.

It became more difficult to concentrate, a sensation crept upon him that was not at all warm or soothing. It burrowed behind his eyes, and within a moment he opened them abruptly. He turned toward his friend.

The older man sat staring at the ground, a shadow had entered his eyes.

"Marco – why on earth is there still all of this *fear?*"

There was a moment of confused silence. A minute went by, then another, and no answer came to either of them.

Suddenly Marco exclaimed, *"But that's it,* Paulo!" His words shook Paulo out of his torpor. "The final obstacle we've been seeking! *Fear* is the basic reason we can't look past our selves, past our lives, to discover what's beyond. Let me explain:

"You see, quite simply – *we still want all this to be real!* We're still afraid to know, to really comprehend, that all we've ever known about the world is not the truth. And I think that while we're still afraid of losing everything we've ever believed in, we'll still need our small selves within the Domain to be our home. We'd feel quite lost without them…

He paused and looked towards Paulo.

"And yet there's still something unclear in all this for me: what could still be stopping us from moving past this fear of not being the selves we've so long imagined?"

A wave of surprise passed over the boy's face, and a hidden knowledge seemed to make itself suddenly clear to him. His thoughts came more easily now, more clearly, as though obstacles were dropping quickly away from their passage. He found himself looking at a painting, a masterpiece, that seemed nearly finished and only needed a few more brush-strokes, a few more thoughts, to be complete. He learned now from this new inner knowledge as he spoke:

"It's actually quite simple, I think, Marco. Zeph's been telling us all along – It's this guilt he's talked about so many times. While we still want to know something apart from our Home, we'll feel guilt, this terrible notion we've done something sinful towards the Kingdom.

"Filled with a shame we just can't stand, we look for some type of protection, like a shield of armor. So we use these bodies and personalities as this shield, and hold on to them with all our might.

We use them like a replacement home while we're lost and think we've found some safety and reality, though actually they're very unsafe. This tiny self and its whole world are like tools we use to keep our heavy fears away."

Paulo stopped. It appeared from the outside that he was listening to something, his head turned to one side and then to another as if words were being spoken to him directly now through the surrounding silence.

"And so –" he continued hesitantly, then more confidently, 'and so while we'd still hold on to the smallest wish to stay a divided being, and give importance to the smallest trace of guilt, we'll keep feeling afraid and even suspicious of Love and everything that stands beyond ourselves. We'll still use these tiny selves to ward against the thing which seems like an even bigger danger, bigger even than the sadness and scariness of our lives here.

"So the answer to our question, what stops us from moving past this fear, well, it's believing that our little self will disappear and just die, and leave us nowhere, and un-living ... It's the powerful thought that a real answer won't be kind at all but terrifying and all-finishing. It's thinking that real knowledge will actually be the end of our body and ourselves. And that's why we don't seem to get anywhere."

There was a pause as Paulo's inner listening faded away.

Marco's face creased into a wide, astonished smile. "Again, my young friend, you've thoroughly outdone me! How an old man like myself can be so privileged to share this road with you. Now tell me, wise-one, what then is the answer to this divine riddle? How shall we overcome this witless fear?"

Paulo thought a moment and looked into the old man's relaxed and cheerful face.

He sought for an answer within his inner hearing, waiting for further special words to come. But nothing came now. No further astonishing words or wisdom came forth, so he looked back at Marco for help.

Abruptly he laughed: a loud and joyous noise erupted from his throat, surprising even himself.

"I think you might've just given us the answer, Marco!"

Marco started and recoiled in surprise.

"No, don't stop – just do it again, Marco. Just smile."

Marco was caught in a moment of intense concentration, his face a picture of bewilderment.

"No, no! Just *smile* – that's all! Just smile, as best you can," Paulo said, grinning from ear to ear, delighting in the new game.

Slowly a new awareness came to Marco's mind and a slight smile began to form on his lips, then broadened into a full and joyous grin. Soon he, too, was laughing, a blissful and warm sound that came from deep within him.

"Oh, yes. Oh, yes, indeed!" he said between merry chuckles. "How silly, how incredibly silly of me."

They stared at each other wide-eyed in a moment of wordless communication. It was so clear to both of them.

"It has always been clear, Paulo," the old man said, greatly relieved to have finally found the one missing piece of the puzzle. "How could we have missed it? The answer, the Key, was there all along! We just weren't ready – that's the only explanation.

"I, for one, couldn't have accepted before that my life was of so little significance, that my world and all I considered myself to be held so little importance. My judgments and thoughts – how important they all were! And all my bother and upset, the guilt and fear …When none of it had any real consequence at all. *Just don't take it seriously!* Of course, that's the perfect answer! Smile at it, smile and laugh happily at everything. You're right, you're so very right – that's all we ever had to do."

Paulo answered, "I think so, Marco. If our little self isn't truth and only fills us with fear and illusion, then we have to learn to take it all much less seriously. That's all. That can be the only answer.

"Can you believe it, Marco?" the boy exclaimed overjoyed. "There was never anything to fear – not really. Fear never had a real reason behind it. Just a strange feeling of distance from our Home was causing all this anguish in our hearts, but nothing more than that. It was all just make-believe … a game even.

"It only needed a little wish to see it all clearly, to understand everything, but a wish we didn't have yet, despite our best trying. To no longer be afraid, we just have to remember that none of this is real or true, and that's okay, not bad. We just have to let truth be what it really is, and to feel happy that this world is not the truth, and that reality is nothing dangerous at all."

Paulo was overjoyed by the fresh new understanding filling his spirit, like water rising from a pure, clear spring.

"We don't need any complicated reasons or shields anymore. What'd we try to protect ourselves against? There *is no* danger coming from Heaven, because nothing ever really happened; no punishment will ever come, because no harm was ever done. *That's* the wonderful Atonement Zeph's been trying to tell us about all along. It's only when we can finally accept this that we can see the tiny self's really nothing at all, just insignificant, because we'll no longer be afraid of its dying. There's nothing at all to be scared of, because there never was any real going away from our birthplace! There was no exile! *We're still at Home!*"

The elderly man stared at the boy's beaming face and felt a new and astonishing lightness enter his heart. Tears welled in his eyes and he allowed the boy's words to penetrate further into the very foundation of his soul.

A moment of joyful silence surrounded the two searchers as they sat there on the bench; and as they looked around them it appeared that the day had suddenly become distinctly less dark and gray. Almost as if the air itself were becoming lighter…

CHAPTER FIFTY-EIGHT

The Myth of the Unkind Father

Marco shook his head in bewilderment. "We've been so mistaken, so incredibly wrong! How... how could all this have happened, all the turmoil, the chaos of our world? What an astoundingly strange path we've been following all this time! How could we have led ourselves so astray?"

"We've already come a long way all on our own – maybe Zeph can help us understand what's going on now," Paulo suggested.

And with that request, the magician appeared to both of them within the space of their quiet, unified mind.

"My friends – welcome now to the final part of your journey!" he announced cheerfully. "I shall always be here, my brothers, helping you to make sense of your path which needs, as you have so beautifully discovered, to be taken ever more lightly. Let me help you now once more. Let me complete a final, unsaid chapter of our story...

"Indeed, once many years ago the strangest of notions occurred to the beloved of the heavenly Father, the idea that we might find something yet greater and better than all his many Gifts if only we left his Home to make our way without him. And we accepted this thought, incredible though it was, with great and solemn belief.

"Once within our minds, this unwholesome desire immediately took on a veritable life of its own and became quickly *self-protective*. It now wished above all to sustain itself, and never return again to its former state of insignificance. The result of this powerful survival intention was the desperate attempt to obscure our self-chosen departure and disguise it as something else. And thus this desire to know something else, to be separated, gave birth to a sentiment unknown till then, terrifying, of mind-controlling intensity, and this was *Guilt*. This was the origin of our conviction in evil, the idea of having betrayed our Creator.

"And so we fled, as swiftly as we could; and in fleeing from this inner torment, we chose to hide in a haven we thought would be outside the sight of the King. Thus was born the *Domain*. In an explosion of fantastic proportions, the need for hiding fabricated an entire world of galaxies and bodies that would serve as a solid shield to understanding and vision. Yes, the little self and its body that have occupied your mind and senses so thoroughly are part of this oblivion, part of this intent to keep the spirit in darkness and ignorance.

"There we had attained it ... *Separation*, at last! But at what terrible cost, for in this dreadful exchange eternal peace itself was lost forever. Death for life, and sadness for joy, our newly gained independence seemed well worth the price we had paid; though who among us really understood it was but cleverly disguised enslavement? No one saw this. To explain our desperate predicament and yet to remain innocent of all responsibility, we portrayed the King himself as the cause, and invented the myth of the Dark Lord. We were not guilty, we were not to blame: our celestial Father was.

"Into our hearts a strange sovereign and protector had now entered; a father whose favor was capricious, whose love was distant and demanded sacrifice. Without self-punishment and reverence, this foreign spiritual lord would refuse his children's homecoming, and at a whim he would sentence them to exclusion and endless pain.

"Just a myth, a children's story, that's all it was; and yet we so firmly believed in this imagined, frightening tale of creation and birth that no opening remained in our minds to hear the truth. Through no fault of our own, but through the unkind will of an unfatherly God we had arrived destitute in the cold, uncaring world of the Domain. There we would wander in confusion and in despair, imploring all the while, 'My Father, why hast thou forsaken me...?"

There was a moment of quiet then.

The magician's voice faded, and Marco and Paulo remained attentive to his last spoken thoughts. Paulo looked up. "He hasn't finished; this isn't where he'd leave us," said the young wood seller. "There's more to come. The magician still has a message he wants to give us."

After some minutes of silent waiting, the sage's voice returned.

"Now, my friends," his voice resounded, "listen carefully to these words as you stand on the threshold of your veritable Home and remember the truth of their meaning:

"There is nothing for you to fear now, for you are not the guilty, evil things you have so long believed. Your Father loves you dearly, and his Love has prevented your dark thoughts from ever becoming reality. Pain is not his wish, nor his creation, and his World of kindness, safety and blessing stands ready to replace the one you have imagined, the moment you will welcome it. Be at peace, my brothers, and remember that peace is your heritage, and your home. Darkness can confuse you but cannot change your reality. You remain as you always were, the beloved and innocent children of your holy, loving Father."

The healing words of the magician remained suspended in the air even as his presence faded from their minds, leaving the old man and the boy on the worn bench by the river to reflect on all the wondrous things they were learning.

Their thoughts were clear and their knowledge closely joined within another, mysterious place. Understanding was present, as if the two brothers were now remembering things they had somehow always known, but had forgotten in the mists of some deep sleep.

The elderly man now leaned gently back in the bench and looked further into his mind, quite unafraid. Then, after some moments he opened his eyes in which shone a fresh joyfulness, and smiled very contentedly. He looked over towards the boy.

Paulo was brimming with life. He stared out over the river now, expectant and curious, quite sure he could feel something else, something powerful and magical all around them. Something almost tangible, and palpable.

"Zeph's right," he murmured, "there really is some kind of special Love present here. Very present, here ... *I feel it*," he said pensively.

The sun was still hidden by strands of gray cloud, the air was cool and damp, and thin tendrils of mist had started to settle along the riverbank, but the old man and the boy could hardly notice these things.

Marco returned now to the conversation, expressing thoughts that came to him from that place of inner remembering.

"We don't really belong in this world, Paulo," he stated soberly. "None of us do, for we are as good as homeless here. We must admit this now, because only this knowledge will take us to our real Home. The Domain is, after all, just a world of shadows and mist, as we have been told. It exists only as a picture in our unified One Mind, as an embodiment of the Separation-thought. And these tiny physical selves that populate it are just ghostly images of the belief in individuality. But nothing really happens here in this place of dreams, and nothing here can be really so important.

"I know all this is extremely hard for us to accept, but it's true nevertheless. This is an essential part of understanding the real nature of things so that we can arrive Home. We have to learn now to look with *proper perspective* at the Domain, as the sage has tried so hard to teach us, but only for one reason, simply for one vital reason: so we can then *let it go*. We will all finally breathe one great sigh of relief from the deepest part of our soul, because we will understand that it has not at all been the truth..."

The young wood seller brought another meaning to Marco's thoughts, speaking now from that same place of boundless intuitive knowledge.

"While we were standing alone and without the magician's help, we couldn't see. We just couldn't face our fear. It's all too much to bear for someone who doesn't join with the sage. Then over time we learned to accept comfort and security from this other warm and wise Voice within our hearts. Only then could we start to think that maybe this world wasn't the whole truth after all.

"And you know what? – it really isn't true! Not the pain, not the sin, not all the upset and tears, not the world – *none* of it!"

The boy's face lit with a glowing happiness, as if the words he spoke reached now inside him and set something free.

"Do you remember where we began, Marco?" he cried excitedly. "This was the starting point for both of us! We looked around in our lives and asked the only question that seemed to make any sense to us: *'Isn't there something else other than these tiresome feelings? Something other than all this ridiculous anguish and shame? Isn't there something other than what I'm seeing here?'*

"Don't you see? It was asking this question that finally got us started opening our hearts. Then it was just being a little honest with ourselves that helped us face the really difficult choice before us. We all have a choice – but we can't possibly make it if we can't see it!

"And then we ended up saying to ourselves: *'No, this can't be right!* This just isn't the way everything is. There *is* something else, even though I don't see it yet.'"

Paulo hesitated several instants, then after a moment of listening inside he finished his thoughts. "And so now we have to learn to turn to this quiet spirit of wonderful kindness in our hearts and start to say, *'I do not know the thing I am. I cannot know. I have been wrong and mistaken, but this is not a sin...'*"

Paulo listened to an inner voice that gently helped him choose his words ..."*Please remind me of what I am, for I would now know ... I am willing to remember and to accept what You say. I have nothing to fear anymore. Please tell me now that I should remember and forget all my doubts...*"

CHAPTER FIFTY-NINE

The Lifting of the Veil

Paulo was vibrant with life, but in his eyes there was a special peacefulness, as if he had found something within him of great freedom and hope. As if a door was opening now in his soul and a fragrant, pure air was wafting through.

"Help me to forget all my doubts … I'm willing to remember now, I'm not afraid … please remind me of what I am," he whispered to himself once more.

The moment was one of exceptional joy, shimmering and expectant. The old man and the boy looked deep into their hearts, both aware that the great Presence they had sought so long on all the obscure pathways of the world was right there, so close now.

As close, in that instant, as their very own heartbeat…

The young sage's apprentice hesitated an instant, then his face started suddenly in confusion and he spoke without turning around.

"Marco! Did you hear that?" Paulo lowered his head in concentration. "Listen a moment inside. Do you hear it, that other strange sound?"

Marco stared longingly into the distance. His spirit dwelled still on their recent extraordinary thoughts. Peace was flowing through his mind like a quiet river, and he listened to the passage of something the current was bringing into his awareness. He too felt a sensation of something opening, burgeoning within him. There was indeed something special, right there…

And then the words broke into their hearts, from some other place within them quite unexpected, welling up and pouring forth upon them in a wave of magnificent harmony and radiance –

"My deeply beloved children ..."

They drew a breath at the same time as the Light-filled sound dawned upon their waiting spirits.

"Beloved children of your Father's Heart..."

The tender words resounded and echoed from a place within them they had closed and forgotten long ago; this wonderful sound that now made their hearts melt with joyful remembrance, and continued in the clearest of golden tones:

"Yes, you are still My beloved Children, as holy, pure and beautiful as when you first lived within My Love."

Their sight was within but their hearts soared to meet the glorious Presence burgeoning all about them. They raised their vision outwards, and then as they turned their faces toward the river they found that the sun had broken through the low clouds and was streaming rays of warm sunshine onto their old wooden bench.

"You are still My dearly beloved Children..." The splendid sound welled up from within them and filled their every sense to completion. They lifted their eyes upward to the heavens and a shaft of brilliant light shone upon them that made their faces glow in radiant happiness. In front of them, the gray mist receded rapidly and a golden luminescence stretched outward from their bench, covering the boats, the river-houses, and finally the fields and forests in the distance. Everywhere they looked the light appeared from beneath the gray and transformed their vision, wiping away the grim sense of wretchedness and imprisonment that had been the eternal dark shadow of the Domain.

Further words now reached to them from that holy place in their hearts that stretched effortlessly and endlessly toward the Truth:

"Yes, forgive your Father, for it was not My Will that My Children wander alone, afraid and cold. Come, return Home now from your

dreams of self-chosen exile. Return your holy minds to Me, and live forevermore within My Joy and Happiness."

Looking around them, everything glowed now with an exceptional warmth, giving all things the appearance of perfect harmony and gentleness. Within this golden vision surrounding them they could find nothing of menacing or harmful intent. No danger existed; all was perfectly calm and gentle. And within this soft and peaceful light arose the words that spoke their hearts' deepest purpose…

"Forgive your Father, for it was only My Will that you be happy and live in perfect peace. Release now all your dreams of sadness and of pain. Come Home, and rest again by My Side."

The two brothers remained perfectly silent on the old wood bench, their breathing slow and deep, quiet and serene. They sat there unmoving, listening in astonishment and wonder, sublimely at home in the ancient Knowing that spoke within them.

Now it was clear, no harm could ever come to them while they remained within this Light, this present memory that their King had bestowed upon them. His gifts of peace and safety, of joy and eternity, had never been removed, and were forever given. No illusion of separation and no insane perception of guilt and fear could ever take them away, no matter how far they dreamed they had wandered from the City. His gifts could be forgotten and hidden, and a thick mist of pain could disguise them, but never could Light and Love be removed. The Door was open, the Knowledge of the King was still present and forever buried within each of them.

Now, they saw, and now they could never forget.

After some time Marco let out a deep, quiet breath and spoke.

"Do you understand, Paulo, we've now broken the Spell, we've gained the Knowing? Our Father does indeed love us; there really is nothing to fear from Him. He was never what we thought at all." He spoke with a new clarity and authority in his voice.

"Now we can listen to the Spell as much as it cries in all its terrifying appearances, and it won't make any difference. We've *seen* the truth. We *cannot* forget. Though we might fail again, it can only be momentary. We have seen that only this Love is true, even behind the frightening appearances of dangers and crises."

"You're right, Marco," the boy said. "Nothing has changed here at all. Look around: the Domain's still just the same. Something inside us in our thoughts has changed, but it's all still the same. Imagine that! The truth was here around us all the time. We've always been more powerful than the Maker, than all the shameful thoughts and feelings that made up his world! We only ever had to really want to see the world around us differently. That's all."

They rose to their feet together and stood there looking calmly over the Eternity lying tranquil and vast, stretching endlessly before them into the pale distance. As they stared, some final words welled up and spoke to them from that place of deepest remembering:

"My Children, the Will of the One People shall be done. Their true Light and Strength will be remembered. Such it was written at the very dawn of time that their Light will one day shine in that place of darkness, and will remind all tired and lonely minds that the time of true hope and peace has finally come."

The boy and the old man remained standing, embraced by the sublime light and warmth of heavenly Love, remembering the truth of complete acceptance into the Kingdom. There was no more to say, and nothing more to do ... there was nothing more to fight for and nothing to strive for, and nothing urgent to achieve. Just something to accept as true.

Their Father's Love was complete and perfect and would remove all sense of pain; His Love was always present and offered and would remove all sense of lack. Now It brought them gently within His whole Embrace. There was no need for change or thought of any kind. Just acceptance unto That Which loved them completely.

CHAPTER SIXTY

Fredo and the Night

Paulo continued to go to the market and sell his wood. He continued chatting with his customers and the villagers, learning of their true nature as his long-lost brothers and sisters; but time was no longer the same. There was no change now to his tranquil experience of life, no alteration of his mood, no disturbance to his perfect peace of mind. Time no longer seemed to exist in quite the same way.

In his vision a golden light suffused his friends and the town, and nothing reached out to him with any harmful intent or distressing purpose. No problem arose that was not solved instantly in his sight, no customer's pain that was not understood and given over to truth, and no lack he saw that was not given full measure of the Love abounding in all things. In all moments and situations, he practiced the only purpose of his heart.

Paulo walked the dark and twisted streets of Towne exactly as before, but his experience was now completely different. He felt *why* there was no reason to be afraid, he felt now *why* his life would always be safe. He knew why happiness was the only proper response to all things: it was a simple knowledge within him. There was no more self-hate, no further desire for separation, and hence no suffering or solitude. Only a simple feeling of oneness and safety.

The boy was now quite aware that the prison he had so long lived in had not been the gray of the Domain at all. Nothing in the Domain had ever been the cause of his sorrow or distress. It was only ever his confused notions of his own being, un-truths and concepts woven out of self-hate and guilt that had hurt him. Imprisoned within his self-concepts, his sense of individuality, he had believed himself to be banished, exiled to an existence of solitude, alone in the minuscule world of his private thoughts, judgments, feelings and experiences. Alone in his body. But he had finally seen, he was not alone.

Only one evening presented him still with a temptation to return to his old ways of thinking. Only one situation still seemed to glimmer with some hope of finding satisfaction within the things of the Domain, the world of deception and pain...

Fredo was looking bothered. He seemed to want to talk with his brother about something but it appeared difficult for him to bring up the subject. They dried the dishes together, and Paulo wondered what could be the matter.

"Paulo, could we take a walk?" he asked.

They strolled to the edge of the Forest and then Fredo tensed. "Paulo, I have something important to ask you. At least, I feel it's important." He hesitated again. "Paulo, you know I've been working with Francesca now for some months. She and I have grown closer, and I have to tell you that I like her very, very much."

Paulo felt this was good. But he wasn't prepared at all for what Fredo said next.

"Paulo, *Francesca still likes you*, not me."

Paulo gazed at Fredo blankly, not understanding.

His brother was trying to hide his distress. "And she still wants *you* to come work at the farm. Things are very busy, and there's work for another person now. She still feels you should come to work at the farm."

Paulo sat down, confused. He saw in his mind that a part of him seemed to leap with joy. "She loves you!" this voice shouted gleefully. "The girl with the gorgeous blue eyes from your dreams, she really loves you after all! Maybe all this was just leading you to a true experience of happiness in the Domain, Paulo, and there's absolutely nothing wrong with that," it proclaimed. And for the first time in months, he seriously wondered what he should do.

Why was this dilemma coming back to plague him? Was there something important after all to learn from an experience with Francesca? This had to mean that there was still something to do there in the Domain, some vital, essential work to do with his brother and Francesca. And, yes, perhaps it was just right for him to have a wonderful, intimate relationship with the lovely girl from the farm.

But I don't want to be hurt again.

Still, what experiences might this hold, things I haven't yet discovered?

Many questions filled his mind, problems he had not thought about for a long time it seemed. So many questions to do with his own life. The questions came back in a way that haunted him with a sense of threat, of something that would drag him into danger, frightening, enticing, and exciting all at the same time.

Perhaps the only real purpose and goal is just to live a good life here, a safe one with security and comfort. Should I take what they offer me, is that my role? He could hear this voice saying: 'You only have one life, and you may as well get what you can and what's offered you. What's wrong with real comfort and pleasure, after all?'

But Paulo had come to understand that this type of comfort could actually be a deep form of sleep, and not life at all, if one was not careful. Focus, Paulo, focus. 'What's my goal? What's my real purpose? Is my own life my purpose?'

Zeph's voice came immediately to help him, "*Paulo, what do you mean by 'your own life'? Be clear as to what you mean.*"

Is my purpose to be with my friends and part of the story of their lives? he continued thinking. What's my role with these people, what can I offer them?

"*Try to think what you can give them that will be most valuable,*" Zeph spoke again. "*Indeed, what is your new role now?*"

Is it best that I serve them at the farm, or in some other way?

So many questions. Focus, Paulo, *focus*.

Paulo felt words within him, and Zeph spoke once more. "Paulo, try to understand, you do not really have any personal interests, not any more, not in the way that you have always conceived of them. You may believe that you can have interests separate from those of others. However there is only one real interest, and it is shared by everyone. Release yourself now from your illusions of need – that will help you, and your friends. That is the service you can render. Listen to the Voice within you, know that your King has given all the People all they really need and want right now."

Paulo tried to listen, and felt some calm enter his mind.

'Even in the darkest of places, the Light is there, for there is nowhere that darkness can hide,' he remembered Zeph telling him once. And the magician now spoke again, "There is no place fear and lack are real; there is no place Love is absent. That is your message. Think on this now."

Paulo had no idea what to do and just looked at his brother. Fredo was tense, his eyes searching Paulo's in the dark for an answer, and Paulo saw in him expectation. And *fear*.

Paulo smiled at him since he loved his brother and wanted him to be well. Then he tried to relax. Fredo would be affected by his answer, he thought, and had his hopes pinned on something special. Fredo knew the answer to the question of farm work would be 'yes' or 'no'. His brother wanted very much to be with Francesca and thought she might learn to love him one day as she loved Paulo now. Paulo's answer, he thought, would quite certainly determine his happiness.

Paulo shook his head slowly.

There was something wrong with this, something wrong with it all, with the question itself. The question was not whether he should accept the job or not. No, it was something else, if the goal was Happiness.

And then he understood. He comprehended the way of true happiness in the Domain, and the problem instantly disappeared.

"Fredo…" he began, and looked toward his brother.

His brother pierced him with a stare, and held his breath in anticipation. Paulo paused, and held his brother gently in his thoughts. "Fredo, I don't know … I don't really know how to answer your question."

The boy appeared confused, and started to look upset as if Paulo was perhaps playing games with him.

"Fredo, I don't think this is the right question. I want you to be free and happy, not in any type of a prison. I ask myself, how can you be really free now? The question, my brother, my friend, is… 'How can you be happy – *no matter what I decide?*'"

Fredo's eyes widened in surprise.

Paulo realized that he loved his brother completely, and did not want to see any possibility of suffering enter his mind. The way Fredo was thinking about the situation he would be hurt no matter which answer Paulo gave. He did not want his brother to be affected now by *anything* he did.

Paulo wanted his brother to know that *nothing* could affect him, and that he was completely free of all needs in this world, because there was nothing outside him that could affect his feelings. Not when his thoughts were placed within his Self, within his True Mind. He wanted Fredo – and Francesca, too – to be able to follow the Golden Path Home with him, and knew that their fears, regrets and needs would only make it more difficult for them to do so.

There was a brilliant, resplendent light all around his brother, around all of them. But focusing on the situation in such a very personal way, thinking of all the personal benefits it would give, would only lead all of them into the Maker's illusions, and pain. This was the way of the Maker, the way he prevented them from accessing the King's Love. There was indeed a great attraction to this separation from Love, but only because the guilt and pain of this condition were so cleverly disguised.

Fredo! he wanted to say – *Wake up!* Please don't look at me this way with such expectation and fear. I can't do for you what you wish, not by answering yes, or no. There's nothing I can do that can change your experience of life. This is not in my power. But it is in yours! Don't let your sight be obscured by the mist, by the small, gleaming hopes of this dark world. There's a universe of light and beauty for you to behold, and it all begins within you. What you're really looking for is not within this situation, but elsewhere. Look elsewhere now, my brother!

His brother's freedom was his own now. Play into Fredo's fears and beliefs that the situation was critical for the sake of happiness and he, Paulo, would be trapped. Help Fredo to understand that neither of them needed to be concerned for their happiness, and they would both be able to breathe freely and joyfully, and the decision would come naturally. There should be only one real goal now, because it would help them all with every decision, no matter how tempting and beguiling the situation: Seek for the love and peace that were already present, and know that no thought of lack or unhappiness was true.

"Fredo," he finally repeated, "how can you be happy – *no matter what I decide*? Asking this question is the only real help I can give us all right now, the only way I can really love you as a brother. You see, I must learn now once and for all that my happiness doesn't come from the magical things that another person might offer me. I have to learn that real joy can only come from the Love that's already within me, and within you, too. And within Francesca."

He waited a moment while Fredo stared at the ground, lost in thought.

"If you want, I can come work at the farm," he continued, "and we'd surely have great fun working together, and of course I'd be very happy spending time with Francesca, and I think she'd like that very much, too. Or I can go my own way still, and perhaps you'd grow closer to Francesca, and perhaps she to you, and I think you'd like that very much. But I don't want either of you to suffer if I do come or if I don't, and you'll be sorrowful if you still think your happiness comes from any of these things."

He looked at his brother and felt very peaceful. "You see, Fredo, my happiness can't really come from just working at the farm with you and having Francesca as my lovely, special companion, as much as I might want to believe that. And it can't come from helping you either." He didn't need to speak the unsaid words, but Fredo understood clearly: neither could *his* happiness really come from such things.

Fredo sat and stared into the deep night surrounding the Forest. He was trying hard to understand the message his brother was trying to share. After a long moment he heaved a peaceful sigh.

"Paulo – I think you must be right," he said. "I can see how I was very anxious about your answer. I wanted to think that Francesca could eventually learn to like me if you didn't come to the farm. But I was also anxious because I wanted Francesca to be happy, and it's obvious she'd be happier if you came to work at the farm. And then of course I thought you'd enjoy more working with us at the farm instead of selling wood, like you've always said.

"But you're right. My joy isn't really going to come from these things. And Francesca's happiness doesn't really depend on your coming to work at the farm, either. Even your freedom, as you say, doesn't depend on leaving the market place."

He looked at Paulo warmly and tried to understand how it would be possible to have no personal interest in this matter, the way his brother had done. *No one's* personal happiness was truly at stake, not his, not Francesca's, nor even his brother's, he reflected.

Fredo looked into the night and somehow it seemed to him just a little less dark, as if there were a brightness in the air now, a lightness there he had not seen before, and he breathed more easily. He felt free, freer than ever before. Relaxed. There was something there, something remarkable and peaceful, just out of sight. *What was it?*

After some time Paulo said, "Here is what I'll do. I'll go and speak with Francesca myself and give her my answer. But you must promise me you'll try to be happy no matter what I decide. Can you do that?"

"Yes, I think so. It doesn't really matter so much what your answer is. I think I know how to be happier now. Thank you, my friend – my *brother*."

Suddenly he wrapped his arms around Paulo and gave him a big hug.

Paulo sat there for some time after Fredo had returned to the house, and reflected on the quietness he felt around him. There seemed to be no more doubts in his mind now; there seemed to be no more questions. There appeared a new type of peacefulness that filled every conceivable part of him. Every problem seemed to have a perfect answer in that instant. As if it had only ever been a matter of knowing the right question.

At market-end the next day, the young wood seller and the girl from the farm walked down from the town-square to the river, and then strolled along the tree-lined bank on its north side. In former times Paulo would have been trembling with nervous excitement to find himself so close to his beloved. But now there was only a quiet confidence, a gentle happiness that helped him at this difficult time to find the words he needed to express his feelings.

"Fredo told me of the developments at the farm," he began. "That's really good, things are going very well for you."

"That's right, yes! And we have place for yet another hand, Paulo," she said excitedly. "What do you think – this would be good, no?" Her cheeks were flushed with a happy anticipation, and her eyes sparkled and drew Paulo around to face her.

"Francesca, I could think of nothing lovelier than to join you and Fredo and your parents at the farm. That's a greatly cherished dream of mine, which you should know."

She gazed back at him and he saw a girl with a deeply held wish, which was the same as his. His heart rejoiced, yet still there was an obstacle. How would she understand?

"Francesca, *would you be able to still wait a little longer?* I can't at this moment give you an answer. But all will be clear very soon. I promise that all shall be very clear in a short time, and we'll both know the answer to the wish we share."

A veil of confusion descended heavily upon her face. Her eyes fell away, and although it seemed to Paulo that she was caught somewhere between anguish and anger, there was something else there also. He watched, and after some minutes of breathless silence her face warmed with blood and she lifted quiet eyes up to his, eyes that held a new spirit he had not seen in her before. And she said,

"Paulo, my … friend, you ask a great deal of me. I'm not by nature one who sits by and waits easily, or peacefully. And I've already waited beyond the measure of time I believed was possible for me. And *still* you say I should wait…"

Paulo could not conceivably guess her thoughts at this moment. He listened more intently than he had ever done before.

"I've waited already … and this time hasn't gone by wasted. In waiting till now, I've had to find my happiness elsewhere, since I couldn't have what my heart yearned for. I've found my happiness, but not within another person, nor within the things of my life…"

Her gaze drifted away an instant, then returned.

"But it's there – somewhere, though just out of sight. I find it at times when my thoughts are quiet as I work … It's joined itself to me at times, and I've come at these moments into more happiness than I've ever known before."

She sighed, not with disappointment, but with a resigned peacefulness. "Perhaps after all my path is one of waiting. That's my role, it would seem. And perhaps, maybe by my waiting I shall learn all the things there are to know in this life, and become one of the truly wise. Then now, perhaps I shall have to learn again."

She looked calmly and steadily at Paulo, and spoke firmly,

"I shall wait longer still. That … is my answer."

Paulo looked at her intently and a warmth welled up in his heart.

The girl shook her head slightly from side to side. "I don't know where you're going, or what you must do that's of such importance. I believe that you're leaving us, though you haven't wanted to say as much. But I do trust you, and know that you speak honestly. This I can tell in a person.

"So, please, leave us, if that's your path. And if that means we're to meet again one day, all and well, and I'll be much the happier. But if not, then I shall learn again, and my lesson shall be a very difficult one. But peace will always prevail, so it is said … And so it shall be." She whispered the last words and as she looked up at him her eyes were moist with emotion.

Paulo found no words to say, he was left quite breathless. He stared back into her shining eyes, and came closer, and then gently took her hand in both of his. Slowly, he brought it up to his face and held his lips to her warm ivory skin. He kissed her hand tenderly and then brushed his fingers lightly across her cheek. She then took both his hands in hers, drawing him forward, placing them around her waist, and rested her hands lightly on his shoulders. They held each other's eyes this way for a long moment, and then came together and kissed; and as they kissed, their love for each other was sealed, bonded forever, beyond every mountain, river or realm.

Paulo rose in the middle of the night, suddenly wide awake.

No one stirred as he crept from the cottage and out into the cool, still night. A half-moon shone palely through a hazy veil of fleeting clouds, and he wandered into the forest, passing quietly among the dark silhouettes of trees, feeling utterly at home. He found a wide flat stone to sit upon and closed his eyes, breathing relaxedly a few times, filling his lungs with the crisp night air.

As he sat, a presence came from deep within and filled him with a sense of wellness and extraordinary safety. He opened his eyes and found he was once more outside the Wall in a broad sweeping field on a moon-less night; a warm breeze whispered through the tall grasses and a million brilliant stars illuminated the heavens. Seated next to him was the magician.

For some time they sat there without talking, until Paulo asked in a murmur, "Is this what it's really like?"

"Yes, Paulo, this is what it's really like," Zeph answered tenderly.

"No more fear, that's all," his teacher continued, "This is what it's like. No more fear and no further questions, your body is no longer the source of your experience; your body's only real purpose you have finally given back to it, a means of giving the message, that there is no prison, there is no exile, and no danger.

"Your spirit is now no longer rooted within the Domain, Paulo. That is why it looks and feels like this. After all," Zeph chuckled, "the infinite and eternal have no need of fear – do they, my young brother?"

Paulo just nodded lightly.

They sat there the two of them for some time, and the warm air lifted and swayed the grassy stems around them, until Paulo at last spoke. "All's really well," he said.

"And it will forever be," Zeph returned, smiling. "It was only ever a bad dream, and perhaps for you it is now over."

They sat there in silence while the stars spiraled majestically and slowly over their heads and the world slumbered deeply under their feet, and then Paulo got up and returned quietly back to the cottage.

CHAPTER SIXTY-ONE

The Blacksmith and the Angel

The next morning Paulo woke early before anyone else, and knew it would be a special day. He looked tenderly on his mother and brother as they slept, closed the cottage door silently, and then left for town, making his way straight down the dusty old path toward the bridge.

The day could not possibly have been more beautiful in his eyes, with a light, cool wind and an early dawn sky that seemed to promise some rain later. He remarked to himself curiously as he went down the rough cobbled road, the path he had walked so very often over the past few years without really knowing where he was really going, that today it seemed to know exactly where his destination lay.

The Golden City. Finally.

Paulo marched quickly down to the riverfront where he knew his friend and fellow traveler would be waiting. Marco looked younger and stronger than ever, and a deep happiness and quiet expectation shone from his eyes.

"Are you ready, little brother? Shall we take the last few steps together?" Marco asked brightly, then studied Paulo further. A frown appeared suddenly on his face, and a question mark came into his eyes.

"Paulo – I don't think you're quite ready to come with me yet. What do you think?"

Paulo looked inside, and Marco was quite right: there remained one final important task. "But I don't think I'll be long. Will you wait here for me?"

Marco nodded in agreement.

The boy strode his way back over the bridge, turned right and followed the narrow trail along the riverbank. Within minutes he had wound his way through the village on the outskirts of Towne and up to the blacksmith's house. The front door was wide open, and Paulo stepped silently over the threshold.

Things lay in disarray everywhere. Furniture was upturned, shelves were on the floor – knives and forks and other objects lay scattered all about. The blacksmith could hardly be seen amongst the mess, huddled in a dark corner of the room on a wooden stool, his head between his legs. His eyes were red and veined, and his face puffed and pale. He had been awake all night – ever since he had returned home from the workshop and found that his wife and children had left him. He had become extremely angry and had spoken very harshly to himself.

Could this be possible?

Have they really gone, have they left me? My wife, my children? Are they no more, are they really gone? It cannot be! I didn't do anything, really I didn't. I'm not the one that did it – it's not me, I promise!

Yes, indeed it's you – filthy, evil creature!

No, I couldn't be the one, it's not possible. Please tell me it wasn't me! Why have they gone, why did she go? It's not me!

It is indeed you, yes! And now you know, you finally know: you are indeed an evil, despicable creature to have made them all go away, to make Love disappear. Why else would Love abandon you? Only you know how terribly, truly evil you are.

No, it can't be true. There must be something else, there must be something wrong. Please, please help me.

The blacksmith had no idea how it had happened, how he had done it, but he knew it was him. And it was such an immensely horrible thought to feel you have destroyed the source of comfort and love, and not know how to make it return.

If only I could make them come back. Where is love ... where is Love? Oh, the pain – it's too much. No, there must be something wrong. It's not possible. Please, please help me find comfort, help me understand.

He thought of his wife, his children. The mother and father he had never known. And more deeply of the King, his true Father. There was an emptiness in his soul, a gaping cavern into which his emotions plunged with no hope of salvation. He was faced with the immensity of his feelings about himself, a sense of evil and horror he could not bear. The pain was excruciating, the darkness a sharp knife severing his heart and soul in pieces, and he knew without a doubt there was no possibility of return from this hell.

It had been at some early hour in the morning that he had fallen to his knees on the floor, his mind a whirlpool of fear and self-hate bringing him outrageous pain. He had to make it stop.

He tried to shake his head clear of the suffering and turmoil. He breathed a few times quietly and slowly, then asked inside, pleaded inside, to find something other than his pain. Just for a brief moment, the barest instant, he was sincere in his asking, available to something other than his suffering.

Just for an instant he was able to see across the barrier of fear, hate and pain in his mind, and look into the place of calm that lay just on the other side. He waited, and then he heard the faintest, vaguest trace of something that was not pain, something quiet, and still.

As soon as he noticed someone had entered the house, he looked up. He glared glassy-eyed through the doorway and rose heavily from the stool but fell heavily against the table. Standing there swaying, he tried to look large and menacing but found it hard to focus. Suddenly he drew himself upright, looked around agitatedly, and then lunged toward a terracotta bowl on the table. He drew his arm back wildly and hurled the bowl with all his might toward the door and the boy. It smashed harmlessly in pieces against the wall over Paulo's shoulder and showered a red dust into the room.

The boy, however, did not move.

"Go away! *Get out of here!* I don't want to see anyone, do you hear me? You've no right to be here. This is my house. Now, *get out!*" he shouted blindly.

Still Paulo did not move. He continued looking quietly at the maddened, unsteady figure.

The blacksmith grabbed another heavy clay bowl. He braced himself this time, propping himself against the table, and now looked more closely at the intruder to take him in. He stopped instantly.

"What – who –? *What's going on*?"

His eyes shot open, his hand began to tremble violently and dropped the bowl which clunked on the wooden floorboards. He was lost in total confusion, for standing in the doorway in the place of the unwelcome stranger he now saw the image of a beautiful being surrounded by light, a golden figure exuding peace and strength – an image, like that of a magnificent Angel.

The blacksmith stood there hypnotized and embraced by the gentle countenance that looked upon him quietly. He could not release his eyes from the sight. The vision made him weak and confused, and then, for the second time that night, he sank forward and on to his knees.

Paulo moved forward slowly and came up to the giant man. Yet all the blacksmith saw was the silent approach of a being of light that stopped just before him. The wood seller looked into the big man's tired and painful eyes and saw a boy, like himself, one who had only ever felt abandonment and betrayal. And the rough man looked back, and saw only an extraordinary presence of Love.

They stared at each other in this way until the large man's eyes started to well with tears. His great chest heaved and coughed as he fought to withhold them, but then they broke through. Soon he was sobbing pitifully and furiously, and a lifetime of disappointment and sadness spent itself in heavy splattering drops upon the dirty wooden floor.

Paulo approached closer and the big man bent forward and lay his mass of tangled black hair on the boy's shoulder. Paulo placed his hands tenderly around his head.

He whispered just several words – words that the aching man could hardly bear to hear. "You have done nothing, my friend. You have done nothing to deserve this pain, I assure you. Love is not gone, and Love has not left you now."

The blacksmith continued to weep.

When after some time his crying waned, Paulo pushed him back gently to look within his eyes. His voice kind but strong, he said to him, "You have not done the terrible thing you believe. You still possess the Love that you thought you lost. Nothing is gone. It is all here, it is still right here. In your heart."

Paulo placed his hand on the big man's chest.

The boy looked directly into the blacksmith's tired, grieving eyes. "The Love you seek is not gone, but you *have* been concealing it. And this has made you do many hateful things. Would you like now to leave your hate and sadness, would you like now to be happier, and peaceful?"

But the tough man was still too absorbed by his emotions and did not hear the question.

Paulo pushed him back further. "Listen to my words. Listen –" he repeated. The blacksmith this time looked back at him and began to calm down.

"Listen to my words. *Try to let go of your pain – for just a moment.*"

Paulo fixed the blacksmith's eyes with his own. He waited until the man was breathing more calmly and began to let go the focus on his hurt.

"Try to understand, *you did not do this most dreadful thing you think.* You have banished Love from your mind, you have sought to impose your will on others, and you have been very vicious and unkind.

"But no matter how your life now appears, you have not destroyed what you think is gone. You must learn this, but you must ask sincerely for Love to replace your anger and sadness. Only *you* can accept Love to replace your hate and pain, do you understand?"

The man looked confused, but then nodded his head.

Paulo continued, "You have been wicked, but only because you have turned away from Love, from the kindness that is still there within you. Your wife and children are gone now. But you can still learn that Love is there. Begin to be kind to yourself, and then teach this kindness to others. Then you shall know that Love has finally returned to you."

Paulo paused to see if the blacksmith was following him. "And you must learn to ask inside for help, as you did this past night. Can you do that?"

The blacksmith nodded again.

The young boy spoke kindly, "Because only when you put aside your pain and ask to see differently can I help you. I cannot come to you when you hold on tightly to your emotions and thoughts, even though I am always there. Relax, and try to step back from your feelings, even just a little, and we will meet. This I promise."

Then Paulo added gently, "And now you know, Love *is* still there. We have finally met, and now you won't forget, right?" Paulo smiled at the great man whose eyes met his at the same height.

The blacksmith looked at him understandingly and made a slight smile in return.

Paulo soon departed, just as quietly as he had come, and the blacksmith sat on the stool for quite some time, lost in thought, and then calmly began to clean up the mess.

Marco was still waiting on the riverbank when Paulo returned from the blacksmith's house.

He placed himself next to his friend on the bench, now finally ready to take the last few steps of the journey Home. They closed their eyes and asked inside for the next path to take, feeling with all the desire they possessed to be present again within the Golden Realm of their King.

They rose and walked toward the market square, passing through its empty early-morning expanse, behind the Town Hall, through the narrow, dark street and toward the magical Great Door. They glanced at the Guards of Fear contentedly asleep, and continued walking on through the giant stone archway, leaving the Domain behind them.

The path was light and easy under their feet, and Paulo could not help but remark how much easier it was than the first time he had attempted to take the journey Home. He passed by the familiar landscape of his lessons with Zeph, there in the distance, the tree under which he had first met the magician, the fields where they had shared so many discussions; and made his way along the golden path which began to shimmer radiantly beneath his feet.

All traces of shadow now disappeared from his vision, and the light, already bright within the Kingdom, became still more vibrant and brilliant as they progressed along the path. Paulo was astonished how intense the light became, and he understood it would have been impossible to approach this brightness while any dark thoughts had remained within him: he would have been far too scared.

The all-surrounding radiance increased in intensity, and at the same time Paulo experienced himself becoming lighter, somehow less encumbered by the weightiness of his body. The countryside of the Kingdom faded gradually into a broad luminosity as they advanced further toward the City, and Paulo lost sight of the hills, the valleys and forests, all things that had once been so familiar. This would have normally frightened him had he been attached to the Domain; but instead of fear, there was the feeling of recognizing something even more familiar, more known than all that had been part of his life before.

He glanced across at Marco and now found that instead of the same old gentleman, there was a resplendent, glowing figure that accompanied him, and looking upon himself he perceived that he, too, had been transformed. He then lost all sight of form and shape for a moment and the two of them experienced a lifting sensation, carrying them upward and forward, as if entering another place altogether different. They traveled some time in this way till finally there was a sense of returning downward, this time to a lying position. They lifted their heads at precisely the same time.

"Welcome, my friends!" they heard spoken warmly. "Welcome Home – *at last!"*

CHAPTER SIXTY-TWO

Always There At Home

A calm, bright voice spoke to them where they lay and they turned to recognize the familiar figure of the magician. Only in place of his traditional blue robe, he now wore a garment that seemed to glow deeply and luminously from within, and Paulo and Marco noticed that they too were clothed in fabrics woven of the same magnificent light, in hues of silver, gold and violet.

The two travelers rose from the ground and looked eagerly about them. The portals of the City stood just before them, wide-open and welcoming, and on the ground near where they had woken lay other beings of light; many, many others, countless others, exactly like Paulo, Marco and Zeph.

The boy gazed about him, astounded. The entire area was illuminated by the radiance of these many thousands of golden beings that surrounded them, all lying on the soft grass in front of the portal of the Golden City. Staring at one who looked familiar, he noticed it was none other than Mr Bravura; and there next to him was Mrs Belladonna. *The Townspeople!* Not far away he found his mother, and then Fredo. All of the Townspeople were in fact there, his customers, the fish-man, and the Blacksmith. Even the Mayor was there, lying serenely quiet on the grass, wearing radiant clothes of light. It was a splendid, remarkable sight, and Paulo looked upon his sleeping brothers and sisters in wonder and awe.

The magician smiled. "You do understand now, my friends – don't you?"

Paulo and Marco looked back at him with amazement in their eyes.

Zeph continued, "Yes – this is precisely where you have been all this time, quietly sleeping at the foot of the Golden Gates, just as your brothers and sisters here. Able in fact to awaken and enter the City anytime you desired, able to awaken from your dark and frightening dreams any time you wished."

"But what could possibly have happened here?" asked Paulo.

"A long time ago, we all gathered together at this place outside the Gates, drawn by an idea: *What might there be aside from Home?* At the precise moment this strange wish entered our thoughts, we fell instantaneously asleep here on the ground where we were standing.

"We fell into a deep sleep, and in this slumbering state we imagined our beloved King had now become a terrible Tyrant and Judge. We saw him condemn our departure from the City as a grave sin, and pursue us into the mists of sleep. We fled, and we discovered within these bleak mists a new world, an entire universe, but one of darkness and ignorance, of exile and abandonment.

"Yes, that is the sum total of the world in which you believed so firmly. Yet now you see the truth: there *is* no Domain. *That place is nothing more than a dream.*

"Here we lay at the steps to the Golden City, and here we slept until an opening, at first small and hesitant, appeared within our deluded minds, and a question appeared: Could a truly beneficent Creator have made such a chaotic, dangerous world for those He loved? And a wish awakened within us to know our real Home once more.

"That desire, to remember his origin, would guide a sleeping brother back to his real Self and to awakening; and this has been your choice. Your remembrance and love of your Home have guided you back here, my friends. The Key was with you all the time. You have always been free to undo your false beliefs and awaken any time you wished."

Paulo spoke, "Then the world I saw was only ever a kind of giant picture we were all dreaming together? And even the person that I thought I was within it, it was a kind of dream-figure? That's really strange. But the Maker, what's he then?" he asked.

"The Maker, as well, was only our fabrication, Paulo; he has no real substance. The Ego-Maker is simply the spirit of the wish for independence from Home. But though he is evil and wicked beyond measure, the Maker is above all *our fabrication* – the result of our own desire for division from the original condition of our creation.

"There is only one spirit of the Maker, and this is the spirit each sleeping brother shares as he sleeps, though it is expressed differently for each one as the individual he knows as himself within his dream. It is the voice that rules his identity and would prevent him from waking to find his one true Self lying here before you – but only while he still wishes to remain within its power.

"When our brothers begin to doubt the Maker's counsel, when the disappointment with their imaginary world becomes truly intolerable, when they have need to remember that there is indeed *another way*, a way of kindness and brotherhood and safety – then will they begin to remember. They will sense the presence of their Father's Love calling them to awaken and remember, and the Maker's voice will over time subside to nothingness.

"As peace of mind then gradually returns, we become aware of the dream while still within it, even as you managed to do while still as 'Paulo' you studied and worked. Eventually we awaken fully to our magnificent Selves, those you see lying here. We awaken to our truth, that of the One Great People, the Christ, formless, undifferentiated and wholly embraced within the Love of our heavenly Father."

Paulo looked about him and now noticed a number of awakened brothers moving around amongst the many sleeping figures. They bent down occasionally here and there, appearing to speak to them.

"They are the Helpers, Paulo," the sage said. "They whisper into our brothers' dozing minds that it is safe to awaken and remember. They remind them that there is nothing to fear. This is the voice that everyone in the Domain hears in the back of his awareness. It reminds him that it is okay to let go of fear, and that he is loved and cared for, no matter what seems to be happening in his nightmare world. You understand now, we cannot stop our brothers from having the nightmares they seek. They shall see the terrible things they wish for themselves and we can only try to remind them that they are free to choose otherwise."

Paulo looked further and found other sleeping brothers whose light seemed to be different, somehow brighter and more peaceful than the others. He looked curiously at one nearby; her face held a distinctly different look from those of the others, not a trace of anguish or agitation could be found anywhere on her features.

Zeph explained, "Those are the brothers who have fully awoken, and have then returned to the dream Kingdom in order to call from that place. They awoke here, and then chose to sleep once more in order to reach out to their sisters and brothers within the dream."

"That's you, right?" Paulo asked, and the wizard just answered with a smile.

Zeph continued his explanation: "No make-believe home of fear and sadness could keep you, my friends, away from this Home of yours, and the Light bathed you even as you dreamed of darkness. It was *all* just a dream. You had never even left the Kingdom of Happiness but had only ever wandered far in a sleep of sadness and guilt, to a tiny place that seemed to be where Love could not enter.

"And yet, even there was the Light that is your Home. You remembered Love and let it light the world that darkness made, for nothing can exclude the Light the King has placed within your mind. Now, you know, you can *never* leave your Home. It was created for you, and always shall be your beloved Home."

The three of them now strolled up the path toward the gates and Zeph opened his arms to show the way, the last few steps.

Inside the giant portal, Paulo and Marco could see moving and blending the golden, silver and orange and deep violet glowing shapes of many brothers. They seemed to merge into one luminous radiance, suffusing and sharing within the same splendid unified light that illuminated the entire Kingdom. Paulo turned his head upwards and found the brilliant light reaching higher and higher, stretching all the way into the heavens above, stretching and spiraling into all directions, the luminous figures dancing and flowing from one beam to another, now together, now apart, till it seemed that every part of the sky was filled with this marvelous motion of light.

Marco turned and looked at Paulo, his face bright with an intense glow of expectation. He stood there a moment, reflecting, and then he understood.

"This is where we part, isn't it, my friend?"

Paulo was awash in radiance, and just smiled. "But remember we are never, ever apart, are we, Marco? I shall be right there with you."

Marco turned and gave one last look before entering through the Gates, and then disappeared into the heart of happiness that was his Father's own. He was once again what he had always been, one of His Father's beloved and holy People.

CHAPTER SIXTY-THREE

A Little Return Visit

Paulo took the magician's hand and without looking back at the Golden Gates they started down the path toward the sun-dappled grassy field where their sleeping brothers lay. Within moments they faded into the glorious, brilliant luminosity that surrounded the Kingdom, and Paulo knew that his body of light was now slumbering peacefully next to those of his brothers.

Before them the path stretched and rolled around the green hills in the dream aspect of the Kingdom. As they strolled Paulo pondered and sought to understand better his new role in the Realm of Happiness. "Zeph, why is it that you don't go into the Domain itself to help our brothers and sisters there?

"It's not that we can't, Paulo, but as you've seen, the Domain itself is a place of sleeping. We cannot stop our brothers from having the dreams they wish, from seeing the terrible things they wish to see and have happen. You have seen that the Domain is a place where the children of the King have gone to *escape* the light and love of the Kingdom. Attaching oneself to that dark place represents a decision *not* to know Love. As tiny as the Domain is, we cannot intrude on our brothers' and sisters' decision to claim it as their misbegotten home in the place of Love – doing so would constitute an attack on the power of their mind.

"It is only when they desire to know the truth with all their heart and soul, to wish that Love be present for them, even for just an instant, that we can help them. But while they still hold tightly onto suffering we cannot help them, for pain is a decision *not* to remember Love. Pain can be useful, in order to help remember when one is choosing against Love. But ultimately only a brother can decide to remember peace instead of pain in order to meet with us."

"You mean, you can only be there for him when you're invited?" Paulo asked. "Because otherwise you'd be saying he can't decide for himself?"

"Yes, exactly. No one can dispossess a brother of his right of choice. The will of the People is very powerful, and can even exclude Love. There is nowhere one can go where Love is not present, but one can banish Love so totally from the mind that a person can become terrified at its approach. Even there in total darkness it is present, but he can choose to be blind to it. We must respect this decision to live in darkness, if that is what a brother chooses, even though we know that darkness is not real or necessary."

"So we wait here, just the other side of the Wall?"

"We must show them that darkness is not the true cause of their experience, nor even what they would really seek for themselves in their right mind. That is why we wait here in the light and call to them, so that they may turn inside and learn to find there what is truly worth discovering. A brother need only contain some doubt about his experience and perceptions within the Domain, and he will begin to sense us here. The freedom to experience real happiness is available to every brother, no matter the seeming harshness of his circumstances. It just requires a little willingness to question the origin of his feelings."

Paulo responded gaily, "When they find us here they can see there's really nothing to fear or be sad about."

The wizard replied, "Precisely. Remember, whenever someone wants, no matter where he is, he can find an old wood bench or a broken stool, look around him and know that *somewhere* there with him, Love is truly present. No matter what turmoil and chaos surround him, no matter what he believes is his failure or crisis or prison, he can feel that something other than his painful condition is also real and present. It can be that easy. Come, let's walk now."

They wandered further down the path, and before long the massive shape of the Wall appeared in the distance, a clear dark line following a ridge of hilltops.

Paulo thought for a moment, then laughed loudly. "Does that now mean that when people make it out here to the Beyonde that I have to jump out of trees and poke funny faces at them – like you did?

Zeph chuckled. "Only if you think it would help them relax. Happiness is what we teach, as well as the release from fear and guilt. It felt right to do it with you, and maybe you'll do it with someone else. But after all, you'll just be you."

They strolled across the same familiar field of their lessons and sat under the same big oak tree where Paulo had first met Zeph, and looked out at the Golden City. Indeed it did not seem distant in the least, Paulo now thought. He could still feel it as if he was right there at the foot of the gates.

"You know, Paulo, with the work that we do, more and more people will be willing to look at the Door that separates them from the Kingdom and start to wonder. They'll discover that it's open and that there's no reason to be afraid of the guards. One day all of our brothers and sisters will pass back through the Door without fear and find what they turned their backs on so long ago. Then we will walk Home together and forget all about the Domain. It will be a distant and dusty thought of something that never really existed anyway, that will then disappear completely forever from our memories."

They remained silent a few moments, peaceful and present to a remarkable, sure future: the last and final judgment, the acceptance by the One People of true love and freedom for all things.

Paulo then said seriously, as seriously as could a young boy, "It's an awfully big task for just you and me to accomplish, Zeph, don't you think?" Paulo knew that time didn't matter much, but still wanted his brothers and sisters to be there with him soon.

"That's why we have company, Paulo. I never said that it would be just you and me. You decided to come back to help and there were others, too, before you. Remember, the Helpers? Look over there," he said, pointing.

Sure enough, emerging from the Forest was a group of people he had never seen before. He looked at their bright faces and saw they were happy, *very* happy people, like Marco and him, and they were smiling and laughing. These were in fact the other brothers and sisters he had seen sleeping at the gates whose auras had appeared brighter than the others. They were meandering between the trees in their direction and clearly in a very playful mood.

As they arrived, Zeph introduced the members of his new family one by one. Paulo looked at each person and felt completely at home with her and him instantaneously. He *knew* them. He greeted each one in turn and they gave him a hug or spoke a word or held his hand for a moment.

"And so you see, my fine young friend," said the magician, "much help is available. You shall not be alone on your quest, we are many out here to assist you. But *you*, on the other hand…"

He looked intently down at the boy and placed a hand on his shoulder, smiling broadly. "I believe that *you* have a special mission to undertake now. Haven't you guessed that? You have some special talents that would best be put into practice elsewhere, don't you think?"

Paulo thought a moment, listening inside, and his face lit with surprise. There *was* indeed a new, unexplored role for himself, he found, and now that he noticed it, it seemed quite clear: his path would not end there just yet with Zeph and the others.

The wizard explained merrily, "It is not your time, nor your place, to stay here with us, not yet. There is other work that only you can do, another special position to fill, one you have waited for very patiently till now. So, go off now on your bright new journey, my fine young man. All our blessings go with you, and we shall see each other soon enough, I'm quite sure."

The wizard accompanied Paulo slowly back toward the Door, as he had done so many times in the past. The boy looked up at the tall, imposing gates, but this time he crossed the threshold into the Domain, into the world of misty grayness, with a profound joy and gratefulness. He entered the gate without a backward glance, breathed deeply once, and disappeared into the very heart of the illusion.

A place lay in wait for him there, he knew, a very special place. And he strode briskly back into Towne with light trailing along his footsteps, making directly for the farm where a certain brother and sister were waiting for him. There, he would live with them, play with them, and take them by the hand, and lead them gently further along the path toward the land of light and glory and love.

Zeph sighed lightly, watching the figure of his young apprentice till it was gone in the distance, then turned away from the Door.

"Come," he said, signaling to the remaining brothers and sisters who had been watching the return ceremony from a distance. "Let's go now and welcome the others who've just arrived from over the Wall. We can't just stand about here, not when there's so much to do. That won't do at all!" he chided laughingly. "Come, let's get going…"

Further Acknowledgements

I would also like to express many thanks to the following people for their help along the bumpy road to completing this work:

D. Patrick Miller, for his valuable suggestions for getting the book back on a viable track at a critical turning point;

Lani Gosset and William Ferguson for believing in *Paulo* from the beginning;

The excellent team at Booksurge for their help in bringing this book into production; and

Patricia Roudil, for her loving companionship, practical suggestions, and boundless patience over many years of uncertainty and time-consuming work.

2449740

Made in the USA